Aspect-Oriented Security Hardening of UML Design Models

Djedjiga Mouheb · Mourad Debbabi
Makan Pourzandi · Lingyu Wang
Mariam Nouh · Raha Ziarati
Dima Alhadidi · Chamseddine Talhi
Vitor Lima

Aspect-Oriented Security Hardening of UML Design Models

 Springer

Djedjiga Mouheb
Concordia University
Montreal, QC
Canada

Mourad Debbabi
Concordia University
Montreal, QC
Canada

Makan Pourzandi
Ericsson Canada Inc.
Montreal, QC
Canada

Lingyu Wang
Concordia University
Montreal, QC
Canada

Mariam Nouh
King Abdulaziz City for Science
   and Technology
Riyadh
Saudi Arabia

Raha Ziarati
Sophos Inc.
Vancouver, BC
Canada

Dima Alhadidi
Zayed University
Dubai
United Arab Emirates

Chamseddine Talhi
École de Technologie Supérieure
Montreal, QC
Canada

Vitor Lima
Montreal, QC
Canada

ISBN 978-3-319-36894-8   ISBN 978-3-319-16106-8   (eBook)
DOI 10.1007/978-3-319-16106-8

Springer Cham Heidelberg New York Dordrecht London
© Springer International Publishing Switzerland 2015
Softcover reprint of the hardcover 1st edition 2015

Printed on acid-free paper

Springer International Publishing AG Switzerland is part of Springer Science+Business Media
(www.springer.com)

Foreword

Today, software is being used virtually everywhere in our society; in vehicles, banking, commerce, media, industrial control systems, and health care, just to mention a few. A large part of our infrastructure, including the communication systems that interconnect people, machines, and devices, are built on and managed through software. As our dependency on this infrastructure increases, so does the need for assurance of the software; to ensure that the software is functioning as intended, and that vulnerabilities are few and appropriately handled.

Assurance and verification of software are becoming essential, not only for IT security, but for communication systems in large. The need for security, as well as the means to verify security, will become even more emphasized with evolvements toward 5G and Internet of things, which come with new requirements on networks and services. Improved and proactive software assurance is also motivated by the fact that security breaches in software systems keep appearing in spite of numerous updates and patches.

Given the complexity and pervasiveness of today's software systems, building secure software is a challenging task, especially as security must be addressed during all phases of the software engineering process rather than added as an afterthought. In many cases, the security of software largely depends on developers' awareness of security requirements. Therefore, to reduce the burden on developers, there is a clear need for practical tools and methods for secure software development.

A promising approach for early security hardening is to leverage prominent modeling languages, such as the Unified Modeling Language (UML) for the specification and strengthening of software security. Indeed, using UML for developing secure software has a practical significance considering the fact that UML is the de-facto standard for object-oriented modeling of software systems and there exist many tools for UML modeling.

Because of the pervasive nature of security, adding security manually into a UML design is tedious, may lead to the introduction of new security vulnerabilities, and security components may become tangled and scattered throughout the whole design. Consequently, the resulting UML design model will most likely become difficult to understand and maintain. In this respect, the aspect-oriented technology emerged as an appealing approach for strengthening software security. This paradigm, which has received considerable attention from researchers and industry, allows a more advanced modularization by separating crosscutting concerns, such as security, from the software functionalities.

This book contributes to methodical engineering of secure software-intensive systems, by extending prominent modeling languages such as UML to address security concerns throughout the development life cycle. Such measures, as well as their extension, are vital in making software-intensive systems reliable, flexible, and highly secure. These are properties necessary for software systems as we come to depend on them as a natural part of our environment.

Stockholm, January 2015   Eva Fogelström
                                                    Director Security, Ericsson Research

Preface

In the coming years, information technology will continue to transform the way we think, work, communicate, and learn. The tremendous success of Internet-related technologies (web services, voice over IP, mobile telephony, etc.) coupled with advances both in hardware and software will invigorate the existing proliferation of software intensive systems. This will allow for new services, applications, and systems that will recede increasingly into the background of our lives. In this setting, the secure engineering of such software-intensive systems becomes a major concern. This is emphasized by the fact that security breaches of software systems keep appearing at an alarming rate in spite of numerous updates and patches that are constantly being issued.

Unfortunately, in many organizations, the emphasis on operational security usually leads most investments to be directed to network security measures, such as firewall, virtual private network, intrusion detection system, etc. However, in spite of significant efforts on network security, the scale and severity of security breaches have been increasing with no victory in sight in this arm race against attackers. Recently, new efforts have emerged in extending the defense by rooting the security in software itself. However, given the complexity and pervasiveness of today's software systems, building secure software is a challenging task. In most cases, the security of software widely depends on developers' awareness of security requirements, which is unfortunately not always present. To reduce the burden on developers, there is a clear need for practical tools and methods for secure software development.

Very often security practices are added to existing software either as an after-thought phase of the software development life cycle, or manually injected into software code or UML models. However, this practice is no longer acceptable for such an important aspect, especially with the increasing complexity and perva-siveness of today's software systems. Therefore, security must be addressed during the early phases of the software engineering process. A promising approach to early security hardening is to leverage prominent modeling languages, such as the Unified Modeling Language (UML) for the specification, verification, and hard-ening of software security. Indeed, using UML for secure software development would have more practical significance considering the fact that UML is the de-facto standard for object-oriented modeling of software systems and there exist many tools for UML modeling. In addition, UML supports standard extension mechanisms that enable the language to be customized for different platforms or domains.

Besides, because of the pervasive nature of security, adding security manually into a UML design is tedious, may lead to additional security vulnerabilities, and security components may become tangled and scattered throughout the whole design. Consequently, the resulting UML design model will most likely become difficult to understand and maintain. In this respect, the aspect-oriented technology emerged as an appealing approach for security hardening. This paradigm has received considerable attention from researchers and industrial practitioners alike. It allows a more advanced modularization by separating crosscutting concerns, such as security, from the software functionalities. Due to the increasing interest, the aspect-oriented technology has stretched over earlier stages of the software development life cycle. Aspect-Oriented Modeling (AOM) applies aspect-oriented techniques to software models with the aim of modularizing crosscutting concerns. It carries over the advantages of aspect-oriented programming to the modeling level. Indeed, handling those concerns at the modeling level would significantly help in alleviating the complexity of software models and facilitate reuse of existing design models.

This book contributes to the secure engineering of software-intensive systems. To this end, it extends current model-driven engineering paradigms and prominent modeling languages, such as UML, to address security concerns throughout the development life cycle. Moreover, it leverages the AOM paradigm for the specification and the systematic execution of security hardening practices on UML models. In this regard, a UML profile has been developed for the specification of security hardening aspects on UML diagrams. In addition, a weaving framework, with the underlying theoretical foundations, has been elaborated for the systematic injection of security aspects into UML models. The book will benefit researchers in academia and industry as well as students in the field of software and systems engineering. The reader will find, in this book, an overview of the research advancements related to model-based software security hardening.

The book is organized as follows: Chapter 1 presents an introduction to software security, model-driven engineering, UML, and aspect-oriented technologies. Chapter 2 provides an overview of UML language. Chapter 3 describes the main concepts of AOM. Chapter 4 explores the area of model-driven architecture with a focus on model transformations. The main approaches that are adopted in the literature for security specification and hardening are presented in Chap. 5. Chapter 6 presents our AOM profile for security aspects specification. Afterwards, Chap. 7 details the design and implementation of the security weaving framework. In addition, several real-life case studies are illustrated to demonstrate the relevance of the proposed framework for security hardening. Chapter 8 elaborates an operational semantics for the matching/weaving processes in activity diagrams. Moreover, Chaps. 9 and 10 elaborate a denotational semantics for aspect matching and weaving in executable models following a continuation-passing style. Finally, a summary and evaluation of the presented work are presented in Chap. 11.

March 2015

Djedjiga Mouheb
Mourad Debbabi
Makan Pourzandi
Lingyu Wang
Mariam Nouh
Raha Ziarati
Dima Alhadidi
Chamseddine Talhi
Vitor Lima

Acknowledgments

We would like to express our deepest gratitude to all the people who contributed to the realization of this work. This book is the result of a fruitful research collaboration between Concordia University and Ericsson Canada under the Collaborative Research and Development (CRD) Grant Program of the Natural Sciences and Engineering Research Council of Canada (NSERC) with additional support from PROMPT Quebec. The project is entitled "Model-Based Engineering of Secure Software and Systems" (MOBS2 Project) and has been executed, while most of the authors were affiliated with Concordia University. We would like to thank, from Ericsson: Anders Caspar who saw early on the potential and importance of this topic and without his support, this project would not have been possible; Rolf Blom whose advice and insights guided us throughout the project; Pierre Boucher whose continuous support for the project made this research a reality; Magnus Buhrgard who helped us to shape the project activities; and finally special thanks to Denis Monette for his precious advice, know-how, support, and good humor.

Acknowledgements

Contents

Acronyms

AAM	Aspect-oriented Architecture Model
Alf	Action Language for Foundational UML
AMW	Atlas Model Weaver
AOEM	Aspect-Oriented Executable Modeling
AOM	Aspect-Oriented Modeling
AOP	Aspect-Oriented Programming
AOSD	Aspect-Oriented Software Development
API	Application Programming Interface
ATL	Atlas Transformation Language
BNF	Backus-Naur Form
BPMN	Business Process Modeling Notation
CASE	Computer Aided and Software Engineering
CORBA	Common Object Request Broker Architecture
CORBA AC	CORBA Access Control
CPS	Continuation-Passing Style
CWM	Common Warehouse Metamodel
DAC	Discretionary Access Control
DSML	Domain Specific Modeling Language
FDAF	Formal Design Analysis Framework
FNE	Framework for Network Enterprises
fUML	Foundational UML
GReCCo	Generic Reusable Concern Composition
HiLA	High-Level Aspect
IDE	Integrated Development Environment
IP	Internet Protocol
IRC	Internet Relay Chat
ISO	International Organization for Standardization
JPM	Join Point Model
M2M	Model-to-Model
M2T	Model-to-Text

MAC	Mandatory Access Control
MDA	Model-Driven Architecture
MDE	Model-Driven Engineering
MDSD	Model Driven Software Development
MOBS2	Model-Based Engineering for Secure Software and Systems
MOF	Meta-Object Facility
MTF	Model Transformation Framework
NIST	National Institute of Standards and Technology
oAW	open Architecture Ware
OCL	Object Constraint Language
OMG	Object Management Group
PLSE	Product Line Software Engineering
QVT	Query/View/Transformation
QVTO	QVT Operational
RAM	Reusable Aspect Model
RBAC	Role-Based Access Control
RFP	Request for Proposal
RSA	Rational Software Architect
SAF	Service Availability Forum
SIP	Session Initiation Protocol
SQL	Structured Query Language
TOCTTOU	Time-of-Check-To-Time-Of-Use
UML	Unified Modeling Language
UWE	UML-based Web Engineering
VPL	View Policy Language
XMI	Extensible Markup Language
XMPP	Extensible Messaging and Presence Protocol
XSLT	EXtensible Stylesheet Language Transformations
XSS	Cross-Site Scripting
xUML	Executable UML

Chapter 1
Introduction

Software-intensive systems have become an inseparable part of our today's lives. Our dependence on software systems is very high in several sectors of our daily activities, such as, telecommunications, financial services, electronics, home appliances, transportation, etc. At the same time, software complexity is increasing drastically. Therefore, software systems become more susceptible to defects and vulnerabilities. In fact, the statistics provided by the National Institute of Standards and Technology (NIST) show that the amount of software security vulnerabilities, collected and analyzed from different sources, raises almost every year (Fig. 1.1).[1] In this setting, the security engineering of such software-intensive systems has become a major concern. This is emphasized by the fact that, in spite of significant efforts on software security from academia and industry, the scale and the severity of security breaches have been increasing with no complete victory against attacks.

1.1 Motivations

Nowadays, software security hardening is generally conducted as an afterthought phase of the software development life cycle, usually during the maintenance and the deployment phases, by applying security updates and patches. In fact, security mechanisms are usually fitted into pre-existing software without the consideration of whether this would jeopardize the main functionality of the software and produce additional vulnerabilities [142]. However, given the complexity and the pervasiveness of modern software systems, adding security mechanisms as an afterthought leads to a huge cost in retrofitting security into the software and further can introduce additional vulnerabilities. Studies have shown that considering security during the early stages of the software development life cycle decreases significantly the cost of the development [58, 99]. For example, a study conducted in [58] estimates that a single security vulnerability costs around $7,000 if it is fixed during the testing phase

---

[1] http://web.nvd.nist.gov/view/vuln/statistics.

© Springer International Publishing Switzerland 2015
D. Mouheb et al., *Aspect-Oriented Security Hardening of UML Design Models*,
DOI 10.1007/978-3-319-16106-8_1

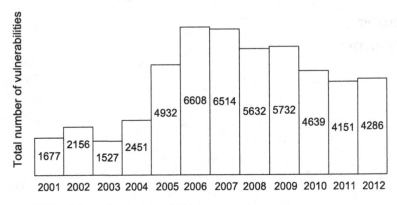

Fig. 1.1 NIST statistics: software vulnerabilities

Stage	Critical Bugs Identified	Cost of Fixing 1 Bug	Cost of Fixing All Bugs Early	Cost of Fixing All Bugs at Coding	Cost of Fixing All Bugs Later
Requirements		$139			
Design	200	$455	$91,000		
Coding	200	$977		$195,400	
Testing	50	$7,136			$356,800
Maintenance	150	$14,102			$2,115,300
Total			$91,000	$195,400	$2,472,100

Source: Cigital, "Case Study: Finding Defects Earlier Yields Enormous Savings"

Fig. 1.2 Cost of fixing vulnerabilities [58]

and can even reach $14,000 if the vulnerability is fixed at the maintenance phase. However, this cost can be reduced to less than $500 if the vulnerability is repaired during the design phase [58]. Given the large number of security vulnerabilities that a software can contain, it is clear that fixing those vulnerabilities early saves a substantial amount of money. As shown in Fig. 1.2, the cost can be reduced by $2.3M for 200 vulnerabilities [58]. Another research suggests that if the cost of solving a vulnerability in the design phase is $1, this cost will increase to $60–$100 to solve the same vulnerability during later phases [99]. Furthermore, approximately 60% of all vulnerabilities are usually introduced into software during the design phase [38]. Therefore, security must be addressed during the early phases of the software engineering process.

A promising approach to early security hardening is to adopt the emerging Model-Driven Software Engineering (MDE) [51] paradigm and prominent modeling languages, such as the Unified Modeling Language (UML) [152]. MDE is a software development methodology that considers software modeling the primary focus of the development process. UML is the de facto standard language for software specification and design. In addition, these paradigms are widely accepted by industry and academia due to their expressiveness, easiness, and tool support.

Furthermore, security is a crosscutting concern that pervades the entire software. Indeed, a security solution is not confined to one element in the software design but may impact several elements. Moreover, one element of the design can integrate several security solutions fixing different security vulnerabilities. Therefore, if the developers add security solutions manually into a UML design, security features may remain tangled and scattered throughout the whole UML design, especially in case of large scale software (e.g., hundreds or thousands of classes). Consequently, the resulting UML design models may become more complex and difficult to understand. Additionally, adding security manually is tedious and generally may lead to other security flaws.

In this respect, Aspect-Oriented Programming (AOP) [114] is an appropriate paradigm for security hardening. AOP has received considerable attention from researchers and industrial practitioners alike. It allows a more advanced modularization by separating crosscutting concerns, such as security, from the software functionalities by introducing new modules, called aspects, that capture generally one concern. The adoption of AOP techniques for developing secure software has become the center of many research activities [35, 49, 56, 130, 141, 172, 199, 207]. This could be justified by the following observations: (i) Aspect-oriented techniques allow security solutions to be carefully and precisely specified in isolation without altering the logic of the software. (ii) Developers can systematically integrate the security solutions into the software without digging into the inner working of those solutions.

In this book, we aim at leveraging this technique to perform security hardening of software at the UML design level through Aspect-Oriented Modeling (AOM) [31, 40, 182]. AOM allows software developers to conceptualize and express concerns in the form of aspects at the modeling stage, and integrate them into their UML diagrams using UML composition techniques. The concepts of AOM are similar to the ones of AOP (pointcut-advice model), namely, adaptations, join points, and pointcuts. An adaptation specifies the modification to be performed on the base model. A join point is a location in the base model where an adaptation should be applied. A pointcut is an expression that designates a set of join points. The process of identifying join points is called matching and the process of composing aspects with base models is called weaving.

Using AOM, security aspects can be precisely defined at UML design level, and systematically injected, at the right places, into UML design models. However, in spite of the increasing interest, to date, there is neither a standard language for specifying UML aspects, nor a standard mechanism for weaving aspects into UML design models. Accordingly, the primary objective of this book is to elaborate an aspect-oriented modeling and weaving framework, with the underlying theoretical foundations, for software security hardening at the UML design level.

Before presenting the proposed framework, we provide, in the following, an overview of the core concepts that are involved in the field of model-based security hardening of software. We first recall some important concepts about software security and the main security requirements. Then, we present an overview of Model-Driven Engineering (MDE) [51] and its main terms and concepts. Afterwards, we provide the necessary background on modeling languages, focusing on the Unified Modeling Language (UML) [152] since it is the de facto standard language for software specification and design. Finally, we introduce the aspect-oriented paradigm, with a focus on Aspect-Oriented Modeling (AOM) [31, 40, 182].

1.2 Software Security

Software security is the process of designing, building, and testing software, such that it becomes resilient against attacks and threats. It gets to the heart of computer security by identifying and expunging problems in the software itself [133]. Secure software should be as vulnerability and defect free as possible. In addition, it should limit the damage resulting from any failure and recover as quickly as possible from this failure. Moreover, it should continue functioning correctly under malicious attacks [38]. In the following, we briefly recall some important concepts and security requirements, which will be considered in the course of this book.

- *Security Policy*: A security policy is a set of rules and guidelines that specify how to achieve the needed security requirements for a system or an organization. It might include rules for virus detection and prevention, granting and revoking access to system resources, protecting critical information from unauthorized users, etc.
- *Security Flaw*: A security flaw is a defect in a program that can cause a system to violate its security requirements. A software defect is the result of encoding human errors into the software.
- *Security Vulnerability*: A security vulnerability is a weakness in a system that could be exploited to violate the system's security policy. It is the result of exploiting a security flaw by an attacker. Examples of flaws that usually lead to vulnerabilities include: memory management errors (e.g., buffer overflow [87]) and input validation errors (e.g., format string, SQL injection, and cross-site scripting [86]).
- *Attack*: An attack or exploit is a technique that takes advantage of a security vulnerability to violate a security policy.
- *Security Hardening*: Security hardening can be defined as any process, methodology, product, or combination that is used to add security functionalities, remove vulnerabilities, and/or prevent their exploitation in a software [140].
- *Security Mechanism*: A security mechanism is a software/hardware solution targeting the enforcement of security policies. Examples of such mechanisms include access control mechanisms such as Role-Based Access Control [83].

Security requirements can be classified into high-level and low-level requirements. High-level security covers requirements such as, confidentiality, integrity, authentication, authorization, availability, etc. Low-level security deals with safety vulnerabilities that can be introduced in the software source code during the implementation phase. Those vulnerabilities depend on the platform and the programming language used for the development of a software system. The most common low-level security vulnerabilities include: buffer and integer overflows, format string errors, memory and file management errors, SQL and command injection, cross-site scripting, directory traversal, clear and set interrupts, TOCTTOU (Time-of-Check-To-Time-Of-Use) errors [46, 210], etc. Since we are dealing with security hardening at design level, we are more interested in high-level security than low-level security. In the following, we provide an overview of the main high-level security requirements that are usually specified and verified on software.

- *Confidentiality*: The International Organization for Standardization (ISO) defines confidentiality as "ensuring that information is accessible only to those authorized to have access" [104]. Enforcing confidentiality is one of the main security services provided by many cryptographic protocols. When properly enforced, it ensures that the data that is sent between participants in a communication session reaches only the intended receivers but unintended parties cannot determine what was sent.
- *Integrity*: It requires that data should not be accidentally or maliciously altered or destroyed. In other words, the data received by the receiver should be exactly the same as the data sent by the sender. The objective of integrity is to ensure the correctness and the accuracy of data. Integrity can be compromised through malicious altering, such as an attacker modifying a message in a communication network, or accidental altering, such as a transmission error or a system crash.
- *Authentication*: The objective of an authentication requirement is to ensure that users are who they claim to be. In other words, authentication provides assurance that an entity is not pretending to have the identity of another entity without being detected. To ensure the authentication property, a system must provide a mechanism to verify the identity of its users before interacting with them.
- *Authorization*: It stipulates which user is allowed to access one or more resources in a system. After a user is authenticated, the authorization process determines whether that user has access to a specified resource. Legal users are granted authorization to the required resources while illegal ones are denied access to the resources. The authorization requirement prevents unauthorized users from obtaining access to inappropriate or confidential data. Authorization and authentication are closely related because any meaningful authorization policy requires authenticated users. Authorization requires that accessing critical information should be controlled. Accordingly, different models of access control have been proposed. The most known models are Role-Based Access Control (RBAC) [83], Mandatory Access Control (MAC) [45], and Discretionary Access Control (DAC) [144]:

  - In the RBAC model, access decisions are based on the roles and the responsibilities of users within an organization. Users and permissions to perform operations on objects are assigned to roles.
  - In the MAC model, security levels (e.g., *unclassified, confidential, secret* and *top secret*) are assigned to each object (*classification*) and each subject (*clearance*). The permission for a subject to access an object depends on the relation between the object's classification and the subject's clearance.

– In the DAC model, access restriction to objects is based on the identity of subjects and/or groups to which they belong. In this model, every object has an owner that controls the permissions to access the object. The owner of an object can make decisions of who else in the system can access that object. In addition, the owner is able to delegate his/her permissions to other users.

1.3 Model-Driven Engineering

Model-Driven Engineering (MDE) [51] is a promising approach adopted for software development. It aims to raise the level of abstraction in program specification by considering models as the primary focus of development. Once designed, the software model is used to direct all the different phases followed for development of the software. These include code generation, verification and testing, maintenance, etc. The main goal of MDE is to increase productivity by automating the development process as much as possible. Moreover, it aims at maximizing compatibility between systems by using standardized models and best practices in the application domain. We start in this section by introducing the main concepts of MDE, which are used in the course of this book.

- *Model*: It is an abstract representation of a specification, a design, or a system, from a particular point of view [192]. A model usually focuses on a certain aspect of the system and omits all other details.
- *Executable model*: It is a model that contains enough details that are required to produce the desired functionality of a single problem domain.
- *Modeling language*: It is a specification language, generally defined by a syntax and a semantics, for expressing models. It can be either graphical or textual. A graphical modeling language uses diagrams to represent concepts and the relationships between them. An example of such language is UML. A textual modeling language uses reserved keywords associated with parameters. An example of such language is Alf language [156] (Sect. 2.7.2).
- *Meta-model*: It is a model of a modeling language. It describes the structure, the semantics, and the constraints for a modeling language. By analogy, a model should conform to its meta-model as a program conforms to the grammar of a particular programming language. A meta-model itself should be expressed in some language, such as Meta-Object Facility (MOF) [151].
- *Meta-Object Facility (MOF)*: It is an OMG standard language for defining meta-models. It is also a meta-model and often called a meta-meta-model.
- *Abstract syntax*: It defines the concepts of a language and their relationships. It is often defined using a meta-model.
- *Concrete syntax*: It defines how elements of a language should be formed. For example, in the case of a graphical language, a concrete syntax defines the graphical appearance of the language concepts and how they may be combined into a model.

- *Semantics*: In the context of MDE, a semantics for a model describes the effect of executing that model.
- *Model transformation*: It is the process of converting one model into another model of the same system based on some transformation rules [148]. More details about this process are provided in Chap. 4.

1.4 Unified Modeling Language

Nowadays, models appear constantly in our routine. Any person, even with no modeling background, is used to read models representing, for example, driving directions, furniture assembling instructions, device safety procedures, etc. Models are an appealing way of representing a system in many different fields. It is not a surprise that modeling languages are becoming more and more important in software engineering. Modeling abstracts a real system to a level where only the essential aspects matter. It provides a means of understanding extremely complex software, as well as it makes the communication among the development team much more efficient and effective [198].

The Unified Modeling Language (UML) is a language and notation system used to specify, construct, visualize, and document models of software systems. Before UML, software developers used to have a collection of mismatched diagram techniques, notation, and semantic approaches [125]. The creation of UML came as a solution in order to have a *unified* notation and semantic model. UML covers a wide range of applications and is suitable for technical (concurrent, distributed, time-critical) systems and so-called commercial systems [205]. It is now used in many different ways by people with very different backgrounds. Weilkiens and Oestereich enumerate some interesting examples of professionals using UML [205]:

- Business planners, as a language to specify the planned operation of a business process, perhaps in concert with a business process language such as the Business Process Modeling Notation (BPMN) [145].
- Consumer device engineers, as a way to outline the requirements for an embedded device and the way it is to be used by an end user.
- Software architects, as an overall design for a major stand-alone software product.
- IT professionals, as an agreed-on set of models to integrate existing applications.
- Database professionals, to manage the integration of databases into a data warehouse, perhaps in concert with a data warehousing language such as the Common Warehouse Metamodel (CWM) [146].
- Software developers, as a way to develop application that are flexible in the face of changing business requirements and implementation infrastructure.

UML is now at version 2.4.1 [152]. A major update has been done at version 2.0 compared to version 1.x. The version 2.0 of UML improved behavioral modeling by deriving all behavioral diagrams from a fundamental definition *behavior*, in contrast to UML 1.x, where different behavioral models were completely independent. It also improved the relationship between structural and behavioral models. Now, UML allows to designate that, for example, a state machine or sequence is the behavior of a class or component. The new version of UML goes beyond the classes and objects modeled by UML 1.x to add the capability to represent not only behavioral models, but also architectural models, business processes and rules, as well as other models used in many different parts of computing and even non-computing disciplines [152]. Chapter 2 is dedicated to the detailed presentation of UML, the main UML diagrams and extension mechanisms.

1.5 Aspect-Oriented Paradigm

Aspect-orientation emerged as a paradigm that allows advanced modularization of crosscutting concerns. A crosscutting concern is a concern that cannot be easily and efficiently modularized into a single entity using object-oriented techniques. Thus, such a concern remains scattered and tangled throughout various places in the application. Scattering means that one concern is located in different modules whereas tangling means that one module contains many concerns. These concerns may vary depending on the application domain; they can be functional or non-functional, high-level or low-level features. Security, logging, and synchronization are some examples of such concerns. The objective of aspect-orientation is to encapsulate those concerns that cross-cut an application into single units of modularization called *aspects*. Then, define a mechanism to compose the different aspects into a coherent program.

The aspect-oriented paradigm originally emerged at the programming level. Various Aspect-Oriented Programming (AOP) [114] models were proposed to achieve the aforementioned goals. The most important models are: Pointcut-Advice [131], Multi-Dimensional Separation of Concerns [159], and Adaptive Programming [158]. In addition, many AOP languages have been developed, such as, AspectJ [113] and HyperJ [160], built on top of the Java programming language, AspectC [61] and AspectC++ [189], built on top of the C and C++ programming languages, etc. However, due to the rise of MDE, aspect-oriented techniques are no longer restricted to the programming stage, but are increasingly adopted at prior stages of the software development life cycle. In this context, Aspect-Oriented Modeling (AOM) aims at applying AOP mechanisms at the modeling level, which encompasses requirements engineering, analysis, and design stages [31].

An appropriateness analysis study of the different AOP models from a security point of view has been conducted in [33]. As a result of this study, the pointcut-advice model was identified as the most appropriate approach for security hardening. Indeed, the pointcut-advice model allows capturing subtle points in the control flow of applications that are important from a security point of view, such as method calls, method executions, getting and setting of attributes, etc. In addition, security behavior can be automatically injected at these points. The main concepts of the pointcut-advice model are the following:

- *Aspect*: An aspect is a unit of modularization that encapsulates a cross-cutting concern of an application. Typically, an aspect contains a set of adaptations, specifying in what way a concern's structure and behavior should be adapted, i.e., enhanced, replaced, or deleted [182].
- *Advice and Introduction*: Advice is a piece of code specifying how the behavior of an application should be adapted at specific points. Whereas, an introduction specifies how the structure of an application should be adapted. In AOM, we use the term *adaptation* to refer to both structural and behavioral modifications.
- *Join Point and Pointcut*: A join point is an event during the execution of a program such as a method call or a method execution. At the modeling level, a join point represents a location in a model where an event happens, such as, a call message in a sequence diagram or an action in an activity diagram. A pointcut is an expression that designates a set of join points.
- *Matching and Weaving*: Matching is the process of selecting the join points that satisfy a given pointcut expression. Whereas, weaving is the process of composing aspects with the base modules. In other words, weaving is the process of applying the aspect adaptations at the matched join points.

1.6 Outline

The remainder of this book is organized as follows:

- Chapter 2 presents the necessary background on Unified Modeling Language (UML). We discuss the benefits of using UML. Then, we present UML structure and its different views and concepts. Afterwards, we present an overview of UML diagrams with examples of the most important ones. We also introduce the main UML extension mechanisms, namely stereotypes, tagged values, and constraints.
- Chapter 3 is dedicated to presenting the main concepts and definitions in the domain of AOP/AOM. We start by recalling the main AOP models. Then, we discuss the appropriateness of these models from a security point of view. Afterwards, we present the basic constructs of the pointcut-advice model since it is the one adopted in this research. Finally, we introduce the main concepts of Aspect-Oriented Modeling (AOM).
- Chapter 4 explores the area of Model-Driven Architecture (MDA) with a focus on model transformations. We discuss the benefits of MDA and the main MDA layers. Then, we describe MDA transformations. Additionally, we explore the different applications of model transformations in various domains. Moreover, we present an overview as well as a comparative study of the different model transformation languages and tools.
- Chapter 5 presents the current literature related to security at the modeling level. We start by surveying the state of the art in this domain. Then, we present the main approaches that are adopted in the literature for security specification

and hardening. The approaches in question are UML artifacts, extending UML meta-language, and creating a new meta-language. In addition, we discuss the usability of each approach for security specification according to a defined set of criteria. Moreover, we investigate the main mechanisms used to address security hardening at the modeling level, namely security design patterns, mechanism-directed meta-languages, and AOM.

- Chapter 6 presents our proposed AOM approach for security hardening of UML design models. We provide details of the defined AOM profile for security aspects specification. This includes the specification of aspect adaptations and a pointcut language proposed to designate UML join points.
- Chapter 7 details the design and the implementation of the security weaving framework. We first provide a high-level overview that summarizes the main steps of the weaving approach. Then, we detail each weaving step, namely, aspect specialization, join point matching, and actual weaving. Moreover, we provide algorithms that implement the different matching and weaving methods in each supported UML diagram. Finally, we present details about our prototype implementation. This includes the authoring of the AOM profile and the implementation of the weaving plug-in. In addition, we illustrate the proposed framework and demonstrate its usefulness for security hardening by several real-life case studies.
- Chapter 8 explores the semantics of the matching and the weaving processes in activity diagrams using deductive proof systems. In addition, we formalize algorithms for matching and weaving and prove the correctness and the completeness of these algorithms with respect to the proposed semantics.
- Chapters 9 and 10 are dedicated for presenting dynamic semantics for aspect matching and weaving based on CPS and defunctionalization. The purpose is to describe the semantics in a precise and elegant way. For clarity and to facilitate understanding, we elaborate the semantics in two steps. First, in Chap. 9, we present the CPS semantics for matching and weaving in λ-calculus. Second, in Chap. 10, we present the CPS semantics in xUML models.
- Finally, Chap. 11 briefly summarizes our contributions. In addition, it provides an evaluation of the proposed framework as well as closing remarks and final conclusions.

Chapter 2
Unified Modeling Language

The Unified Modeling Language (UML) [152] is a general-purpose modeling language in the field of software engineering. It was created and standardized by the Object Management Group (OMG) in 1997. UML came as a solution to provide a *unified* modeling notation and semantic models. The objective of UML is to provide system architects, software engineers, and software developers with tools to specify, construct, visualize, and document models of object-oriented software systems. It is now considered the de facto language for software specification and design. Currently, UML is at version 2.4.1 [152]. A major update has been done at version 2.0 compared to version 1.x. UML 2.0 has been enhanced with significantly more precise definitions of its abstract syntax rules and semantics, a more modular language structure, and a greatly improved capability for modeling large-scale systems [152]. In addition, UML now is defined in terms of Meta-Object Facility (MOF) [151], which makes it compliant with other meta-models defined by OMG.

In the following sections, we present an overview of UML background. Section 2.1 recalls the usefulness of a unified modeling language. Section 2.2 presents the structure of UML language. The different UML views and concepts are presented in Sect. 2.3. In Sect. 2.4, we overview the main UML diagrams. Additionally, in Sect. 2.5, we present the standard UML extension mechanisms, i.e., stereotypes, tagged values, and constraints, followed by an overview of the OCL language in Sect. 2.6. Section 2.7 provides the necessary background on Executable UML and related standards, i.e., Foundational UML and Alf language. Finally, we conclude this chapter in Sect. 2.8.

2.1 Why Unified Modeling Language?

One of the objectives of modeling software systems is helping developers express and discuss the problems and solutions involved in building a system. Usually, in large sized systems, each developer is responsible for a certain component of the system. However, the developer will need to have a good understanding of the other

© Springer International Publishing Switzerland 2015   11
D. Mouheb et al., *Aspect-Oriented Security Hardening of UML Design Models*,
DOI 10.1007/978-3-319-16106-8_2

components as well. In order to accomplish this, having a unified modeling language that is widely used will facilitate the interaction between developers. Additionally, this will result in reducing the development cost. For instance, if different modeling languages are used by developers of different components for the same system, it will require each of them more time to understand the details of the other's components. Moreover, if a unified modeling language is used, it will ease the process of integrating a new member into the development team, which will make the development wheel move faster [166].

2.2 UML Structure

UML is an extremely extensive language. However, once its structure and concepts are known, the size of the language no longer represents a problem. To be able to understand the structure of the UML language, it is better to look at it from two different dimensions (see Fig. 2.1).

First, one needs to distinguish between *structural* and *behavioral* elements. The former represents the structure of the system while the latter is used to represent the exact behavior of a given function in that system. The *Others* column presents elements that refer to both structure and behavior [204].

In the second dimension, it is necessary to differentiate between *Models* and *Diagrams*. A Model represents the complete description of the system, while a diagram represents part of the model from a certain point of view. For example, Fig. 2.2 represents two diagrams for the same model. The top diagram shows the classes with their attributes and the name of the associations between them, while

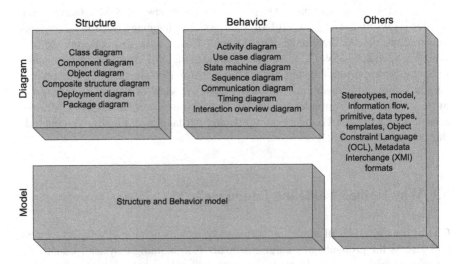

Fig. 2.1 The structure of UML [204]

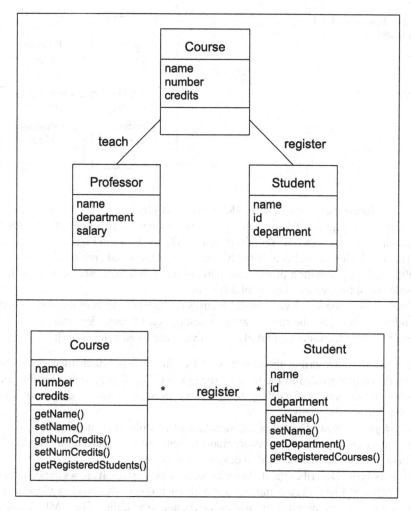

Fig. 2.2 Example of two different diagrams of the same model

the bottom diagram shows a different view of the model from the perspective of the student with a complete list of attributes, operations, and association information.

2.3 UML Views and Concepts

There are many ways to break up UML diagrams into perspectives or views that capture a particular aspect of a system. In order to better understand the different functionalities and usages of UML diagrams, the classification of Philippe Kruchten

Fig. 2.3 Kruchten's 4 + 1
view model

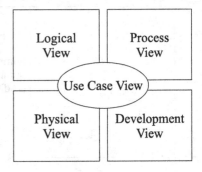

who introduced the 4 + 1 view model is adopted [167]. The 4 + 1 view model
organizes a description of a software architecture using five concurrent views, each
of which addresses a specific set of concerns [167], as shown in Fig. 2.3.

The 4 + 1 view model is adopted by many developers and architects because it
facilitates the examination of different parts of an architecture, and minimizes the
complexity of the overall viewing of a system.

Each view in the 4 + 1 view model focuses on certain aspects of the system and
intentionally conceals the rest. A general description of each view and the corresponding UML diagrams supported by each view are listed below [167]:

- *Logical View*: Describes the object model of the design, which focuses on the
  functionality provided to the user by the system. The logical view contains the
  following diagrams: *class diagrams, object diagrams, sequence diagrams, and
  collaboration diagrams.*
- *Development View*: Describes the structure of modules and files in the system.
  It is more concerned with software management and its organization. The UML
  Package diagrams can be used to describe this view.
- *Process View*: Describes the dynamic aspects of the system. It shows the different
  processes and how they communicate with each other. The process view deals
  with concurrency, distribution, performance, and availability. The UML *Activity
  diagrams* represent this view.
- *Physical View*: Describes the mapping of the software to the hardware. In other
  words, it is concerned with how the application is going to be installed and executed
  in the physical layer. *Deployment diagrams* are used to depict this view.
- *Use Case View*: This view is also called the *Scenario view*. It uses elements from
  all other views to describe the functionality of the system and illustrate what the
  system is supposed to do. The UML *Use Case diagrams* are used to describe
  this view.

2.4 UML Diagrams

The visual notation of UML models is expressed in a rich set of diagrams. UML 2 consists of fourteen diagram types describing different views of a software system. The OMG's UML specification classifies UML diagrams into two main categories: *structural* and *behavioral* diagrams (Fig. 2.4). Structural diagrams describe the static structure of objects in a system as well as the relationships and the dependencies between the objects. Behavioral diagrams describe the dynamic behavior of objects in a system.

Unhelkar [198] proposed an additional classification for UML diagrams based on the *time* dependency of each diagram (Fig. 2.5). He suggests that UML models can have either a *static* or a *dynamic* nature. Dynamic models are those which display various states of elements and the events that cause state changes, and those diagrams which are *frozen* in time are then static.

Table 2.1 provides a brief description of each UML diagram.

To illustrate the different applications of UML diagrams, Fig. 2.6 depicts a hypothetical situation where the system needs to implement two use cases (*login* and *logout*). This requirement is shown in Fig. 2.6a by the *Use Case diagram*. In order to implement these use cases, a developer can decide to define two classes which are: *User* and *Authenticator*. The static structure of these classes is shown in Fig. 2.6b as a *Class diagram*. The interaction among the instances of the classes in the login scenario is presented as a *Sequence diagram* in Fig. 2.6c. This diagram shows that a database with user credentials should also be implemented in this system. Finally, internal behavior of the authenticator is specified using a *State Machine Diagram*.

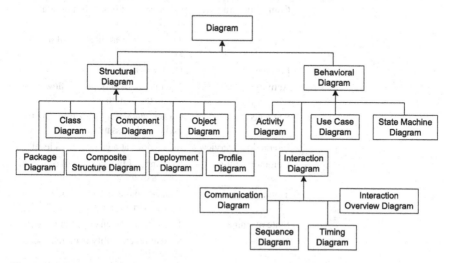

Fig. 2.4 Taxonomy of UML diagrams

Fig. 2.5 Diagrams
classification including
structural and behavioral
views as well as their static
versus dynamic nature [198]

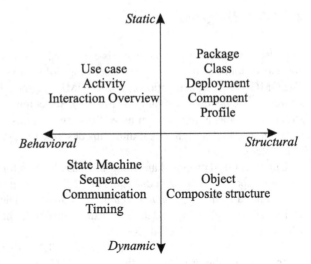

Static

Package
Class
Deployment
Component
Profile

Use case
Activity
Interaction Overview

Behavioral   Structural

State Machine
Sequence
Communication
Timing

Object
Composite structure

Dynamic

Table 2.1 UML diagrams

UML diagram	Specifies
Class	Classes, entities, business domain, databases, etc.
Package	The organization of packages, sub-systems
Object	Objects and their relationships at one point in time
Component	Software and hardware elements that make up a system
Composite structure	Component of object behavior at run-time
Deployment	The hardware architecture of a system
Profile	UML extensions
Activity	A sequence of actions of a flow within the system
Sequence	Object interactions over time and the exchanged messages
Interaction overview	Interactions at a general high level
Communication	Exchange of messages between objects over time
Timing	Changes in the state or value of elements in a timeline
State machine	The behavior of an object at run-time
Use case	System functionality from the user's viewpoint

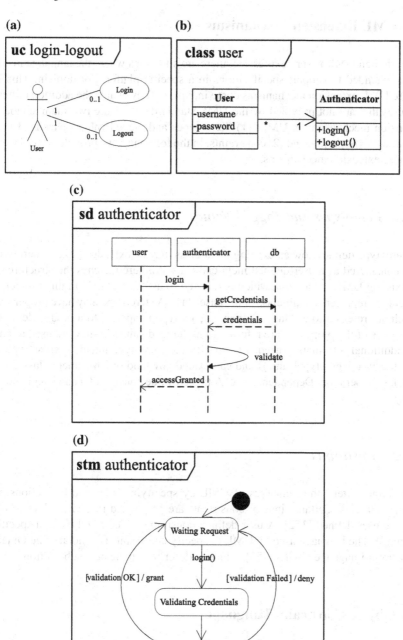

Fig. 2.6 Examples of using UML diagrams

2.5 UML Extension Mechanisms

Even though UML is very expressive, there are situations where the language needs to be extended to support specifications in a specific platform or domain. This is where UML extension mechanisms come into play. They enable the addition of new features that are not provided by the UML standard. There are two main standard extension mechanisms in UML: (1) Stereotypes and tagged values, packaged in a so-called *UML profile*, and (2) constraints. In the following, we provide an overview of these extension mechanisms.

2.5.1 Stereotypes and Tagged Values

A stereotype defines how an existing meta-class may be extended [152]. Therefore, it is considered as a user-defined meta-class. Its structure matches the structure of an existing UML meta-class, which is referred to as "base class". In this respect, a stereotype represents a sub-class of the base class. A stereotype may have properties, which are referred to as "tags". When a stereotype is applied to a model element, the values of the properties are referred to as "tagged values". They are used to add the additional information needed to specify the stereotype intent. A stereotype is denoted by ⟨⟨StereotypeName⟩⟩ and can extend any kind of UML meta-class, such as, Class, Operation, Dependency, etc. A tagged value consists of a name and one or many values.

2.5.2 Constraints

Constraints extend the semantics of UML by specifying rules and restrictions on model elements. Certain kinds of constraints are predefined in UML, while others may be user-defined [152]. A user-defined constraint is described using a specific language. The language used by UML to specify constraints is generally the Object Constraint Language (OCL) [153], which is described in the next sub-section.

2.6 Object-Constraint Language

The Object Constraint Language (OCL) [153] is a formal language used to specify expressions on UML models. These expressions typically specify constraints that must hold for the system being modeled or queries over objects described in a model. OCL is mainly used to specify application-dependent constraints for UML models. In addition, it is used to specify invariants of the UML meta-language.

More precisely, the main purposes for which OCL can be used are to: (1) query UML elements, (2) specify invariants on classes and types in the class model, (3) specify type invariants for stereotypes, (4) describe pre and post conditions on operations, and (5) describe guards [153]. OCL is a pure specification language; the evaluation of OCL expressions over UML elements cannot change anything in the model. This means that when an OCL expression is evaluated, it simply returns a value. It cannot have any effect on the state of the system even though an OCL expression can be used to specify a state change (e.g., a post-condition) [153].

2.7 Executable UML

UML provides software designers with graphical modeling notations to specify, construct, visualize, and document the artifacts of a software system. However, the standard notations of UML are not always sufficient to capture the detailed software behavior, such as variable and attribute assignments, operation calls, transition effects, etc. As a result, the models specified using UML notations remain abstract and high level. In addition, the standard UML specification does not offer precise and complete execution semantics for UML elements. In fact, the semantics is defined informally in English. Consequently, it is not possible to define fully executable UML models that can be simulated and validated before development. Furthermore, in the security context, some vulnerabilities, such as the ones related to data flow, cannot be easily detected on high-level models since these vulnerabilities involve variables and their data values. Accordingly, it is important to have detailed and executable specifications to be able to detect and fix such vulnerabilities.

Fortunately, the Object Management Group (OMG) proposed a new standard called Semantics of a Foundational Subset for Executable UML Models [157]. This standard defines the precise execution semantics for a selected subset of UML, the so-called foundational UML (fUML) [157]. However, fUML provides only the abstract syntax of executable UML and does not specify how executable models should be formed. Consequently, the creation of executable models remains a difficult task, especially for large-size executable UML models. For these reasons, OMG defined another standard, called Action Language for Foundational UML (Alf) [156], to provide a concrete syntax for fUML. In the following, we present the main elements of fUML. Afterwards, we provide a brief introduction to Alf language.

2.7.1 Foundational UML

Foundational UML (fUML) [157] is an executable subset of the standard UML that can be used to specify, in an operational style, the structural and the behavioral semantics of a system. The main elements of fUML are activities, actions, structures, and asynchronous communications [157]. In the following, we present the basic features of activities and actions as they are used in Chap. 10.

Activities are specifications of control flow and data flow dependencies between functions or processes in a system. An activity is composed of nodes connected by edges (control flows and object flows) in the form of a complete flow graph. A control flow specifies the sequencing of activity nodes. An object flow provides a path for passing objects or data between activity nodes. There are mainly three kinds of activity nodes: action nodes, object nodes, and control nodes. Actions are fundamental units of executable behaviors that represent single steps within activities. They operate on control and data they receive through their incoming edges, and provide control and data to other actions through their outgoing edges. Foundational UML supports various kinds of actions, which can be classified into four groups:

- *Invocations actions*: Include invocations of behaviors such as activities, invocations of operations, and communication actions such as sending of signals and accepting of events.
- *Object actions*: Include creating objects and destroying objects.
- *Structural feature actions*: Include reading structural features, adding, removing, and clearing structural feature values.
- *Link actions*: Include reading links, creating new links, destroying existing links, and clearing associations.

Object nodes are used to hold data temporarily as the data wait to move through the control flow graph. There are two main kinds of object nodes: activity parameter nodes and input/output pins. Activity parameter nodes hold inputs and outputs to activities, while pins hold inputs and outputs to actions. Control nodes are nodes that coordinate flows in an activity. The main control nodes are initial node, final node, fork node, join node, decision node, and merge node. The initial/final node starts/terminates the activity execution. The fork and join nodes are used to model concurrency and synchronization. The decision and merge nodes are used to model branching.

An activity execution can be described in terms of tokens' flow. A token is a locus of control or a container for an object/data that may be present at an activity node. For example, Fig. 2.7[1] illustrates a simple activity, which is invoked with an argument of 1 for its input parameter. Consequently, a data token with a value of 1 is placed on the input activity parameter node. Then, that data token flows to the input pin of the action A along the object flow a. Consequently, the action A fires and produces a result as a data token. Then, this data token flows to the output activity parameter node along the object flow c. In addition, the action A produces a control token, which flows to the action B along the control flow b. Finally, the action B accepts the control token and fires, producing a data token that flows to the output activity parameter node along the object flow d.

---

[1] http://www.omg.org/news/meetings/tc/agendas/va/xUML_pdf/Seidewitz_Tutorial.pdf.

```
result = DoSomething (1, output);
```

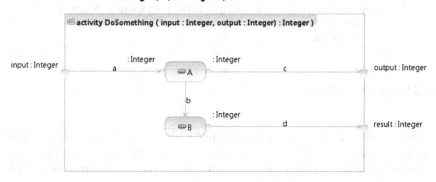

Fig. 2.7 Example of an activity

2.7.2 Action Language for Foundational UML

Action Language for Foundational UML (Alf) [156] is a textual representation for specifying executable fUML behaviors within a UML model. Such a text may specify only parts of a UML model, or it may specify an entire UML model, at least within the limits of the fUML subset [156]. The key components of Alf are: (1) An abstract syntax, which is a MOF meta-model that defines the concepts of Alf and their relationships, (2) a concrete syntax, which is a BNF specification for fUML model elements, (3) a semantics, which is defined by mapping Alf abstract syntax meta-model to fUML abstract syntax meta-model, and (4) a standard model library, which consists of primitive types and behaviors from fUML model library, collection functions similar to OCL ones, and collection classes such as Set, List, etc. In addition of being a standard, Alf is highly expressive and provides a compact representation for specifying precise and detailed behaviors. Alf is composed of three main constructs:

- *Expressions*: An expression is a behavioral unit that evaluates to a (possibly empty) collection of values. Expressions may also have side effects, such as changing the value of an attribute of an object. Alf expressions may be used in any place where a UML value specification may be defined. For example, they may be used as the body of a UML opaque expression or may be compiled into an equivalent UML activity to act as the specification of such an expression.
- *Statements*: A statement is a behavior that is executed for its effect and does not have values. Statements are the primary units of sequencing and control in Alf. Alf statements may be used to define the detailed behavior of a UML action or a complete UML behavior within a UML model.

```
Activity DoSomething(in input : Integer, out output : Integer) : Integer {
        output = A(input);
        return B();
}
```

Fig. 2.8 Example of Alf code

- *Units*: A unit is a namespace defined using Alf notation. Units are lexically independent segments of Alf text that provide a level of granularity similar to typical
  programming language text files [156]. Alf units may be used to represent a model
  element, e.g., class and activity, within a UML model, or may be used to represent
  an entire UML model.

The execution semantics of Alf is given by mapping Alf abstract syntax to fUML.
The result of executing an Alf code is thus given by the semantics of the fUML model
to which it is mapped [156]. Figure 2.8[2] shows an example of Alf code, which has
the same execution semantics as the fUML model presented in Fig. 2.7.

2.8 Conclusion

UML was defined as a unified language and notation to specify, construct, visualize,
and document models of software systems. It is considered the de facto standard
language for software specification and design. In this chapter, we have presented
an overview of UML language. We mainly presented the UML structure, the $4 + 1$
view model, and the different UML diagrams. We have seen that there is a wide
range of UML diagrams with different capabilities. It is possible to see that each
diagram has a different purpose and a precise strength for particular tasks inside
the software development process. Choosing the right set of diagrams to model a
system is very important to make the design understandable and approachable [198].
Additionally, we have presented an overview of the main standard ways of extending
UML language to customize it to a particular domain.

---

[2] http://www.omg.org/news/meetings/tc/agendas/va/xUML_pdf/Seidewitz_Tutorial.pdf.

Chapter 3
Aspect-Oriented Paradigm

Object-Oriented Programming (OOP) has become the dominant programming paradigm during the last few decades. It introduced the idea of using *objects* to represent different components of a given system by breaking down a problem into separate objects, and having each object grouping together data and behaviors into a single entity. Such an approach aids in writing complex applications while maintaining comprehensible source code [77]. However,some requirements do not decompose efficiently into a single entity, and thus scatter in various places in the application source code. To this end, Aspect-Oriented Programming is introduced to solve this issue and separately allows for the specification of the different concerns of a system [77].

Aspect-Oriented Programming (AOP) [114] is based on the idea of *separation of cross-cutting concerns*. In other words, it separately specifies the different concerns that cross-cut the application source code in many places, and then defines a mechanism, called *weaving*, to compose the different parts into a coherent program. These concerns may vary depending on the application domain; they can be functional or non-functional, they may be high-level or low-level features. The objective of aspect-orientation is to realize these scattered concerns into single elements, called *aspects*, and eject them from the various locations of the program [77]. AOP techniques have emerged into various families of programming languages. They can be defined over different languages, such as C, C++, PHP, and Java.

Many approaches were proposed in the literature to achieve the goals of AOP, such as *Pointcut-Advice* [131], *Multi-Dimensional Separation of Concerns* [159], and *Adaptive Programming* [158] models. According to the study conducted in [33], the pointcut-advice model is the most appropriate one for security hardening.

The remainder of this chapter is organized as follows. In Sect. 3.1, we present an overview of the main AOP models. In Sect. 3.2, we discuss the appropriateness of these AOP models from a security perspective. Section 3.3 presents the main constructs of the pointcut-advice model. Section 3.4 introduces the main concepts of AOM. Finally, Sect. 3.5 concludes this chapter.

© Springer International Publishing Switzerland 2015
D. Mouheb et al., *Aspect-Oriented Security Hardening of UML Design Models*,
DOI 10.1007/978-3-319-16106-8_3

3.1 AOP Models

Various AOP models have been proposed to achieve the goals of AOP. The most important ones are: Pointcut-Advice [131], Multi-Dimensional Separation of Concerns [159], and Adaptive Programming [158] models. In the following, an overview of each model is presented.

3.1.1 Pointcut-Advice Model

The fundamental concepts of the pointcut-advice model are: join points, pointcuts, and advices. A join point is an event during the execution of a program such as a method call or a method execution. A pointcut is an expression that designates a set of join points. An advice is a piece of code specifying how the behavior of an application should be adapted at specific points. Advice code can be executed before, after, or around a specific join point. Before-advice and after-advice are executed before and after the intercepted join point, respectively. Whereas, around-advice executes in place of the intercepted join point. Moreover, the computation of the original join point can be executed within the body of the around-advice using a special construct named proceed. AspectJ [113] is the most known representative of the pointcut-advice model. Figure 3.1 shows a tracing aspect written in AspectJ where the pointcut ptrace picks out any call to any method. Before-advice and after-advice are used to display the start time and the end time respectively.

Around-advice must be declared with a return type, like a method because it is allowed to return a value. Within the body of around-advice, the computation of the original join point can be executed with the special syntax proceed(...). The proceed form takes as arguments the context exposed by the pointcut of the around-advice, and returns whatever the around-advice is declared to return. Accordingly, the around-advice, shown in Fig. 3.2, doubles the second argument to foo whenever it is called, and then halves its result.

```
public aspect TracingAspect
{
  pointcut ptrace(): call (* *.*(..));
  before(): ptrace()
  {
    System.out.println(" Start Time: "+System.currentTimeMillis());
  }
  after(): ptrace()
  {
    System.out.println(" End Time: "+System.currentTimeMillis());
  }
}
```

Fig. 3.1 AspectJ tracing example

```
aspect A
{
 int around(int i): call(int C.foo(Object,int)) && args(i)
   {
    int newi = proceed(i*2)
    return newi/2;
    }
  }
```

Fig. 3.2 AspectJ around-advice with proceed

Matching is the process of selecting the join points that satisfy a given pointcut expression. Whereas, weaving is the process of injecting the advice behaviour specified in the aspect at the identified join points. Commonly, the inputs to the weaving process are the application and the aspect programs, and the produced result is the combined programs. Figure 3.3 shows a high-level representation of an aspect and the result of the weaving process.

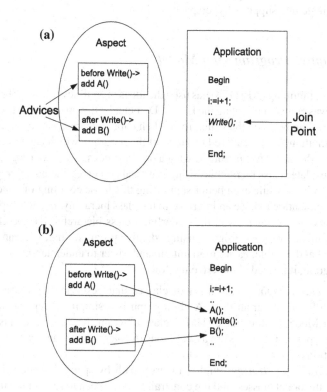

Fig. 3.3 Example of an aspect. **a** Before weaving. **b** After weaving

3.1.2 Multi-Dimensional Separation of Concerns Model

Separation of concerns aims to identify, encapsulate, and manipulate those parts of software that are relevant to a particular concept. Traditionally, most languages and modularization approaches support only one dominant kind of modularization, e.g., class in object-oriented languages. However, one needs different decompositions according to different concerns at different times. Then, once a system has been decomposed, extensive refactoring and reengineering are needed to remodularize it [159]. Multi-Dimensional Separation of Concerns (MDSOC) [159] allows simultaneous separation according to multiple, arbitrary kinds (dimensions) of concerns, with on-demand remodularization. The latter allows a developer to choose, at any time, the best modularization, based on any or all of the concerns, for the development task at hand. At the same time,these concerns can overlap and interact. This model treats all concerns as first-class and co-equal, including components and aspects,allowing them to be encapsulated and composed at will. This is in contrast to most aspect-oriented models, which enable aspects to be composed with components but do not support composition of components (or aspects) with one another. Hyperspaces constitute an approach to achieve MDSOC. HyperJ [160] is the most known language that supports hyperspaces in Java.

3.1.3 Adaptive Programming Model

Adaptive programming (AP) [158] has used the ideas of AOP several years before the name AOP was coined. Following the Law of Demeter [20], a programming style rule for loose coupling between the structure and behavior concerns, can result in a large number of small methods scattered throughout the program, which can make it hard to understand the high-level picture of what a program does. Adaptive programming, which encapsulates class hierarchies using traversal strategies and adaptive visitors, avoids this problem while even better supporting this loose coupling of concerns. It enables an application to have an interface to the class hierarchy, i.e., the application is not sensitive to the changes in the underlying class hierarchy. By specifying as little as possible about your program using adaptive programming, you can make it more general and flexible, easier to maintain, and easier to understand.

In a program, it is needed to derive the following:

- *Derive a class graph*: Create a set of classes that best captures the necessary structure of your program data. A class graph is a simplified representation of a Unified Modeling Language (UML) class diagram. Its nodes are classes and primitive types and its edges are associations (has-a relations) and generalizations (is-a relations).
- *Derive a traversal strategy*: Find a traversal path by specifying the root of the traversal, the target classes, and the constraints in between to restrict the traversal.
- *Derive a visitor method*: Attach specific behavior to certain classes that are visited along each traversal.

DJ [158] is a Java library for adaptive programming that allows traversal strategies to be constructed and interpreted dynamically at runtime. DJ allows traversing a graph object according to the traversal strategy and allows specifying a visitor to be executed before or after specific nodes.

3.2 AOP and Security

Several approaches have investigated the use of AOP for security. These approaches can be categorized into the following groups: (1) languages targeting security [22, 23, 120], (2) case studies that explore the usefulness of AOP for developing and injecting security concerns into software code [49, 101, 171, 187, 207], and (3) new security-related pointcuts to enrich the expressiveness of the join point model [37, 122, 130]. Moreover, an appropriateness analysis study of the most used AOP models from a security point of view has been conducted in [33]. The studied models are the pointcut-advice, the multi-dimensional separation of concerns, and the adaptive programming models.

All the aforementioned AOP models are candidates to separate crosscutting concerns in general but a model might be more appropriate than another when it comes to security hardening. In this respect, the authors in [33] have analyzed common practices in security hardening inspired from CERT coding rules [18, 19, 21] and US Department of Homeland Security coding rules [24] where they are representations of knowledge gained from real-world experiences about potential vulnerabilities that exist in programming languages. The expressiveness of the aforementioned AOP models is challenged to describe these practices. Depending on this analysis, the following results have been concluded.

The MDSOC has a serious limitation from a security perspective. It does not allow adding a functionality before, after, or around field accesses. Authorization to a given field in a given class is a simple security example that we cannot handle with HyperJ [160], which is a representative for the MDSOC model. The MDSOC model works at method granularity and consequently it cannot operate within method bodies. HyperJ does not support pulling apart of code within method bodies. Picking out multiple concerns within method bodies is required in many situations to enforce security. The adaptive programming is concerned with the loose coupling between structure and behavior and focuses on certain kinds of concerns. DJ [158], which is a representative for adaptive programming model, is unable to replace a method by a more secure one.

The pointcut-advice model is the most popular model. It offers better granularity than MDSOC and considers more general kinds of concerns than the adaptive programming. Furthermore, the pointcut-advice model extensively adapts the pull approach. It allows tracking subtle points in the control flow of applications that are important from a security point of view, such as method calls, method executions, getting and setting of attributes, etc. In addition, security behavior can be

automatically injected at these points. Hence, the pointcut-advice model was identified as the most appropriate approach for security hardening.

3.3 Basic Constructs of the Pointcut-Advice Model

As mentioned previously, the pointcut-advice model is considered the most
appropriate approach for security hardening. In this section, we explain the basic
concepts of this model through AspectJ language [113], which is the most known
representative of this model. The pointcut-advice model is based on the following
set of constructs:

3.3.1 Aspects

Aspects are elements that encapsulate concerns that cross-cut the core components
of a given application. It is composed of two kinds of crosscutting elements: (1)
Dynamic crosscutting, which defines additional behaviour to run at certain well-
defined points in the execution of programs, and (2) static crosscutting, which defines
elements that affect the static type signature of programs. Similar to a Java class, an
aspect can contain both fields and methods but it cannot be explicitly instantiated.

3.3.2 Join Points

A join point is a well-defined point in the execution of a program. A join point model
provides a common frame of reference that makes it possible to define the dynamic
structure of crosscutting concerns. Different kinds of join points are supported in
AspectJ language, as shown in Table 3.1.

3.3.3 Pointcuts

A pointcut is an expression that picks out join points and exposes data from the
execution context of those join points. Pointcuts are used primarily by advice.
They can be composed with boolean operators (&&, ||, and !) to build up other
pointcuts. For instance, the pointcut designator `call(void Point.f(int))`
matches all method call join points where the signature of the called method is
`void Point.f(int)`. AspectJ supports both named and anonymous pointcuts.
Named pointcuts are declared with the keyword `pointcut` and can be referred to
by its name in several places in an aspect. Anonymous pointcuts cannot be referred
to because they have no names. The primitive pointcuts provided by the language

Table 3.1 AspectJ join points

Joinpoint	Meaning
Method call	Matches when a method is called, not including super calls of non-static methods
Method execution	Matches when the body of code for an actual method executes
Constructor call	Matches when an object is built and that object's initial constructor is called
Constructor execution	Matches when the body of code for an actual constructor executes, after its this or super constructor call
Static initializer execution	Matches when the static initializer for a class executes
Object pre-initialization	Before the object initialization code for a particular class runs. This encompasses the time between the start of its first called constructor and the start of its parent's constructor
Object initialization	Matches when the object initialization code for a particular class runs. This encompasses the time between the return of its parent's constructor and the return of its first called constructor
Field reference	Matches when a non-constant field is referenced
Field set	Matches when a field is assigned to
Exception-handler	Matches when an exception handler executes
Advice execution	Matches when the body of code for a piece of advice executes

are presented in Table 3.2 following the documentation on the Eclipse site [162]. The patterns used as parts of the syntax of AspectJ pointcuts are described in Fig. 3.4.

In many cases, the AspectJ compiler can determine statically if a piece of advice should be executed at all the matched join points. In these cases, no dynamic test is required to determine if the advice code should be executed or not. On the other hand, there are cases where static analysis cannot determine the applicability of the advice as in the case of the cflow pointcut. In such a situation, residual testing code is added to guard the execution of the advice. The aforementioned AspectJ pointcuts can be classified into three types:

- Kinded pointcuts match directly a granular bytecode instruction or a set of bytecode instructions. For instance, a call pointcut matches the invoke bytecode instructions and an execution pointcut matches a bounded region of bytecode instructions in a method or a constructor execution.
- Scope matching pointcuts target a set of join points within a certain scope in the program. There are two kinds of scopes: a static scope and a dynamic scope. A static scope is a syntactic location in a program such as a class or a package. The dynamic scope is a location in the control flow of a method call or a method execution. The aim of such pointcuts is to restrict join point location lookup inside a program. The pointcuts that belong to this class are *within*, *withincode* and *cflow*.
- Context matching pointcuts focus on providing contextual information such as object values during runtime. These pointcuts are generally used in conjunction with kinded pointcuts. The pointcuts that belong to this class are: *args*, *target* and *this*.

Table 3.2 AspectJ pointcuts

Pointcut	Meaning
call(*MethodPat*)	Picks out each method call join point whose signature matches *MethodPat*
execution(*MethodPat*)	Picks out each method execution join point whose signature matches *MethodPat*
call(*ConstructorPat*)	Picks out each constructor call join point whose signature matches *ConstructorPat*
execution(*ConstructorPat*)	Picks out each constructor execution join point whose signature matches *ConstructorPat*
staticinitialization(*TypePat*)	Picks out each static initializer execution join point whose signature matches *TypePat*
preinitialization(*ConstructorPat*)	Picks out each object pre-initialization join point whose signature matches *ConstructorPat*
initialization(*ConstructorPat*)	Picks out each object initialization join point whose signature matches *ConstructorPat*
get(*FieldPat*)	Picks out each field reference join point whose signature matches *FieldPat*
set(*FieldPat*)	Picks out each field set join point whose signature matches *FieldPat*
handler(*TypePat*)	Picks out each exception handler join point whose signature matches *TypePat*
adviceexecution( )	Picks out all advice execution join points
within(*TypePat*)	Picks out each join point where the executing code is defined in a type matched by *TypePat*
withincode(*MethodPat*)	Picks out each join point where the executing code is defined in a method whose signature matches *MethodPat*
withincode(*ConstructorPat*)	Picks out each join point where the executing code is defined in a constructor whose signature matches *ConstructorPat*
cflow(*Pointcut*)	Picks out each join point in the control flow of any join point *j* picked out by *Pointcut*, including *j* itself
cflowbelow(*Pointcut*)	Picks out each join point in the control flow of any join point *j* picked out by (*Pointcut*), but not *j* itself
this(*Type* or *Id*)	Picks out each join point where the currently executing object is an instance of *Type* or of the type of the identifier *Id*
target(*Type* or *Id*)	Picks out each join point where the target object is an instance of *Type*, or of the type of the identifier *Id*
args(*Type* or *Id*, ...)	Picks out each join point where the arguments are instances of *Type* or type of the identifier *Id*
if(*BooleanExpression*)	Picks out each join point where the boolean expression evaluates to true

MethodPat	::= [*ModifiersPat*] *TypePat* [*TypePat*.] *IdPat* (*TypePat*|.., ...) [throws *ThrowsPat*]
ConstructPat	::= [*ModifiersPat*] [*TypePat*.] new (*TypePat*|.., ...) [throws *ThrowsPat*]
FieldPat	::= [*ModifiersPat*] *TypePat* [*TypePat*.] *IdPat*
TypePat	::= *IdPat* [+] [[] ...] | ! *TypePat* | *TypePat* && *TypePat* | *TypePat* || *TypePat* | (*TypePat*)

Fig. 3.4 AspectJ pointcut patterns

3.3.4 Advices

Advice is a method-like construct used to declare that certain piece of code should execute at particular join points defined by a pointcut. Advice declarations define advice by associating code with a pointcut, and the time when the code should be executed. AspectJ supports before-advice, after-advice, and around-advice. Before-advice runs when a join point is reached but before a program proceeds with this join point. After-advice runs after a program proceeds with a join point. While before-advice is relatively unproblematic, there can be three interpretations of after-advice: after the execution of a join point completes normally, after it throws an exception, or after it does either one. AspectJ allows after-advice for any of these situations. Before-advice and after-advice are strictly additive, meaning the code in the advice declaration runs just before or just after the normal computation at a join point. On the other hand, around-advice provides a way to preempt the normal computation at a join point and to continue a program just after it. Within the body of the around-advice, the computation of the original join point can be executed with the special syntax proceed(...). Each piece of advice is of the form

[strictfp] *AdviceSpec* [throws *TypeList*]: *Pointcut* {*Body*}

The strictfp modifier is the only modifier allowed on advice. It has the effect of making all floating-point expressions within the advice be FP-strict. An advice declaration must include a throws clause listing the checked exceptions the body may throw. This list of checked exceptions must be compatible with each target join point of the advice, or an error is signalled by the compiler. The forms of *AdviceSpec* are:

- before(*Formals*)
- after(*Formals*) returning [(*Formal*)]

- after(*Formals*) throwing [(*Formal*)]
- after(*Formals*)
- *Type* around(*Formals*)

where *Formal* refers to a variable binding like those used for method parameters of the form (*Type Variable-Name*) whereas *Formals* refers to a comma-delimited list of *Formals*. Since more than one piece of advice may apply at the same join point, the programmer can explicitly define a precedence order between aspects.

3.3.5 Introductions

Up until now, we have only seen constructs that allow implementing dynamic crosscuttings that change the way a program executes. AspectJ also allows implementing static crosscuttings that affect the static structure of programs. This is done using forms called introduction. An introduction is a member of an aspect, but it defines or modifies a member of another type (class). With introduction we can:

- Add methods to an existing class.
- Add fields to an existing class.
- Extend an existing class with another.
- Implement an interface in an existing class.
- Convert checked exceptions into unchecked exceptions.

Introduction is a powerful mechanism for capturing crosscutting concerns because it does not only change the behavior of components in an application, but also changes their relationships.

3.4 Aspect-Oriented Modeling

Due to the rise of Model-Driven Engineering, aspect-oriented techniques are no longer restricted to the programming stage, but are increasingly adopted at prior stages of the software development life cycle. In this context, Aspect-Oriented Modeling (AOM) aims at applying AOP mechanisms at the modeling level, which encompasses requirements engineering, analysis, and design stages [31].

The concepts of AOM are similar to the ones of AOP, namely:

- An aspect is a unit of modularization that encapsulates a cross-cutting concern of an application. Typically, an aspect contains a set of adaptations, specifying in what way a concern's structure and behavior should be adapted, i.e., enhanced, replaced, or deleted
- An adaptation specifies the modification to be performed on the base model. We distinguish between structural and behavioural adaptations. A structural adaptation is similar to an introduction in AOP languages (e.g., AspectJ) in the sense that it

affects the structural part of a software system. A behavioral adaptation is similar to an advice in AOP languages since it affects the behavioral part of a system.
- A join point is a location in the base model where an adaptation should be applied.
- A pointcut is an expression that designates a set of join points.

3.5 Conclusion

In this chapter, we have reviewed the main concepts of aspect-oriented programming and discussed the most-used AOP models, namely the pointcut-advice model, the multi- dimensional separation of concerns model, and the adaptive programming model. Following the success of AOP techniques in modularizing crosscutting concerns at the implementation level, various contributions worked on abstracting the AOP concepts and adopting them to the design level as well. Moreover, the applicability of aspect-oriented techniques to specify security requirements and hardening mechanisms has been heavily studied in the literature both at the design and implementation levels. In this context, we have discussed the appropriateness of the AOP models from a security point of view. The pointcut-advice model is considered the most appropriate one for security hardening. As such, we have presented an overview of the main constructs of this model, namely, join points, pointcuts, advices and introductions.

Chapter 4
Model-Driven Architecture and Model Transformations

Model Driven Architecture (MDA) [148] is a well-known approach that facilitates the development of software systems. It is an OMG initiative to Model-Driven Engineering (MDE), with the goal of separating business decisions from underlying platform technologies. Model transformation is the process of converting one model to another model of the same system [148]. This process takes, as input, one or more models that conform to specific meta-models, and produces, as output, one or more models that conform to specific meta-models. The goal underlying the use of a model transformation is to save time and efforts and reduce errors by automating the modification of models as much as possible. Model transformation is an essential part of MDA. In this context, model transformations are mainly used to convert a model of a certain layer into another layer, such as transforming a platform-independent model into a platform-specific model. However, model transformations are also useful for transforming models within the same layer, such as to perform model weaving as we will see in Chap. 7.

Within the MDA approach, model transformation can be divided into two categories: Model-to-Model transformation (M2M) and Model-to-Text transformation (M2T) [148]. The former is used to transform models from PIM (Platform-Independent Model) level to PSM (Platform-Specific Model) level, while the latter is used to transform models from PSM level to code level. In this research, we are interested in the first type, i.e., model-to-model transformation. Thus, throughout this book, when we say model transformation we are referring to model-to-model transformation in particular.

A model transformation is specified as a set of mappings. Each mapping consists of a set of refinements of model elements, addition of further details to a model, or conversion between different kinds of models. There are four different transformation approaches [148]: (1) Manual transformation, (2) transformation using a UML profile, (3) transformation using patterns and markings, and (4) automatic transformation using tools and transformation languages. In this research, we are interested in the automatic transformation.

Many classifications of model transformation approaches exist in the literature [63,135,186]. Some classify them according to the nature of the transformation

© Springer International Publishing Switzerland 2015
D. Mouheb et al., *Aspect-Oriented Security Hardening of UML Design Models*,
DOI 10.1007/978-3-319-16106-8_4

language, whether it is declarative, imperative, or hybrid (combination of declarative and imperative). Others base the classification on the techniques used to implement such transformation. Either by direct manipulation of the model using general purpose programming language, or by dealing with some intermediate representation of the model, or by using dedicated model transformation languages or meta-modeling languages.

Czarnecki and Helsen [63] provide a classification of model transformation approaches that has been adopted by many people in the software engineering community. In the following, we give a summary of their classification while pointing out the strengths and limitations of each approach.

- *Direct Manipulation Approach*: This approach adopts object-oriented techniques to transform models using general purpose programming language, such as Java. This programming language will manipulate the internal representation of the models using specialized application programming interfaces (APIs). Since this approach uses any general purpose object-oriented language, the overhead of learning new language is minimal. However, since the language is not specially designed to handle model transformation, many properties and features, such as scheduling processes, are implemented from scratch.
- *Relational Approach*: This approach is considered a declarative approach where the types of the source and target elements need to be explicitly specified along with a constrained relation between them. Thus, this approach does not allow in-place transformation. One implementation of this approach is the use of logical programming languages. In relational approaches, target elements are created implicitly, unlike the first approach where target elements need to be explicitly created. For instance, when the transformation is executed the different relations are verified and then the target model contents are automatically created [64].
- *Graph Transformation Based Approach*: It is a declarative approach based on the theoretical work done on graph transformation. It depends on two patterns, left hand side (LHS), and right hand side (RHS) patterns. The LHS pattern is used as a matching pattern against the model we need to transform. While the RHS pattern will replace the matched patterns in that model. The main limitation is the non-determinism of rule scheduling [107] as we will explain in Sect. 4.6.
- *Structure Driven Approach*: The structure driven approach consist of two phases. The first phase where the hierarchical structure of the target model is being created. The second phase where we set the different attributes and references in the target model. In this approach, the user specifies the transformation rules, however, he/she does not have any control over the rule scheduling as it is determined by the framework. OptimalJ [7] is an example of an implementation of the structure driven approach.
- *Hybrid Approach*: The hybrid approach is a combination of any of the previously mentioned approaches. For example, the standard language QVT [150] is considered a hybrid approach as it contains three components such that two of them adopt a relational approach, while the third is operational. Another example of a hybrid approach is ATL [1] where a single ATL transformation rule may be fully declarative, hybrid, or fully imperative.

In this chapter, we explore the area of model transformation presented by the Object Management Group (OMG) as part of the MDA framework in [148]. First, in Sect. 4.1, we describe the main MDA layers. In Sect. 4.2, we recall the main benefits of using the MDA approach. Afterwards, we provide an overview of the different kinds of MDA transformations in Sect. 4.3. In Sect. 4.4, the different applications of model transformations in different domains are described. In Sect. 4.5, the different model transformation languages and tools are studied. Finally, we summarize this chapter in Sect. 4.7.

4.1 MDA Layers

The MDA approach defines four layers that aim at separating the application logic from any underlying technology platform. These layers are defined as follows [148]:

4.1.1 Computation Independent Model (CIM)

CIM model captures the user requirements and specifies what functionalities the system should have without indicating any information about how it will achieve these functionalities. In other words, at CIM level, the business requirements and the domain of the system are described and all the structural details and the information about the target platform are hidden as they are still undetermined.

4.1.2 Platform Independent Model (PIM)

PIM model is a business-oriented model that abstracts from platform issues, which can survive the different technology changes. Additionally, PIM model satisfies the main goals of MDA, portability and reusability. Moreover, at the PIM level, the focus is on the operation of the system while hiding all the details that are required for a particular platform. In other words, only the part of the specification that does not change from one platform to another is shown.

4.1.3 Platform Specific Model (PSM)

PSM is derived from the PIM level by adding some platform-specific characteristics to it. In this level, it is defined how the different functionalities in the PIM level are realized on a certain computing platform. It is important to mention that it is possible to generate multiple PSMs from one PIM, each of which corresponds to a different platform.

4.1.4 Implementation Specific Model (ISM)

ISM is the actual generation of the executable code. Since the PSM already contains all the details regarding the target platform, the generation of the code is somewhat straightforward.

4.2 MDA Benefits

Following the MDA approach, while developing software and systems, is beneficial in many ways. According to [203], the main advantages and benefits of using the MDA approach is to achieve the following:

- *Portability*: Within MDA, portability is achieved through the development of the PIM, which is, by definition, platform-independent. Using the PIM, and by providing the corresponding transformation rules, the same PIM can be transformed to multiple PSMs, hence, being portable from one platform to another.
- *Productivity*: In MDA, the focus of the developers is to design the PIM and from which the PSM and code will be automatically generated. Therefore, developers need not to worry about the implementation and platform details as they will be added later by the PIM to PSM transformation. According to [119], this can improve productivity in two ways: The developers will have less work to do as the details of the implementation do not require to be specified as they will be added later by the transformation definitions. Likewise, at the code level, the developers will have less code to write as most of the code will be automatically generated from the PIM and PSM levels. Therefore, by shifting the focus from writing code to designing PIMs, the developers will have the opportunity to pay more attention to solve the business problem at hand. To summarize, improving productivity requires the use of tools that can automate the transformations from PIM to PSM and later to code.
- *Cross-platform Interoperability*: Interoperability property defines the ability of different systems to inter-operate and work together. MDA makes the concept of cross-platform interoperability possible through the establishment of the PIM. In MDA, one PIM is used to generate multiple PSMs, each of which is targeting a different platform. Therefore, two different PSMs can interoperate as they both originate from the same PIM. This is made possible by building bridges and establishing links between the two PSMs. By having these bridges established, the two PSMs that are targeted for different platforms can actually communicate.
- *Maintenance and Documentation*: As the PIM is used to generate the PSM and the code afterwards, the generated code will be an exact representation of the model. Therefore, the PIM can be considered as a high-level documentation that is needed for any software system nowadays. However, the PIM will not be discarded after generating the code but it will be maintained so that any future modifications to the system will be made by modifying the PIM and regenerating the new PSM and code [119].

4.3 MDA Transformations

The MDA guide [148] defines model transformation as: "the process of converting one model to another model of the same system". This process takes as input one or more models that conforms to a specific meta-model and produces as output one or more models that conforms to a given meta-model. Additionally, it is important to mention that the transformation itself is also considered a model, i.e. it conforms to a given meta-model.

Moreover, when transforming a PIM into a particular PSM, the input to the transformation, along with the PIM, is a set of mapping rules that specify how each element in the PIM will be transformed to the target PSM. The result of the transformation along with the PSM is a record of transformation. The record of transformation contains a map from elements of the PIM to the corresponding elements of the PSM. Also, it shows which parts of the mapping were used for each part of the transformation.

When referring to model transformations, it is necessary to distinguish between two types of transformations: model-to-model and model-to-code transformation. Moreover, we usually refer to model-to-code transformations as model-to-text since non-code artifacts may be generated, such as XML and documentation [63].

In the following, we present some definitions and key concepts relevant to model transformations:

- *Endogenous and Exogenous transformations*: Endogenous transformations are transformations of models that conform to the same meta-model. In other words, both the input and output model(s) conform to the exact meta-model. On the other hand, exogenous transformations are transformations of models that conform to different meta-models [135].
- *In-Place, Unidirectional and Bidirectional transformations*: In-place transformation is a transformation that affects the same model. In other words, there is no source model and target model, but only one model that is being modified by the transformation. However, the unidirectional transformation must have source and target models where the target model is generated or updated based on the source model. In other words, the execution of the transformation can be done in one direction only. In contrast, bidirectional transformation is when the execution can be done in both directions, that is transform the source model to the target model and transform the target model to the source model [135].
- *Transformation Definition and Transformation Rules*: As mentioned previously, model transformation is the process of generating a target model from a source model. This transformation is specified in what is called transformation definition. Transformation definition consists of a set of rules, each of which specifies how the elements in the source model will be transformed into elements in the target model.
- *Horizontal and Vertical Transformation*: MDA supports two different directions of transformations; horizontal and vertical transformations. Horizontal transformations may occur inside a single layer of abstraction, that is, the level of abstraction

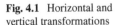 **Fig. 4.1** Horizontal and
vertical transformations

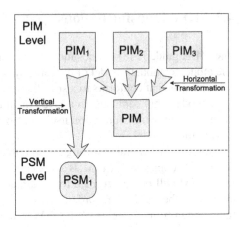

of the source and target model are always the same. For example, merging a group
of PIMs or PSMs together will result of a new model where its level of abstraction
remains the same. However, vertical transformation is when there is progression
from one level of abstraction to a more specialized level, such as going from PIM
level to PSM, where more information about a specific platform is added (Fig. 4.1).

4.4 Applications of Model Transformations

Model transformation (MT) has become a useful technique that can be incorporated
in various development methodologies. In this section, we highlight some important
scenarios of model transformations in different application domains.

In the context of Model Driven Software Development (MDSD) [190], a software
system is developed through an iterative modeling process where the system model
is refined repeatedly until it reaches a stage where sufficient details to implement the
system are specified [150]. The refinement process aims at transforming the system
from abstract models to more concrete ones.

Another example where model transformation becomes useful is when adopting
Aspect-Oriented Software Development (AOSD) methodology [41]. AOSD is an
emerging technology where the aim is to isolate non-functional requirements from
the system main functionalities. However, at some point these isolated concerns need
to be composed "woven" with the primary concern to produce a working system.
Similarly, in the context of Product Line Software Engineering (PLSE) [168], which
is a software development technology targeting the creation of a portfolio of closely
related products that share common assets with variations in features and functions.
In PLSE, the different features that compose a given product need to be integrated
together to produce the final product. This integration of different software features

can also be considered as a transformation process. Figure 4.2 illustrates the refinement and composition processes in different software development methodologies.

Moreover, software refactoring, code generation, and model translation are more examples of applications to model transformation. Software refactoring is a software transformation that preserves the software behavior, but enhances its internal structure such that it makes it easier to understand and maintain. Additionally, model translation is when the source model expressed in one language is transformed to another model expressed in different language; for example, transforming UML models to artifacts that can be analyzed formally using formal analysis tools [90]. Table 4.1 summarizes the examples of model transformation applications with the corresponding direction of the transformation.

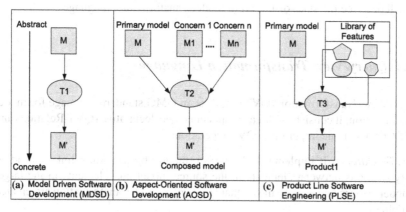

Fig. 4.2 Transformation examples

Table 4.1 Examples of model transformation

Example	Transformation direction
Software refinement (MDSD)	Vertical
Aspect weaving (AOSD)	Horizontal
Feature integration (PLSE)	Horizontal
Software refactoring	Horizontal
Code generation	Vertical
Model translation	Vertical

4.5 Model Transformation Languages and Tools

With the increasing interest in the MDA approach, many model transformation techniques and languages have been proposed. Model transformations can be achieved using different approaches, one approach suggests the use of APIs combined with a general purpose programming language. For example, the Java meta-data interface (JMI) [25] is one of the existing APIs that facilitates model access and manipulation. Using this method there is no overhead to learn a new language since known object-oriented languages can be used. However, since the language is not designed to handel model manipulation, all transformation rules and transformation scheduling must be implemented from scratch [107]. Therefore, transformation languages should be the solution as they have better performance and portability. In the sequel, we will describe the state-of-the-art in model transformation languages.

4.5.1 Query/View/Transformation Language

Query/View/Transformation (QVT) [150] is an OMG standard language for model transformation. It consists of three components: two declarative (QVT-Relations and QVT-Core) and one imperative (QVT-Operational):

- *QVT-Relations*: It implements the transformation by providing links that identify relations between elements in the source model and elements in the target model. Traces between elements that are involved in a transformation are created implicitly.
- *QVT-Core*: It is a small language that only supports pattern matching. Thus, its semantics can be defined in a simple way. However, QVT-Core does not have a full implementation and it is not as expressive as QVT-Relations.
- *QVT-Operational*: It is an imperative language that is designed for writing unidirectional transformations.

QVT-Relations and QVT-Core languages are good for simple transformations where the source model and the target model have a similar structure. However, when it comes to more sophisticated transformations where elements in the target model are built with no direct correspondence with elements in the source model, declarative languages can be a limitation. Thus, the need for an imperative language becomes a must. Therefore, QVT proposed the third language, which is QVT-Operational [108]. QVT integrates also OCL language that it extends with imperative features. The Eclipse modeling framework provides an implementation of QVT-Operational through its M2M open source project.[1] Unlike other tools and languages that only support some concepts of the QVT standard, Eclipse QVT-Operational (QVTO) implements the final adopted specification.

---

[1] http://projects.eclipse.org/projects/modeling.mmt.

4.5.2 Atlas Transformation Language

The Atlas Transformation Language (ATL) [1] is a hybrid language that is a mix of declarative and imperative constructs. It consists of three components: Atlas Model Weaver (AMW) [80], ATL, and ATL Virtual Machine. AMW creates links between model elements and saves them in a separate model, commonly referred to as the *weaving model*. ATL is the transformation language; it supports unidirectional transformations and it is used to write ATL programs, which are executed by the ATL virtual machine. ATL is not compliant with QVT, although, it implements similar concepts and functionalities.

4.5.3 Open Architecture Ware

Open Architecture Ware (oAW) [6] is a framework that supports model transformations using a language called *Xtend*.[2] The latter supports transformation of models by running a sequence of statements. These statements are called within a workflow and executed by a workflow engine. Moreover, oAW provides special support for aspect-orientation [114] through a model weaver called XWeave [97].

4.5.4 IBM Model Transformation Framework

IBM Model Transformation Framework (MTF) [70] allows the specification of model transformations as a set of relations between models. These relations are expressed using a language called Relation Definition Language (RDL) [70]. For example, a relation can be established between classes that have a matching attribute. These relations are then parsed and evaluated by a transformation engine. MTF supports bi-directional transformations, i.e., transforming the source model to the target model and vice versa.

4.5.5 Kermeta

Kermeta [17] is a modeling and programming language for meta-model engineering. It is considered the first executable meta-language that can be used for different purposes, such as model and meta-model prototyping and simulation, verification and validation of models against meta-models, model transformations, and aspect weaving [17].

---

[2] http://www.eclipse.org/xtend/.

4.6 Comparative Study of Model Transformation Languages

The field of model transformation is relatively new and thus the support for transformation languages is increasing through time. In the previous subsections, we highlighted some of the existing transformation approaches and languages while pointing out the different features that each of them provide.

As our objective in this research work is to provide a methodology for automatic integration of security concerns "aspects" into design models, the technology of model transformation can be of a great value. Moreover, one of the great challenges we faced was to select the appropriate language from the pool of available transformation languages that best suits our needs. To do so, we identify some characteristics that are desirable in the transformation language. The following is a description of these characteristics:

Transformation Approach: While studying the existing transformation languages, we found them to be either declarative, imperative, object-oriented, or hybrid. Declarative languages are good for simple transformation that is based on establishing relations between the input and output models. Imperative languages are more suited for complex transformations as they describe the different steps that need to be executed to transform the source model into the target model. Hybrid languages are those who combine both declarative and imperative constructs. Indeed, the process of weaving aspects into base models is not always based on establishing direct relations between the models. In fact, it may require complex operations that declarative languages fail to achieve. Thus, imperative or perhaps hybrid approaches will give us more expressiveness in terms of language constructs when dealing with aspects weaving.

Rule Scheduling: It is the order in which transformation rules are applied on the models while executing the transformation. As defined in [63], rule scheduling in transformation languages can be categorized as follows: (1) *Implicit scheduling*, which is based on the implicit relations between rules, (2) *Explicit scheduling*, which is based on explicit specification of rule ordering. Additionally, explicit scheduling can be further classified into *explicit internal* and *explicit external* scheduling. While the former is defined using explicit rule invocations, the latter depends on defining the scheduling logic outside the transformation rules by the means of some special language. Furthermore, in the context of aspect weaving, we need to have full control over the order in which the rules are applied. Such control will help in handling different issues, such as conflicting advices where the application of one advice depends on the application of the other.

Traceability Support: The tool has to provide support for traceability between models. It should provide a trace record that shows links between elements in the source model to elements in the target model. This is important to be able to track what aspect applied what modification on the base model. In addition, traceability is of high value for documentation purposes.

Standardization: The Object Management Group (OMG) defined QVT (Query/ View/Transformation) as a standard language for model transformations. It is important to choose a language that is based on a standard and thus support all other relevant

Table 4.2 Comparison of model transformation languages and tools

Language/Tool	Approach	Rule scheduling	Traceability	Standardization
QVTO	Imperative	Explicit internal	Yes	Yes
ATL	Hybrid	Explicit internal	Yes	No
OAW	Imperative	Explicit external	No	No
MTF	Declarative	Implicit	Yes	No
Kermeta	Imperative	Explicit internal	No	No
Graph-based language	Declarative	Explicit external	No	No
General-purpose programming language	Imperative	Explicit internal	No	No

standards, such as UML, MOF, OCL, etc. This will provide portability for the weaver through different UML case tools, which provide support for OMG standards.

Table 4.2 summarizes the different transformation languages. By comparing the different languages/tools with regards to the aforementioned characteristics, we conclude that QVTO is the best language to use as it meets our needs for model weaving.

4.7 Conclusion

In this chapter, we have presented the background related to MDA and model transformations. We have shown the benefits of such technology through its different applications in various domains. Moreover, we have presented an overview of existing transformation languages and tools. Additionally, a comparison between these tools with respect to a set of defined criteria is presented. As a result, we have decided to use *QVT Operational* as the adopted language in our approach.

Chapter 5
Model-Based Security

This chapter presents the background related to security at the modeling level. We start in Sect. 5.1 by investigating security specification approaches for UML design. Three main approaches have been adopted in literature for security specification: (1) using UML artifacts, (2) extending UML meta-language, and (3) creating a new meta-language. In Sect. 5.2, we evaluate the usability of these approaches for security specification according to a set of defined criteria. Afterwards, in Sect. 5.3, we overview the main design mechanisms that are typically adopted for security hardening at the modeling level. These are security design patterns, mechanism-directed meta-languages, and aspect-oriented modeling. We also highlight the challenges related to the use of these mechanisms in UML design. In Sect. 5.4, we present the research contributions that address security specification and hardening in UML design. Finally, we conclude this chapter by a discussion on the relevance of these mechanisms for security hardening.

5.1 Security Specification for UML Design

There are three main approaches that are usually adopted for security specification in UML: using UML artifacts, extending UML meta-language, and creating a new meta-language. Thus, a subsection is dedicated to present each approach and show how it can be used for security specification.

5.1.1 Security Specification Using UML Artifacts

In this section, we show how stereotypes and tagged values, OCL, and behavior diagrams can be used for security specification and design.

© Springer International Publishing Switzerland 2015
D. Mouheb et al., *Aspect-Oriented Security Hardening of UML Design Models*,
DOI 10.1007/978-3-319-16106-8_5

5.1.1.1 Stereotypes and Tagged Values

Description: *Stereotypes* are provided as a mechanism for extending UML meta-language. Therefore, a stereotype is considered as a user-defined meta-element. Its structure matches the structure of an existing UML meta-element which is referred to as "base class". In that sense, a stereotype represents a subclass (subtype) of the base class. It has the same form but with a different intent. A stereotype can have tagged values used to define the additional information needed to specify the new stereotype intent. Besides, constraints can be defined on both the base class attributes as well as the tagged values. Code generators and other tools, such as those used for verification and validation, reserve special treatment to stereotypes.

Use for Security Specification: Security requirements are specified by attaching stereotypes along with their associated tagged values to selected elements of the design (e.g., subsystems, classes, etc.). Thus, a "security" profile should be created by some security expert for the specification of these stereotypes. The compiler used to parse the UML diagram is then modified such that it can read and interpret the stereotypes annotating the design. This interpretation consists in generating a formal representation of the security requirement corresponding to the security annotation. This security requirement is generated on the basis of the intent of the security expert while taking into consideration the specificities of the analyzed design. In addition, a formal semantics is associated with the design. Then, the formal security requirement together with the formal semantics are provided as inputs to a verification tool (usually a model checker or a theorem prover). The result of verifying the security requirement on the design is translated into some representation that non-security expert developer can understand. Some stereotypes are parameterized over the adversary type. These stereotypes are used to specify security properties that need to be verified against a specification of an attacker (adversary). Faire exchange, secrecy,

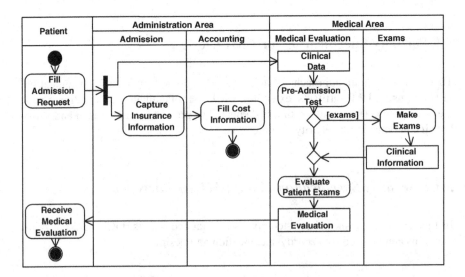

Fig. 5.1 An activity diagram: admission of patients in a medical institution

and authenticity are examples of these properties. The adversary type specifies the adversary's computation capabilities and initial knowledge.

Figure 5.2 shows how stereotypes can be used to specify security requirements on UML design of Fig. 5.1. The used stereotypes are Privacy, Auditing, Access Control, Critical, Integrity, and NonRepud. For example, the stereotype Privacy is attached to the Patient partition to specify that unauthorized disclosure of sensitive information about the patient is not permitted.

5.1.1.2 Object Constraint Language (OCL)

Description: OCL is a formal language used to express constraints over UML diagrams. These constraints mainly specify those conditions that must be satisfied by the system being modeled. OCL is mainly used to specify application-specific requirements for UML models. In addition, it is used to specify invariants of UML meta-language. More precisely, the main purposes for which OCL can be used are the followings: (1) to specify invariants on classes and types in the meta-language, (2) to specify type invariant for Stereotypes, (3) to describe pre and post conditions on operations and methods, and (4) to describe guards [153].

Use for Security Specification: Since OCL is a language for constraints specification, it is natural to be used for security specification. According to the main usability purposes listed above, OCL has been used for security specification following three main directions. First, for the security profiles extending UML for security

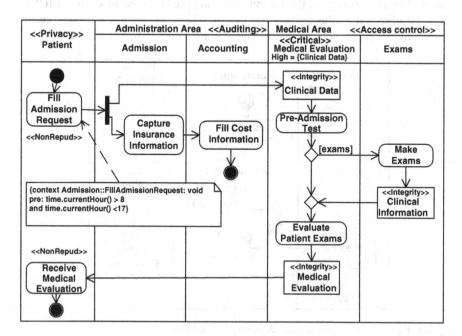

Fig. 5.2 An example of specifying security using stereotypes

specification, OCL is used to define constraints on elements described by stereotypes and tagged values. Second, for those stereotypes used for the specification of
access control properties, OCL can be used by the designer to define access control constraints (preconditions and authorization guards). Third, some OCL extensions [214] allow the specification of temporal logic formulas and thus are used
to specify security requirements in temporal logics, e.g., LTL, CTL, etc. Figure 5.2
shows how OCL can be used to specify a constraint on the action "Fill admission
request". This constraint restricts the execution of this action to working hours. This
will protect the system from malicious use during nights. The condition starts by
specifying its context, i.e., the method on which it is applied, which is the method
`FillAdmissionRequest` of the class `Admission`. Then the constraint specifies the precondition to be satisfied before executing the controlled method.

5.1.1.3 Behavior Diagrams

Description: Behavior diagrams are UML diagrams used to depict the behavioral
features of the system under design. These include activity, state machine, and use
case diagrams as well as four interaction diagrams. The later are those diagrams
used to specify interactions between objects inside the system. Interaction diagrams
include communication, interaction overview, sequence, and timing diagrams.
Use for Security Specification: Behavior diagrams can be used for security specification in two ways. The first one is to specify the behavior that 'MUST' be
observed by the system and the second one is to specify the behavior that 'MUST
NOT' be observed by the system. The later has been investigated by some recent
contributions [215] where the used diagrams are called "Abuse cases diagrams".

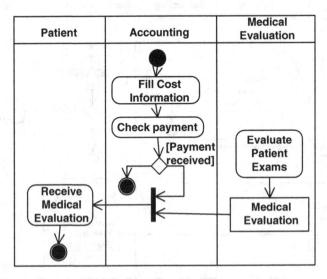

Fig. 5.3 Fair exchange requirement inside medical applications

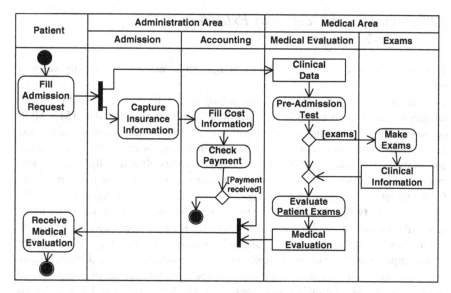

Fig. 5.4 Enforcing the security requirement of Fig. 5.3 in the activity diagram of Fig. 5.1

Figure 5.3 shows an example of an activity diagram specifying the behavior that must be followed by the system after filling the cost information until sending the medical evaluation to the patient. This behavior is required for enforcing faire exchange between patients and the medical institution. Enforcing this behavior inside the original design of Fig. 5.1 results in the new design presented in Fig. 5.4. This represents one possible scenario of using behavior diagrams to enforce security requirements. A non-security expert designer will use this "safe design" and integrate it inside its original design. Another possible scenario is when the behavior diagram, specifying a security requirement, is used to verify, through model checking or theorem proving, whether the design satisfies or not the security requirement. In this case, the diagram is translated into a (1) transition system (finite state machine or automata, etc.) or (2) a logic formula, both expressed in the input language of the target verification tool. Indeed, many contributions establishing the correspondence between transition systems and temporal logics can be found in language theory [50]. A third possible scenario is the use of behavior diagrams to specify security aspects. Indeed, aspects [114] are usually defined by specifying a behavior that is inserted before or after some execution point. Thus this behavior can be easily specified by a behavioral diagram. However, the weaving of aspects and the original design can be performed on the level of design by weaving UML diagrams or postponed to the implementation phase. In the later case, the weaving is performed on selected files of the source code and the actual aspects expressed in existing aspect languages, e.g., AspectJ, and resulting from the refinement of their initial behavior diagrams.

5.1.2 Security Specification by Extending UML Meta-language

This section shows how UML meta-language can be extended to specify security policies.

Description: In this approach, UML meta-language is directly extended by a meta-language specification language as the Meta-Object Facility (MOF) [151]. MOF defines a simple meta-meta-model, and the associated semantics, allowing the description of meta-models in various domains including the domain of object design and analysis. Extending UML meta-language (metamodel) is usually needed when extension mechanisms provided by UML (mainly stereotypes) are not appropriate for the target extension or when the resulting complexity is not tolerated.

Use for Security Specification: The two reasons stated above are the same motivating the extension of UML meta-language for security specification. Although, stereotypes allow the specification of a wide range of security requirements, they are not appropriate for specifying structured security policies: Those that are usually specified using well structured specification languages. Access control properties and security aspects are the main requirements for which it is better to have dedicated meta-elements than using standard UML meta-elements annotated by stereotypes and tagged values.

5.1.3 Security Specification by Creating New Meta-languages

This section shows how new meta-languages can be proposed for specifying security policies.

Description: In this approach, a new meta-language is defined using a meta-language specification language as MOF. The motivations of crating a new meta-language are the same as those of extending UML meta-language. The vocabulary used by the meta-elements defined by the new meta-language have domain-specific intuition and are much more precise than the one used for UML meta-elements. Thus, the interfaces needed for manipulating the new meta-elements are too simpler compared to those required for UML design.

Table 5.1 Usability evaluation of security specification approaches

	Stereotypes and tagged values	OCL	Behavior diagrams	Extending UML Meta-language	Creating new Meta-languages
Expressiveness	All_Reqs, All_Logics	All_Reqs, All_Logics	Static_Reqs, LTL_Logic	Static_Reqs, All_Logics	All_Reqs, All_Logics
Tool support	Standard	Highly Portable	Standard	Highly Portable	Weakly Portable
Verifiability	Comp_Verif	Good_Verif	Good_Verif	Good_Verif	
Complexity	Low_Comp to High_Comp	Acceptable_Comp	Low_Comp	Acceptable_Comp	Acceptable_Comp

Use for Security Specification: The motivations of creating new meta-languages for security specification are exactly the same of extending UML meta-language for security specification. Indeed, the approach is used for the same objectives and allows the specification of almost the same security requirements.

5.2 Usability Discussion

This section discusses the usability of each security specification approach on the light of our survey of the state of the art. First, we define a set of usability criteria that will be used later to discuss the different security specification approaches presented in the previous section. For the first approach, we discussed separately the usability of each of the three UML artifacts used for security specification. The results of the usability discussion of all the approaches are summarized in Table 5.1.

5.2.1 Usability Criteria

Inspired by the state of the art of software usability and software security requirements specification, we defined the following usability criteria:

- *Expressiveness*: Refers to the ability of specifying security requirements. This is a discriminatory criterion since it leads to the rejection of any approach that fails to specify the desired security requirements. Regarding this criterion, any specification approach will be given two ranks. The first rank is related to the covered security requirements and can take one of the following values:

  – *Static_Reqs*: if it allows the specification of the majority of statically enforceable security requirements.
  – *Dynamic_Reqs*: if it allows the specification of the majority of dynamically enforceable security requirements.
  – *All_Reqs*: if it allows the specification of almost all the security requirements.

  The second rank is related to the logic classification of the security requirements that can be specified. It can take one of the following values:

  – *LTL_Logic*: if the security requirements belonging to LTL logic can be specified by the evaluated approach.
  – *CTL_Logic*: if the security requirements belonging to CTL logic can be specified by the evaluated approach.
  – *All_logics*: if the specifiable security requirements can belong to any logic class.

- *Tool Support*: Refers to the availability of tools for specification and verification of security requirements, which is of paramount importance. Tools are mainly used to (1) artifact the specification and (2) compile and store the specification in a useful intermediate representation (for verification and/or code generation). Tool support will be ranked by using one of the following three values: (1) *Standard* when tools are provided by any standard UML modeling framework, (2) *HighlyPortable* when they are not supported by all standard UML frameworks but can be easily ported (e.g., plugged in), or (3) *WeaklyPortable* when the tools are almost unportable.

- *Verifiability*: Refers to the efforts needed to verify the design against the security requirements. These cover (1) associating a semantics to UML design, (2) formally specifying security requirements, (3) actually verifying the design against the security requirements, and (4) interpreting and presenting the verification results. Verifiability will be ranked using one of the following three values: (1) *Comp_Verif* for complex verifiability, (2) *Good_Verif* for verifiability with acceptable efforts, and (3) *Ease_Verif* for easy verifiability.

- *Complexity*: Refers to the amount of security-relevant information added to a UML design and its impact on its readability. Complexity will be evaluated using one of the following three values: (1) *High_Comp* when the added security information seriously deteriorates the readability of the design, (2) *Acceptable_Comp* when it is tolerated, or (3) *Low_Comp* when it is negligible compared to the original design complexity.

5.2.2 Security Specification Using UML Artifacts

5.2.2.1 Stereotypes and Tagged Values

In the following we discuss the usability of stereotypes and tagged values for security specification.

- *Expressiveness*: UML artifacts provided by standard UML, mainly stereotypes and tagged values, are the most used by the majority of the contributions. Among these contributions, we can cite: UMLSec [110] by Jürjens which provides a UML profile and an open-source tool for specifying security requirements such as secrecy, integrity, authenticity, faire exchange, role-based access control, secure communication links, and secure information flow. Stereotypes are used by Pavlich-Mariscal et al. [164] and Basin et al. [127] for specifying access control policies and by Montangero et al. [137] for modeling authentication protocols. These contributions show that various security requirements have been specified using stereotypes and tagged values.

- *Tool Support*: Stereotypes and tagged values have an excellent tool support since any standard UML modeling framework supports profile specification.

- *Verifiability*: A lot of work is done in background to generate a formal semantics for UML design, formally specify the security requirement, verify the property against the design, and show the verification result to the end user (UML designer). The later usually consists in displaying counter examples and providing advices to improve the design and fix the vulnerabilities.

- *Complexity*: The complexity of the information added for security specification, depends on the number of stereotypes and tagged values attached to each UML element. For example, if different security stereotypes are associated with the same UML element then it will be complex for the user to select all these stereotypes and edit the associated tagged values. In this case, the security profile designer has the responsibility of compacting as possible the architecture of his profile design.

5.2.2.2 OCL

OCL is also used by many of the surveyed contributions to express formal constraints in the specification of security properties. This is due to the fact that OCL is part of UML standard, and by its formal nature, it allows precise specification of security constraints. The approach of Painchaud et al. (SOCLe project) [161] is based on temporal logic extension of OCL for security specification. OCL has been also used by [127] to specify additional authorization constraints related to the state of the system. As we mentioned above, it is natural to use OCL for security specification. However, it is important here to distinguish between using OCL as a support for some security specification artifact as stereotypes and behavior diagrams, and using it as security specification language. In the former case, the use of OCL improves the usability of any specification artifact by allowing the definition of constraints over UML design entities. Accordingly, we focused our usability evaluation on the later case. In the following, we discuss the usability of OCL for security specification.

- *Expressiveness*: As a security specification language, the standard OCL [153] is limited to specifying pre and post conditions and invariants that should be satisfied by the application behavior. However, some OCL extensions allow the specification of temporal logic properties.
- *Tool Support*: Standard OCL benefits from the support of different tools provided by standard UML modeling frameworks. However, the usability of OCL extensions is limited by the availability of tools supporting the specification and the compilation of security requirements.
- *Verifiability*: Once compiled and analyzed by the tool, security requirements specified using OCL extensions are systematically provided as input formulas for verification tools (model checkers and/or theorem provers). However, as for stereotypes, a lot of work is done in background to generate a formal semantics for UML design, verify the properties against the design, and show the verification result to the end user (UML designer).
- *Complexity*: The complexity introduced by this approach depends on the number of OCL expressions added to specify security properties and weather they are crosscutting the application functionalities design or separated from them.

5.2.2.3 Behavior Diagrams

We notice the lack of using behavioral diagrams for security specification among the surveyed approaches. In fact, only the approach of Zisman [215] that proposes the modeling of abuse cases to represent possible attack scenarios and potential threats to the system security. In the following we discuss the usability of behavior diagrams for security specification. We distinguish in our discussion between the use of behavior diagrams to specify security requirements for the sake of verification and their use to specify security aspects for the sake of security enforcement or hardening.

- *Expressiveness*: Is limited to specify those security requirements that are naturally expressible via transition systems. These include mainly attack scenarios and dynamically enforceable security requirements. As for security aspects specification, behavior diagrams are very useful for specifying advices behavior. However, stereotypes should be defined to allow the specification of patterns needed for the definition of pointcuts.
- *Tool Support*: Behavior diagrams benefit from a wide tool support. However, tool support for this approach depends also on the tool support of stereotypes.
- *Verifiability*: When used for security requirements specification, behavior diagrams are translated to transition systems or logical formulas in order to be verified on the system design. While the former translation is almost systematic, the later is limited to those diagrams satisfying some structural constraints (e.g., determinism) and constrained by the availability of translation algorithms in language and logic theory. As for stereotypes and OCL, a lot of work is done in background to generate a formal semantics for UML design, verify the properties against the design, and show the verification result to the end user (UML designer). When used for security aspects specification, as for the first approach, a lot of work is done in background to (1) identify diagram entities (e.g., methods/actions) matching the specified patterns and (2) weaving diagrams specifying advices and those specifying the system behavior.
- *Complexity*: Relatively acceptable since the behavior diagrams specifying security requirements are separated from those specifying the system behavior and are easily distinguishable from them. The complexity of security aspects specification is comparable to that of security requirements specification.

5.2.3 Extending UML Meta-language

Only few contributions [164] have investigated the extension of UML meta-language for security specification. This is due to the fact that this kind of modification requires a high expertise and knowledge of UML meta-language and its objectives. Indeed, the extension may require the modification of the whole meta-language which is too complex. In the following, we discuss the usability of extending UML meta-language for security specification.

- *Expressiveness*: Comparable to that of stereotypes.
- *Tool Support*: The extension is heavyweight so that "may require one to extend the CASE-tool itself, in particular the storage components, i.e., the repository, and the visualization components" [127]. This impacts negatively the portability of any extension since any UML modeling framework is heavily modified to allow the use of the new meta-elements and their interpretation.
- *Verifiability*: A lot of work is done in background to generate a formal semantics for UML design, verify the properties against the design, and show the verification result to the end user. However, if the extension targets some low-level policy specification language or AOP language, then the effort spent in background is limited to parsing the specification and translating it to the target language.
- *Complexity*: The complexity is comparable to that of using behavior diagrams.

5.2.4 Creating a New Meta-language

As for the previous approach, only few contributions [127] have investigated the creation of new meta-languages for security specification. In the following we discuss the usability of creating a new meta-language for security specification.

- *Expressiveness*: Comparable to the expressiveness of extending UML meta-language.
- *Tool Support*: Better than that of extending UML meta-language and comparable to that of stereotypes. In addition, the compiler needed to parse the specification can be easily plugged into the UML modeling framework.
- *Verifiability*: Better than that of extending UML meta-language. Indeed, the security specification is exclusively based on the new meta-elements and thus is easier to parse and translate.
- *Complexity*: Comparable to the complexity of extending UML meta-language.

5.3 Model-Based Security Hardening Mechanisms

Three main approaches are usually followed for the specification of security hardening mechanisms at UML design level. These approaches are design patterns, mechanism-directed meta-languages, and aspect-oriented modeling. In the following, we introduce these approaches and then highlight the challenges related to their use in UML design.

5.3.1 Security Design Patterns

Design patterns are defined as generic reusable solutions to solve recurring problems
in software design. The idea of a pattern was first introduced as an architectural
concept by Alexander et al. [30] and was later adopted in the software engineering
community. One of the main goals of design patterns is to help designers in applying
good practices in software development. Indeed, design patterns capture the knowledge of experts in a well-structured form that facilitates its reuse by designers. In
recent years, the application of the pattern concept in the field of information security
has been widely investigated. In this context, a security design pattern describes a
particular recurring security problem that arises in a specific context. In addition, it
presents a well-proven generic scheme for a security solution [184]. Like design patterns, security patterns encapsulate the knowledge of security experts in the form of
proven solutions to common problems. Thus, developers can benefit from the skills
and the experience of security experts.

5.3.2 Mechanism-Directed Meta-languages

Following the same intuition of design patterns, many contributions have proposed
extensions of UML metamodel, each of which is dedicated to the design of a specific security hardening solution. UML extension mechanisms that are adopted are
mainly UML profiles (stereotypes and tagged values). The adoption of these extension mechanisms is motivated by their expressiveness to specify a wide range of
security requirements. In addition, UML standard extension mechanisms benefit
from a good tool support since any UML modeling framework supports the standard
profile specification. Accordingly, many UML extensions have been proposed in the
literature for specifying security requirements. The majority of these languages target RBAC security policies [27, 32, 72, 128, 174]. Other security requirements, such
as authentication, have been also addressed [137].

5.3.3 Aspect-Oriented Modeling

The applicability of aspect-oriented techniques to specify security requirements and
hardening mechanisms has been heavily studied in the literature both at the implementation and design levels [35, 49, 56, 93, 111, 141, 164, 172, 173, 199, 207, 211].
Indeed, aspect-oriented techniques support the idea of separating crosscutting concerns from the application core functionality. Since security is a crosscutting concern
that pervades the entire software, it is natural to consider Aspect-Oriented Modeling (AOM) as a mechanism for security hardening at the modeling level. In fact, a
security hardening solution consists of specifying the needed security functionalities

and the locations where these functionalities should be applied. In addition, these security functionalities should be systematically injected into the base models at specified locations, which could be achieved using AOM.

5.3.4 Challenges

The designer of security hardening mechanisms, using UML, has to deal with the following challenges:

- *Non-Standardization*: There is a lack of standardization efforts regarding the design of security hardening mechanisms. Consequently, for the same security policy, different security experts can adopt different designs (e.g., pattern, aspect). As a result, this will limit the adoption of these solutions and may confuse the end-designer when having to choose between different solutions.
- *Adaptability to Users' Design*: The security mechanism design provided by the security expert is sometimes application-independent. This way, it will be generic enough to be adapted to the design of the end-user. However, since this adaptation/specialization will be performed by a non-security expert designer, it should be as systematic and as easy as possible. It may be required that a well-detailed procedure should accompany the security solution.
- *Maintainability of Design and Security Mechanisms*: During the development process, the design models as well as the security solution may be in continuous modification. Consequently, the security hardening solution should take into consideration the appearance of new elements and the disappearance of others. Indeed, the appearance of some elements necessitates applying the security solution to these elements without reapplying it to the existing elements that are already covered by the solution. If some elements will be dropped from the design while they have been covered by the solution, then the corresponding security elements should be, in turn, dropped from the design. Similar maintenance modifications should be applied when the security solution itself is updated.
- *Validation*: Security mechanisms are supposed to enforce the security policies they are designed for. However, validating this claim is far from being a straightforward task. Thus, rigorous verification and validation techniques should be applied on the proposed security mechanism design.

5.4 Related Work on Model-Based Security

In this section, we present the state-of-the-art initiatives on security specification and hardening at the design level. We classify the related work according to the adopted mechanisms into three main categories: (1) Security design patterns, (2) mechanism-directed meta-languages, and (3) aspect-oriented modeling.

5.4.1 Security Design Patterns

Several security design patterns have been proposed in order to guide software engineers in designing security models at different phases of the software development life cycle. A detailed study of different security patterns can be found in [42, 115, 123, 185, 209]. We present in the following an overview of the existing patterns. Kienzle et al. [115] present 29 security patterns for web applications. The patterns are classified into two categories: structural and procedural patterns. The structural patterns include diagrams that describe both the structure and the interaction of the design pattern. On the other hand, the procedural patterns are used to improve the development process of security-critical software. Romanosky [179] presents eight security design patterns that represent a collection of security practices. The proposed patterns address high-level security concerns, such as, how to provide secure communication in the presence of untrusted third-party, how to make a system fails securely, etc. The discussion however has focused on architectural and procedural guidelines more than on security patterns. Brown et al. [109] introduce the authenticator pattern, which describes a general mechanism to provide identification and authentication from a client to a server. This pattern has been later extended by Fernandez and Warrier [82] for authentication and authorization.

The Open Group [48] presents a catalog of thirteen architectural-level and design-level security patterns that are based on architectural framework standards. It also presents a systematic methodology for using those security patterns to design a system, which has good availability and protection properties. Fernández [81] provides a methodology to build secure systems using patterns. The main idea of this approach is that security principles should be applied through the use of security patterns at every stage of the software development process, i.e., requirements, analysis, design, and implementation. At the end of each stage, audits are performed to verify that the security policies are being followed. Chan and Kwok [54] propose an object-oriented design pattern that models the main entities of security design, such as, vulnerabilities, threats, risks, impact of loss and countermeasures for different parts of an e-commerce system.

Schumacher et al. [184] present a list of forty-six patterns for integrating security in systems engineering. The proposed patterns are at different levels of abstraction. They range from high-level patterns targeting the development of secure applications, to low-level patterns addressing the security of operating systems. An IP telephony case study is provided to illustrate the application of the patterns. Dougherty et al. [73] propose security patterns that are categorized according to their level of abstraction into: architectural-level, design-level, and implementation-level patterns. The security design patterns are proposed as extensions to the existing design patterns (e.g., factory and strategy design patterns) by adding security-specific functionalities.

Yoshioka et al. [209] provide a survey of security patterns according to the different phases of the software development life cycle. During the requirement phase, the different assets of the system are identified as well as the purpose of protecting them. Additionally, the security requirements are specified alongside the system requirements. During the design phase, various security functions are designed as patterns to protect the assets that are identified in the requirement phase. For instance, such patterns may cover functions such as authentication, authorization, and access control. Finally, implementation-level security patterns are needed to guide programmers while writing programs with guidelines illustrating the required techniques to write secure programs.

5.4.2 Mechanism-Directed Meta-languages

Considerable work has been done in the literature to provide UML metamodel extensions for the integration of security into various stages of the software development life cycle. In the following, we present a brief summary of those contributions. The UMLSec approach [110] is among the first efforts in extending UML for the development of security-critical systems. It provides a UML profile where general security requirements, e.g., secrecy, integrity, fair exchange, are encapsulated using UML stereotypes and tagged values. It also defines a formal semantics to evaluate UML diagrams against weaknesses. In order to analyze security specifications, the behavior of a potential adversary, that can attack various parts of a system, is formally modeled.

Basin et al. [128] propose an approach to model RBAC policies for model-driven systems. This approach proposes a general schema, in which systems modeling languages are combined with security modeling languages by defining *dialects*. These dialects identify the protected resources from elements of the system modeling language. This approach defines a general meta-model for generating security modeling languages. SecureUML [127] is one instance of these languages defined for modeling RBAC policies. It has an abstract syntax that is independent of any modeling language and a concrete syntax that is defined as a UML extension using stereotypes and tagged values. From models in the combined languages, access control infrastructures are automatically generated using MDA-based transformation mechanisms [148]. However, SecureUML only focuses on specifying the RBAC model.

The approach of Doan et al. [72] incorporates RBAC, MAC, and lifetimes into UML for time-sensitive application design. The main focus of this approach is that the process of designing and integrating security in a software application captures not only the current design state, but allows tracking the entire design evolution process via the creation and the maintenance of a set of design instances over time. The design tracking allows a software/security engineer to recover to an earlier design version that satisfies specific security constraints.

Zisman [215] proposes a framework to support the design and the verification of secure peer-to-peer applications. Design models and security requirements are specified using the UMLSec approach [110]. The modeling of abuse cases to represent possible attack scenarios and potential threats helps designers to identify the security properties to be verified in the system. In addition, this approach facilitates expressing the properties to be verified by defining a graphical template language. It also allows the verification of the models against the specified properties and visualization of the verification results.

Montangero et al. (For-LySa, DEGAS project) [137] present two UML profiles to model authentication protocols: (1) the *Static For-LySa profile*, which describes how the authentication protocol concepts (e.g., principals, keys, messages) can be modeled using UML class diagrams, and (2) the *For-LySa profile*, which models the dynamic aspects of the protocol in sequence diagrams, as well as the information needed to analyze the protocol. In order to validate a protocol, For-LySa defines a specification language together with its semantics to write pre/post conditions and invariant constraints.

Ray et al. [174] address the issue of integrating different access control policies, such as RBAC and MAC, into a single hybrid model. This approach uses parameterized UML diagrams to model RBAC and MAC frameworks and then compose them manually to produce a hybrid access control policy. It is the first approach that attempts to combine different access control policies. However, it focuses only on how to model these policies in UML without considering how they can be used to design a secure software system.

Painchaud et al. (SOCLe project) [161] provide a framework that integrates security into the design of software applications. It also includes the verification of UML specifications and a graphical user interface that allows the designer to visualize the verification results. In this approach, security policies are specified using the OCL language.

Alghathbar and Wijeskera [32] propose a framework, called AuthUML, to incorporate access control policies into use case diagrams. The aim of AuthUML is analyzing access control policies during the early stages of the development life cycle before proceeding to the design to ensure consistent, conflict-free, and complete requirements.

Popp et al. [169] propose an extension to the conventional process of developing use case oriented processes. In addition to modeling security properties with UML, this approach provides a method to incorporate these security aspects into a use case oriented development process.

Ledru et al. (EDEMOI project) [124] aim at modeling and analyzing airport security. Security properties are first extracted from natural language standards and documents, then integrated into UML diagrams as stereotypes in a UML profile. UML specifications are then translated into formal models for verification purposes. This approach is not general enough to be used for software development.

Ahn and Shin [27] propose a technique to describe the RBAC model with three views using UML diagrams: static view, functional view, and dynamic view. This approach focuses only on the way that UML elements can be used to model RBAC policies rather than taking a larger view of examining secure software design. It does not provide a systematic modeling approach that can be used by developers to create applications with RBAC models.

Epstein and Sandhu's work [78] is one of the first approaches that investigate the possibility of using UML to model RBAC policies. However, it is limited to only one specific RBAC model, which is the RBAC Framework for Network Enterprises

(FNE) [195]. The FNE model contains seven abstract layers that are divided in two different groups. This approach allows to present each of the FNE model's layers using UML notation by defining new stereotypes. This approach can assist the role engineering process, however, it does not include subtle properties of RBAC, such as separation of duty constraints, and it does not provide a method for deriving roles.

Brose et al. [52] extend UML models to support the automatic generation of access control policies for CORBA-based systems. They specify both permissions and prohibitions on accessing system's objects since the analysis phase in use case diagrams. UML design models are used to generate the specification of access control policies in VPL (View Policy Language) that is deployed together with the CORBA application.

Vivas et al. [200] propose a UML-based approach for the development of business process-driven systems where security requirements are integrated into the business model. Security requirements are first stated at a high level of abstraction within a functional representation of the system using tagged values. Next, the UML speci-fication is translated into XMI representation. Finally, the resulting specification is translated into a formal notation for consistency checking, verification, validation, and simulation.

5.4.3 Aspect-Oriented Modeling

The application of AOM to security has generated a lot of research interest in the last few years. Various contributions that aim at modeling security concerns as aspects have been published recently. In the following, we present a brief overview of these contributions. Pavlich-Mariscal et al. [163] propose a new UML artifact called *Role Slice* to capture RBAC [83] policies within UML class models. A role slice diagram contains information on a role's permissions that cut across all classes in an application. RBAC constraints are represented within a role slice diagram using UML stereotypes. Moreover, this approach proposes algorithms that map access control policies, provided in role slice diagrams, to AOP security enforcement code implemented in AspectJ. In another effort [164], Pavlich-Mariscal et al. propose an aspect-oriented approach to model access control policies. They augment UML metamodel with new diagrams that are separated from the main UML design to represent Role-Based Access Control (RBAC) [83], Mandatory Access Control (MAC) [45] and Discretionary Access Control (DAC) [144] models. The separated security diagrams are then composed with the main design using UML composition techniques. However, this approach is limited to access control and specifies only the structural part of the access control policy without considering its behavior.

Ray et al. [173] propose an AOM approach for enforcing access control policies. An access control aspect is represented as a pattern using UML diagram templates. Other functional design concerns are specified in a separate model referred to as a primary model. A composition mechanism is used to integrate access control features within the primary model. The composition mechanism involves the instantiation of the aspect to obtain a context-specific aspect, then composing context-specific aspects with the primary model. This approach also is limited to access control and specifies only the structural part of the access control policy. In another work [89], the authors propose Aspect-oriented Architecture Models (AAMs) that show how different concerns can be described independently of any underlying technology. AAM models consist of: (1) A set of aspect models, (2) a primary architecture model, and (3) composition directives that define how aspect models are composed with the primary model. Aspect models are defined as general patterns represented using UML diagram templates. These patterns are instantiated by binding the template parameters to actual application values to produce context-specific aspects before composing them with the primary model.

Zhang et al. [211] propose an aspect-oriented modeling of access control in Web applications. The approach extends UML-based Web Engineering (UWE) method by specifying the detailed behavior of each navigation node using a state machine. Access control to navigation nodes is specified by refining the default state machines by a state machine modeling the access control rules. This approach extends the UWE metamodel to support aspects. In their AOM approach, an aspect contains navigation nodes that are associated with the same access control rules. Access control rules are defined in the aspect containing those navigation nodes.

Gao et al. [93] propose an aspect-oriented design approach for CORBA AC, a reference model for enforcing access control in middleware applications. The RBAC model is used to implement a functional CORBA AC mechanism. In this approach, the RBAC core model is specified as the base model and each RBAC concern is specified as an aspect. Thus, the approach presents four aspects: role hierarchy aspect, static constraints aspect, temporal constraints aspect, and spatial constraints aspect. This approach uses AspectJ [113] and its weaving rules for the implementation of the CORBA AC model.

Georg et al. [94] propose an aspect-oriented approach for modeling access control. In this approach, aspects are patterns specifying structures and behaviors. An aspect is defined in terms of structures of meta-roles called (meta-) Role Models [94]. Two views are supported by an aspect: static and interaction views. These views are described using two types of role models: Static Role Models (SRMs) and Interaction Role Models (IRMs). Weaving is considered as a special case of UML model transformation using design patterns. In another contribution, Georg et al. [95] propose an aspect-oriented risk-driven methodology for designing secure applications. The proposed methodology starts by identifying the assets of the application that need to be protected. Then, typical attack scenarios are defined and modeled as aspects. The attack model is composed with the application base model to produce the misuse model. After evaluating the application against the defined attacks, and if the application presents a security risk, then a security mechanism, specified also as an aspect, is incorporated into the application. Finally, the resulting system is analyzed to give assurance that it is indeed resilient to the attack.

Jürjens and Houmb [111] present an AOM approach for developing and analyzing security-critical systems at both modeling and implementation levels. In this approach, security aspects are specified as UMLSec [110] stereotypes that are woven into base models. The resulting UML models and the generated code are verified against the specified security requirements using automated theorem provers [102].

Dai et al. [65] propose an aspect-oriented framework called the Formal Design Analysis Framework (FDAF). The latter supports the design and the analysis of non-functional requirements defined as reusable aspects for distributed real-time systems using UML and formal methods. The FDAF approach presents a UML extension to capture performance aspect information in UML models as stereotypes. Then, it automatically transforms UML design into formal models to be able to analyze the response time.

5.4.4 Comparative Study

We have conducted a comparative study (Table 5.2) of the aforementioned approaches according to a set of defined criteria, such as, the supported security requirements, the mechanisms used for the specification of those requirements, formalization of the approach, existence of a tool support, etc. From this study, we have observed the following:

- The focus of many surveyed projects is on the specification of security policies, and sometimes analyzing UML models against the specified policies. There is a lack of approaches for the enforcement of such policies in software systems.
- Most of the approaches adopt Role Based Access Control (RBAC), with an addition of different flavors of access control based on labels, that is, Mandatory Access Control (MAC). However, with the growing complexity of software, UML models must embed more complex security policies.
- The OCL language is employed in many of the surveyed projects for expressing formal constraints in the specification of security policies. Tagged values are also used for expressing access control properties.
- We have noticed the absence of expressiveness, applicability, and learning curve in the majority of approaches. These criteria are important and must be taken into account in future methodologies. As the final users of these methods will be human developers, these criteria can decide whether this approach is realistic or not.
- The approach [164] uses UML stereotypes to represent security policies and then uses AOP to enforce those policies at execution time. The approach transparently enforces access control in software components by implementing/weaving the access control aspect based on roles defined at the design stage. In our opinion, this approach provides the right trade-off between security needs and ease of use through demanding relatively smaller effort from the developers and providing high level of abstraction of the security policies. However, further extension of this work is still necessary for better expressing more security policies.
- In regards to secure code generation, further efforts are needed for reducing the performance overhead of deploying these mechanisms in code. To the best of our knowledge, the generation of efficient code has not been addressed in any of the surveyed approaches.

Table 5.2 Comparative study of existing approaches

Approaches	Security policies	Security policy specification	Constraint specification	Formal semantics	Code generation	V&V	Applicability	Expressiveness	Learning curve	Usage in industry
[110]	General security requirements	Stereotypes		✓	✓	✓	✓			✓
[164]	RBAC/MAC/DAC	New diagrams, stereotypes		✓	✓					
[215]		Based on UMLSec		✓		✓				
[127]	RBAC	Stereotypes	OCL	✓		✓				
[72]	RBAC/MAC	Tagged values		✓	✓	✓				
[137]	Authentication	Stereotypes	Simple language			✓				
[173]	RBAC/MAC	Parameterized UML diagrams	OCL, diagram templates							
[32]	Access control, flow control	Predicates	OCL							
[169]	Access rights	Based on UMLSec	OCL							
[161]			OCL	✓		✓				
[124]		Stereotypes		✓		✓				
[78]	Subset of RBAC	Stereotypes	Natural language							
[27]	RBAC	Stereotypes	OCL							
[52]	Access control	Stereotypes	Natural language		✓					
[200]		Tagged values		✓		✓				

5.5 Conclusion

We have presented in this chapter existing approaches for specifying and hardening security at the design level. We distinguish between those approaches that are based on the artifacts provided by the standard UML specification and those that require explicit extension of the UML meta-language. This mainly allows one to understand when it is better to use UML artifacts and when it is useful to extend UML meta-language. Moreover, we have investigated the mechanisms used for security hardening at UML design: security design patterns, mechanism-directed meta-languages, and aspect-oriented modeling. We have seen that security design patterns mainly provide textual descriptions for solving a given security problem. Although this approach provides reusable solutions to integrate security best practices early during the software development process, it has some shortcomings. In fact, security design patterns are provided as high-level and abstract solutions; information about the behavior of security solutions is generally missing in these patterns. In addition, they generally lack the structure and the methodologies needed for their application. Moreover, although they are meant to be applied at the design stage, some of the patterns are provided as directions written in English, which makes them hard to implement by designers and limits their adoption by industry.

Furthermore, we observed that existing contributions that adopt the use of dedicated meta-models mainly focus on specifying security requirements and sometimes analyzing UML models against the specified requirements. How to systematically enforce the specified requirements is not their main concern. In addition, the majority of these approaches target mainly RBAC model. However, with the growing complexity of software, UML models must embed more complex security policies as well. Furthermore, this approach seems to be ineffective for non-security experts as it requires continuous interaction with security experts during software design in order to ensure the appropriate enforcement of security requirements.

The adoption of AOM for security specification and enforcement overcomes the limitations observed in the previous approaches. Indeed, using AOM, security experts independently specify security enforcement mechanisms as aspects. Moreover, this approach provides a way to automate the process of integrating those security mechanisms within the application base models. However, this approach suffers from the lack of standardization for aspects specification and weaving. In addition, the adoption of AOM for security hardening requires a well-defined procedure for the specialization of the generic aspects designed by security experts. Moreover, from the state-of-the-art related to AOM and security, we noticed that the majority of existing approaches are limited to mainly specifying access control policies. Additionally, they are limited in the supported UML diagrams; sometimes, only the structural part of a security solution is specified without considering its behavior. In the following chapters, we will address these issues by providing a more expressive and generic AOM approach for specifying and systematically integrating security aspects into both structural and behavioral UML diagrams.

Chapter 6
Security Aspect Specification

As mentioned in the introduction of this book, security should be addressed during the early phases of the software development life cycle. From the state-of-the-art survey presented in Chap. 5, we have concluded that AOM is the most appropriate approach to achieve this objective. In this context, we propose, in this chapter, an AOM approach for specifying and systematically integrating security solutions into UML design models, and therefore enabling secure code generation. The targeted security concerns are those high-level requirements that are usually specified and verified on software, and for which a security solution can be provided as an aspect. Examples of such requirements are: confidentiality, integrity, authentication, authorization, access control, etc. In the proposed approach, the security expert specifies the needed security solutions as application-independent aspects. In addition, he/she specifies how these aspects should be integrated into the design models. The developer then specializes the application-independent aspects to his/her design. Finally, our framework automatically injects the application-dependent aspects at the appropriate locations in the design models.

In this chapter, we focus on the specification of security aspects. To this end, we devise a UML profile that assists security experts in specifying security solutions as aspects. The proposed profile covers the main UML diagrams that are used in software design, i.e., class diagrams, state machine diagrams, sequence diagrams, and activity diagrams. In addition, it covers most common AOP adaptations, i.e., adding new elements *before*, *after*, or *around* specific points, and removing existing elements. Moreover, we define a high-level and user-friendly pointcut language to designate the locations where aspect adaptations should be injected into base models.

The remainder of this chapter is organized as follows. Section 6.1 summarizes our approach for specifying and weaving aspects into UML design models. Afterwards, we present our AOM profile in Sect. 6.2. The related work on AOM is given in Sect. 6.3. Finally, Sect. 6.4 concludes this chapter.

© Springer International Publishing Switzerland 2015
D. Mouheb et al., *Aspect-Oriented Security Hardening of UML Design Models*,
DOI 10.1007/978-3-319-16106-8_6

6.1 Proposed AOM Approach for Security Hardening

In this section, we present an overview of our proposed AOM approach for security
hardening of software. The proposed approach assists security experts in designing security solutions in a precise way without altering the software functionalities.
In addition, the proposed approach allows developers with limited security knowledge to reuse those solutions with minimal intervention. The approach architecture
is depicted in Fig. 6.1. The main steps of the proposed approach are the following:

- *Security Aspect Specification*: A security expert designs security solutions as
  application-independent aspects. By analogy, these aspects are generic templates
  representing the security features independently of the application specificities and
  presented in a security aspects library. This design decision is useful in order to
  support reusability of aspects in different application domains. Since there is no
  standard language to specify aspects in UML, a UML profile is developed as part of
  our framework in order to assist security experts in designing security aspects. This
  profile is designed to allow as many modification capabilities as possible. These
  capabilities include the common modification capabilities characterizing the most
  prominent AOP languages (AspectJ [113] and AspectC++ [189]). As part of this
  UML profile, we have developed a high-level language to specify the pointcuts
  that designate the locations in the base model where the aspect adaptations should
  be performed. The details about the design of this profile are provided in Sect. 6.2.

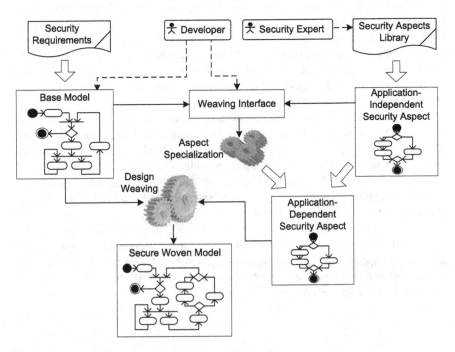

Fig. 6.1 Specification and weaving of UML security aspects

- *Security Aspect Specialization*: The developer has the possibility to specialize the application-independent aspects provided by the security expert according to the application-dependent security requirements and needs. To specialize the aspects, we provide a weaving interface, in which only the generic pointcuts are exposed to the developers. By doing so, the complexity of the security solutions is kept hidden from the developers. More details about security aspects specialization are presented in Sect. 7.2.
- *Join Point Matching*: A security aspect mainly consists of a set of adaptations that should be performed at some specific points (called join points in AOP) of UML design. Based on the pointcuts specified in the aspect by the security expert and specialized by the developer, our framework identifies, without any developer interaction, the join points from the base model where the aspect adaptations should be performed. More details about join point matching are presented in Sect. 7.3.
- *Security Aspect Weaving*: This represents the automatic injection of the security solutions into the design models at the identified join points. To provide a portable solution, we adopt a model-to-model transformation language; the QVT language [150]. QVT is an OMG standard compatible with UML and supports a large set of modifications on UML models. For each aspect adaptation and the corresponding base model elements, a set of QVT transformation rules are generated. The details about the aspect weaving step are provided in Sect. 7.4.

This chapter focuses on describing the security aspect specification step. The remaining steps of our security hardening approach, i.e., security aspect specialization, join point matching, and security aspect weaving are detailed in Chap. 7.

6.2 A UML Profile for Aspect-Oriented Modeling

This section presents our AOM profile that extends UML for security aspects specification. An aspect represents a non-functional requirement. It contains a set of adaptations and pointcuts. An adaptation specifies the modification that an aspect performs on the base model. A pointcut specifies the locations in the base model where an adaptation should be performed. The elements of this profile will be used by security experts to specify security solutions for well-known security problems. However, the profile is generic enough to be used for specifying non-security aspects. In our AOM profile, an aspect is represented as a stereotyped package (Fig. 6.2). For example, Fig. 6.3 shows a partial specification of an aspect designed to enforce RBAC mechanisms.[1] The RBAC aspect is modeled as a package stereotyped ≪*aspect*≫. In the following subsections, we show how adaptations and pointcuts can be specified using our AOM profile.

---

[1] The full specification of the RBAC aspect is presented in Sect. 7.6.1.2.

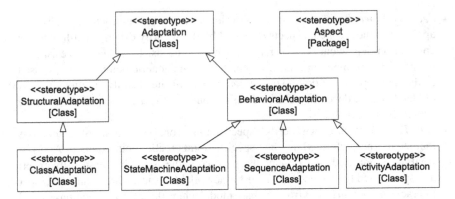

Fig. 6.2 Meta-model for specifying aspects and their adaptations

<<aspect>> RBACAspect		
<<classAdaptation>> RoleAddition	<<sequenceAdaptation>> CheckAcess	**Role**
		name
<<add>> AddRole() {name = Role} {type = Class} {position = Inside} {pointcut = SubscriberPackagePointcut}	<<add>> AddCheckAccess() {name = CheckAccess} {type = InteractionUse} {position = Before} {pointcut = SensitiveMethodPointcut}	grantPermission() revokePermission() checkAccess() getPermissions()
<<pointcut>>SubscriberPackagePointcut() {textExpression = package(SubscriberPackage)} ⋮	<<pointcut>> SensitiveMethodPointcut() {textExpression = message_call(SensitiveMethod) && message_source(User) && message_target(Resource) }	

Fig. 6.3 Partial view of the RBAC aspect

6.2.1 Aspect Adaptations

As mentioned earlier, an adaptation specifies the modification that an aspect performs on the base model. We classify adaptations according to the covered diagrams and the modification rules that specify the effect of adaptations on the base model. UML allows the specification of a software from multiple points of view using different types of diagrams, such as, class diagrams, activity diagrams, sequence diagrams, etc. Unfortunately, most of existing AOM approaches specify aspects within the same modeling view (e.g., structural, behavioral). In this research, we propose an AOM approach that covers both structural and behavioral views of a system. Notice that this does not mean that we cover all existing UML diagrams. Instead, we focus on those diagrams that are the most used by developers: class diagrams, sequence diagrams, state machine diagrams, and activity diagrams. Figure 6.2 presents our specification of adaptations. We define two types of adaptations: structural and behavioral adaptations.

6.2.1.1   Structural Adaptations

Structural adaptations specify the modifications that affect structural diagrams. We focus on class diagrams since they are the most used structural diagrams in software design. A class diagram adaptation is similar to an introduction in AOP languages (e.g., AspectJ). A structural adaptation is modeled as an abstract meta-element named *StructuralAdaptation*. It is specialized by the meta-element *ClassAdaptation* used to specify class diagram adaptations, which contain adaptation rules for class diagram elements (see Sect. 6.2.2). Notice that the meta-element *StructuralAdaptation* can be specialized to model adaptations for other structural diagrams, such as, component diagrams, deployment diagrams, etc. As an example of a structural adaptation, *RoleAddition* in Fig. 6.3 is a class adaptation (stereotype ≪*ClassAdaptation*≫) used for the integration of a class named *Role* into a package, designated by the pointcut *SubscriberPackagePointcut*, as well as the adaptation rules that are required to the adoption of an RBAC solution. The definition and the specification of adaptation rules will be presented later in this section.

6.2.1.2   Behavioral Adaptations

Behavioral adaptations specify the modifications that affect behavioral diagrams. In our approach, we support the behavioral diagrams that are the most used for the specification of a system behavior, mainly, state machine diagrams, sequence diagrams, and activity diagrams. A behavioral adaptation is similar to an advice in AOP languages (e.g., AspectJ). A behavioral adaptation is modeled as an abstract meta-element named *BehavioralAdaptation*. We specialize the meta-element *BehavioralAdaptation* by three meta-elements: *StateMachineAdaptation*, *SequenceAdaptation*, and *ActivityAdaptation* that are used to specify adaptations for state machine diagrams, sequence diagrams, and activity diagrams respectively. As for the meta-element *StructuralAdaptation*, the meta-element *BehavioralAdaptation* can also be extended to model adaptations for other behavioral diagrams, such as, communication diagrams, interaction overview diagrams, etc. As an example of a behavioral adaptation, *CheckAccess* in Fig. 6.3 is a sequence adaptation (stereotype ≪*SequenceAdaptation*≫) defining the adaptation rules required to inject the behavior needed to check user permissions before any call to a sensitive method.

6.2.2 Aspect Adaptation Rules

An adaptation rule specifies the effect that an aspect performs on the base model elements. We support two types of adaptation rules: *Adding* a new element to the base model and *removing* an existing element from the base model. Figure 6.4 depicts our specified meta-model for adaptation rules.

6.2.2.1 Adding a New Element

The addition of a new diagram element to the base model is modeled as a special kind of operation, to which a stereotype ≪*Add*≫ is applied. We use the same specification for adding any kind of UML element, either structural or behavioral. Three tagged values are attached to the stereotype ≪*Add*≫:

- *Name*: The name of the element to be added to the base model.
- *Type*: The type of the element to be added to the base model. The values of this tag are provided in the enumerations *ClassElementType*, *StateMachineElementType*, *SequenceElementType*, and *ActivityElementType*.
- *Position*: The position where the new element needs to be added. The values of this tag are given in the enumeration *PositionType*. This tag is needed for some

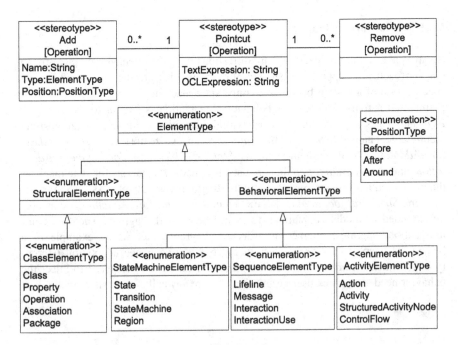

Fig. 6.4 Meta-model for specifying adaptation rules

elements (e.g., a message, an action) to state where exactly the new element should be added (e.g., *before/after* a join point). For some other elements (e.g., a class, an operation), this tag is optional since these kinds of elements are always added inside a join point.

The location where the new element should be added is specified by the meta-element *Pointcut* (see Sect. 6.2.3). For example, in Fig. 6.3, the operation *AddRole()* stereotyped ≪*Add*≫ is an adaptation rule belonging to the class adaptation *RoleAddition*. It adds a new class, named *Role*, to the package *SubscriberPackage*, matched by the pointcut *SubsriberPackagePointcut*. The class *Role* is defined inside the RBAC aspect.

6.2.2.2   Removing an Existing Element

The deletion of an existing element from the base model is modeled as a special kind of operation stereotyped ≪*Remove*≫. The set of elements that should be removed are given by a pointcut expression specified by the meta-element *Pointcut* (see Sect. 6.2.3). The same specification is used for removing any kind of UML element, either structural or behavioral. No tagged value is required for the specification of a *Remove* adaptation rule; the pointcut specification is enough to select the elements that should be removed.

The proposed profile for the specification of adaptations and their adaptation rules is expressive enough to cover the common AOP adaptations; i.e., introductions and *before/after/around* advices. For example, the profile allows to specify the addition of a new class to an existing package, a new attribute or an operation to an existing class, or a new association between two existing classes. In addition, we can remove an existing class, an attribute or an operation from an existing class, or an association between two existing classes. As for behavioral modifications, the profile allows to specify the injection of any UML behavior *before*, *after*, or *around* any behavioral UML element matched by the concerned pointcut. For example, the profile allows to specify the addition of an interaction fragment *before/after/around* a specific message in a sequence diagram, or an action *before/after/around* a specific action in an activity diagram. Moreover, the proposed adaptation rules are generic; they can be used to specify any security solution for any design. Table 6.1 summarizes the main adaptation rules that are supported by our approach.

6.2.3   Pointcuts

A pointcut is an expression that designates a set of join points. To specify pointcuts, we propose a pointcut language in a textual representation rather than using UML notations. This choice is motivated by the expressiveness and the easiness of the textual representation comparing to UML. For example, expressing logical pointcuts

Table 6.1 Supported adaptation rules

UML diagram	Supported adaptation rules
Class diagram	Adding/removing a class
	Adding/removing an attribute
	Adding/removing an operation
	Adding/removing an association
	Adding/removing a package
State machine diagram	Adding/removing a state machine
	Adding/removing a state
	Adding/removing a transition
	Adding/removing a region
Sequence diagram	Adding/removing an interaction
	Adding/removing an interaction use
	Adding/removing a lifeline
	Adding/removing a message
Activity diagram	Adding/removing an activity
	Adding/removing an action
	Adding/removing a structured activity node
	Adding/removing a control flow

in a textual way is more readable than expressing them in UML. In our approach, a pointcut is modeled as a meta-element stereotyped ≪*Pointcut*≫ with two tagged values (Fig. 6.4):

- *TextExpression*: The pointcut expression specified in our proposed textual pointcut language.
- *OCLExpression*: An OCL expression equivalent to the textual one, which will be automatically generated during the weaving process as we will see in Chap. 7.

The textual pointcuts are high-level and easy to write and understand. However, they cannot be directly used to query UML elements and select the appropriate join points. Thus, in our framework, we translate the textual pointcut expressions into OCL expressions to query UML elements. By doing so, we benefit from the expressiveness of the OCL language and, at the same time, we eliminate the overhead of writing such complex expressions from the developers. More details about the generation of OCL expressions from the textual ones are provided in Chap. 7.

Since the targeted join points are UML elements, pointcuts should be defined based on designators that are specific to UML. To this end, we define a pointcut language that provides UML-specific pointcut designators needed to select UML join points. The proposed pointcut language covers all the kinds of join points where our supported adaptations are performed. In the following, we present the primitive pointcut designators for the main UML diagrams that are supported by our approach, i.e., class diagrams, state machine diagrams, sequence diagrams, and activity diagrams.

Those primitives can be composed with logical operators (AND, OR, and NOT) to build other pointcuts.

6.2.3.1   Class Diagram Pointcuts

Table 6.2 presents the pointcut primitives that are proposed to designate class diagram elements. We choose the main elements that are usually used in class diagrams, i.e., class, attribute, operation, association, and package. Class diagram elements are

Table 6.2   Class diagram pointcuts—part 1

Join point	Pointcut designator	Description
Class	Class(NamePattern)	Selects a class based on its name
	Inside_Package(PackagePointcut)	Selects a class that belongs to a specific package matched by *PackagePointcut*
	Contains_Attribute(AttributePointcut)	Selects a class that contains a specific attribute matched by *AttributePointcut*
	Contains_Operation(Operation-Pointcut)	Selects a class that contains a specific operation matched by *OperationPointcut*
	Associated_With(ClassPointcut)	Selects a class that is associated with a specific class matched by *ClassPointcut*
Attribute	Attribute(NamePattern)	Selects an attribute based on its name
	Inside_Class(ClassPointcut)	Selects an attribute that belongs to a specific class matched by *ClassPointcut*
	Of_Type(TypePattern)	Selects an attribute that is of a certain type
	Of_Visibility(VisibilityKind)	Selects an attribute that is of a certain visibility (e.g., public, private)
Operation	Operation(NamePattern)	Selects an operation based on its name
	Inside_Class(ClassPointcut)	Selects an operation that belongs to a specific class matched by *ClassPointcut*
	Args(TypePattern1, TypePattern2,…)	Selects an operation based on the type of its arguments
	Of_Visibility(VisibilityKind)	Selects an operation that is of a certain visibility (e.g., public, private)
Association	Association(NamePattern)	Selects an association based on its name
	Between(ClassPointcut, ClassPointcut)	Selects an association that is between certain classes
	Member_Ends(AttributePointcut, AttributePointcut)	Selects an association based on its member ends
	Aggregation_Kind(AggregationKind)	Selects an association based on its aggregation kind (e.g., composite)
Package	Package(NamePattern)	Selects a package based on its name
	Inside_Package(PackagePointcut)	Selects a package that belongs to a specific package matched by *PackagePointcut*
	Contains_Class(ClassPointcut)	Selects a package that contains a specific class matched by *ClassPointcut*

designated either by their main properties, e.g., name, type, visibility, container, and owned elements, or by other associated elements. For example, the following pointcut expression designates a class, named *c1*, that is inside a package *p1*, and contains an operation *op1*:

```
Class(c1) && Inside_Package(p1) && Contains_Operation(op1)
```

Moreover, if we want to designate all classes that contain either private attributes or private operations, then the following pointcut is an example of such expression:

```
Class(*) && (Contains_Attribute(Of_Visibility(Private)) ||
      Contains_Operation(Of_Visibility(Private)))
```

Note that the symbol "*" is used to designate all the elements of a particular type regardless of their names, as it is used in AspectJ [113].

6.2.3.2 State Machine Diagram Pointcuts

Table 6.3 presents the pointcut primitives proposed to designate the elements of state machine diagrams. We choose the main elements that are usually used in state machine diagrams, i.e., state machine, region, state, and transition. A state machine diagram element is designated either by its name, container, owned elements, specified elements (in case of a state machine), incoming/outgoing transitions (in case of a state), or source/target states (in case of a transition). For example, the following pointcut expression designates a state, named *s1*, with an incoming transition *t1*, and that belongs to a state machine *sm1*:

```
State(s1) && Incoming(t1) && Inside_State_Machine(sm1).
```

6.2.3.3 Sequence Diagram Pointcuts

Table 6.4 presents the primitives proposed to designate sequence diagram elements. We choose the main elements that are commonly used in sequence diagrams, i.e., interaction, message, and lifeline. A sequence diagram element is designated either by its name, type, container, owned elements, specified elements (in case of an interaction), or source/target lifelines (in case of a message). For example, the pointcut *SensitiveMethodPointcut* in Fig. 6.3 is a conjunction of three pointcuts: (1) *Message_Call(SensitiveMethod)* selects any message that calls *SensitiveMethod()*, (2) *Message_Source(User)* selects any message whose source is of type *User*, and (3) *Message_Target(Resource)* selects any message whose target is of type *Resource*. The conjunction of these three pointcuts allows the selection of all message calls to *SensitiveMethod()* from a *User* instance to a *Resource* instance.

Table 6.3 State machine diagram pointcuts

Join point	Pointcut designator	Description
State machine	State_Machine(NamePattern)	Selects a state machine diagram based on its name
	Contains_Region(Region-Pointcut)	Selects a state machine that contains a specific region matched by *RegionPointcut*
	Contains_State(StatePointcut)	Selects a state machine that contains a specific state matched by *StatePointcut*
	Contains_Transition(Transition-Pointcut)	Selects a state machine that contains a specific transition matched by *TransitionPointcut*
	Specifies_Class(ClassPointcut)	Selects a state machine that specifies a specific class matched by *ClassPointcut*
Region	Region(NamePattern)	Selects a region based on its name
	Inside_State_Machine(State-MachinePointcut)	Selects a region that belongs to a specific state machine matched by *StateMachinePointcut*
	Inside_State(StatePointcut)	Selects a region that belongs to a specific state matched by *StatePointcut*
	Contains_State(StatePointcut)	Selects a region that contains a specific state matched by *StatePointcut*
	Contains_Transition(Transition-Pointcut)	Selects a region that contains a specific transition matched by *TransitionPointcut*
State	State(NamePattern)	Selects a state based on its name
	Inside_Region(RegionPointcut)	Selects a state that belongs to a specific region matched by *RegionPointcut*
	Inside_State(StatePointcut)	Selects a state that belongs to a specific state matched by *StatePointcut*
	Inside_State_Machine(State-MachinePointcut)	Selects a state that belongs to a specific state machine matched by *StateMachinePointcut*
	Incoming(TransitionPointcut)	Selects a state that has a specific incoming transition matched by *TransitionPointcut*
	Outgoing(TransitionPointcut)	Selects a state that has a specific outgoing transition matched by *TransitionPointcut*
	Contains_State(StatePointcut)	Selects a state that contains a specific state matched by *StatePointcut*
	Contains_Transition(Transi-tionPointcut)	Selects a state that contains a specific transition matched by *TransitionPointcut*
Transition	Transition(NamePattern)	Selects a transition based on its name
	Inside_Region(RegionPointcut)	Selects a transition that belongs to a specific region matched by *RegionPointcut*
	Inside_State(StatePointcut)	Selects a transition that belongs to a specific state matched by *StatePointcut*
	Inside_State_Machine(State-MachinePointcut)	Selects a transition that belongs to a specific state machine matched by *StateMachinePointcut*
	Source_State(StatePointcut)	Selects a transition that has a specific source state matched by *StatePointcut*
	Target_State(StatePointcut)	Selects a transition that has a specific target state matched by *StatePointcut*

Table 6.4 Sequence diagram pointcuts

Join point	Pointcut designator	Description
Interaction	Interaction(NamePattern)	Selects an interaction based on its name
	Contains_Message(Message-Pointcut)	Selects an interaction that contains a specific message matched by *MessagePointcut*
	Contains_Lifeline(Lifeline-Pointcut)	Selects an interaction that contains a specific lifeline matched by *LifelinePointcut*
	Specifies_Operation(Operation-Pointcut)	Selects an interaction that specifies the behavior of a specific operation matched by *OperationPointcut*
Message	Message_Call(NamePattern)	Selects a message call, either synchronous or asynchronous, based on its name
	Message_Syn_Call(NamePattern)	Selects a message that specifies a synchronous call
	Message_Asyn_Call(Name-Pattern)	Selects a message that specifies an asynchronous call
	Reply_Message(NamePattern)	Selects a reply message based on its name
	Create_Message(NamePattern)	Selects a message that creates an object
	Destroy_Message(NamePattern)	Selects a message that destroys an object
	Message_Source(TypePattern)	Selects a message whose source is of a certain type
	Message_Target(TypePattern)	Selects a message whose target is of a certain type
	Inside_Interaction(Interaction-Pointcut)	Selects a message that belongs to a specific interaction matched by *InteractionPointcut*
Lifeline	Lifeline(NamePattern)	Selects a lifeline based on its name
	Inside_Interaction(Interaction-Pointcut)	Selects a lifeline that belongs to a specific interaction matched by *InteractionPointcut*
	Covered_By_Fragment(Name-Pattern)	Selects a lifeline that is covered by a specific interaction fragment
	Contains_Execution(NamePattern)	Selects a lifeline that contains a specific execution specification

6.2.3.4 Activity Diagram Pointcuts

Table 6.5 presents the primitives proposed to designate the elements of activity diagrams. We choose the main elements that are commonly used in activity diagrams, i.e., activity, action, and edge. An activity diagram element is designated either by its name, type, container, owned elements, specified elements (in case of an activity), incoming/outgoing edges (in case of an action), or source/target actions (in case of an edge). For example, the following pointcut expression designates a call operation

Table 6.5 Activity diagram pointcuts

Join point	Pointcut designator	Description
Activity	Activity(NamePattern)	Selects an activity based on its name
	Contains_Action(ActionPointcut)	Selects an activity that contains a specific action matched by *ActionPointcut*
	Contains_Edge(EdgePointcut)	Selects an activity that contains a specific activity edge matched by *EdgePointcut*
	Specifies_Operation(Operation-Pointcut)	Selects an activity that specifies the behavior of a specific operation matched by *OperationPointcut*
Action	Action(NamePattern)	Selects an action based on its name
	Call_Operation_Action(Name-Pattern)	Selects an action that performs an operation call
	Call_Behavior_Action(Name-Pattern)	Selects an action that performs a behavior call
	Create_Action(NamePattern)	Selects an action that creates an object
	Destroy_Action(NamePattern)	Selects an action that destroys an object
	Read_Action(NamePattern)	Selects an action that reads the value(s) of a structural feature
	Write_Action(NamePattern)	Selects an action that updates the value(s) of a structural feature
	Inside_Activity(ActivityPointcut)	Selects an action that belongs to a specific activity
	Input(TypePattern, …)	Selects an action based on the type of its input pins
	Output(TypePattern, …)	Selects an action based on the type of its output pins
Control Node	Initial(NamePattern)	Selects an initial node based on its name
	Final(NamePattern)	Selects an activity final node based on its name
	Flowfinal(NamePattern)	Selects a flow final node based on its name
	Fork(NamePattern)	Selects a fork node based on its name
	Join(NamePattern)	Selects a join node based on its name
	Decision(NamePattern)	Selects a decision node based on its name
	Merge(NamePattern)	Selects a merge node based on its name
Activity Edge	Edge(NamePattern)	Selects an edge based on its name
	Inside_Activity(ActivityPointcut)	Selects an edge that belongs to a specific activity
	Source_Action(ActionPointcut)	Selects an edge that has a specific source
	Target_Action(ActionPointcut)	Selects an edge that has a specific target

action, named *a1*, that belongs to an activity *act1*: *Call_Operation_Action(a1)* && *Inside_Activity(act1)*.

6.3 Related Work on AOM

During the last decade, AOM has become the center of many research activities. Following the success of AOP techniques in modularizing crosscutting concerns at the implementation level, considerable number of contributions worked on abstracting AOP concepts and adopting them at different specification and design languages. An overview and a comparison of the existing approaches are presented in [31, 170, 182]. In the following, we provide a summary of the main approaches.

Kienzle et al. [116, 117] have proposed Reusable Aspect Models (RAM); an AOM approach that specifies a concern using class, state machine, and sequence diagrams. One of the goals of the RAM approach is to support aspect reusability, i.e., build aspects with complex functionalities by reusing simple ones, by means of aspect dependency chains. A weaver is implemented using Kompose [85] for weaving class diagrams and Geko [138] for weaving state machine diagrams and sequence diagrams.

The High-Level Aspects (HiLA) approach [212] extends UML state machines for specifying history-dependent and concurrent behaviors. Join points in HiLA capture points when a transition is being fired. Pointcuts may also contain constraints, i.e., advices are only executed when the constraints are satisfied. To increase reusability, aspects are specified as UML templates, which are then specialized to the designer's application. HiLA also allows transformational aspects, i.e., aspects that can match a sub-structure of the base state machine and replace them by the advice.

Klein et al. [118] have proposed various formal definitions of join points in sequence diagrams. Aspects are specified as pairs of UML 2.0 sequence diagrams: One sequence diagram for pointcuts and the other one for advice specification. Join points can be either a single element or a collection of elements. This approach also provides a formal definition of a new composition operator for sequence diagrams, called an amalgamated sum, and describes its implementation using Kermeta.[2]

Tkatchenko and Kiczales [196] have added a join point model (JPM) to UML metamodel. They have covered three UML diagrams, namely, class diagrams, state machine diagrams, and sequence diagrams. For class diagrams, the considered join points are class and operation elements. For sequence diagrams, they have considered messages and lifelines as join points. For state machine diagrams, states and call triggers have been considered as join points. Comparing with our approach, we cover a wider range of diagrams and UML elements as join points. In addition, the matching process in this approach is based only on direct name matching or on signature comparison.

---

[2] http://www.kermeta.org/.

Clark et al. [59] have proposed an AOM approach called Theme/UML. This approach is a symmetric one, i.e., there is no distinction between the base model and the crosscutting concerns. It is a general-purpose AOM language. Aspects are modeled as templates that are bound to base elements through binding relationships. Package and class diagrams are used for modeling structural adaptations and sequence diagrams are used for modeling behavioral adaptations. This approach is possibly the most mature and the most well-engineered approach to AOM. However, its main intent is the identification of aspects in the requirements analysis phase and mapping those aspects to the design.

Some contributions have focused on abstracting AspectJ [113] into the modeling level [79, 191, 208]. Evermann [79] has proposed a UML profile for AspectJ based on the existing UML metamodel. An aspect is specified as a stereotyped class. Pointcuts are modeled as stereotyped attributes, while advices are modeled as stereotyped operations. In contrast to previous work on AspectJ profiles, this is possibly the most complete specification so far. Stein et al. [191] have proposed one of the earlier profiles for AspectJ. Pointcuts and advices are specified as stereotyped operations. Join points are considered as messages in collaboration diagrams. The introduction of new class elements or associations is specified using UML diagram templates. Weaving of advices and introductions into base models is modeled as relationships in collaboration diagrams denoting the crosscutting effects of aspects on their base classes.

Yan et al. [208] have adopted the extension of UML metamodel by introducing an AspectJ metamodel in order to support AspectJ software modeling. First, a metamodel for Java was designed by tailoring UML meta-classes to Java. Then, the Java metamodel was extended into AspectJ metamodel. This work aims at narrowing the gap between conceptual modeling of aspects and their concrete implementation in AspectJ. The same approach of extending UML metamodel for aspect specification was also proposed by Chavez and Lucena [55]. However, the main limitation of such an approach is the fact that extending UML metamodel requires either modifying existing UML case tools, or implementing new ones in order to provide support for the newly defined meta-classes.

One of the initial proposals in this field is the one of Aldawud et al. [28]. It provides a UML profile for aspect specification by applying stereotypes on classes. Later, it has been extended to support pointcut and advice specification [29]. Crosscutting associations are used to show how aspect elements relate to base model elements. This profile is very generic and captures only few concepts of AOP. Other contributions in this area [43, 44, 91, 112, 139, 165] have provided extensions of the UML language for modeling aspects using standard UML extension mechanisms. However, the majority of these approaches are programming language dependent and specify only few concepts of AOP.

6.4 Conclusion

In this chapter, we have presented an AOM approach for specifying and weaving security aspects into UML design models. This approach is well suited for job separation: security experts provide high-level security solutions including the details on how to apply them in UML diagrams and the designers apply them in their design by adapting them to the design context. With our approach, even the designers with limited security knowledge can use the security solutions to enforce the needed security requirements in a systematic way in their design. As another result of our contribution, security solutions can be integrated into software from the early phases of the development life cycle. This in turn helps accelerating the development of secure applications and reducing errors and costs.

Different mechanisms can be used to specify aspects at the model level. Some contributions suggest extending UML metamodel by adding new meta-classes or creating new meta-models to specify aspect-oriented concepts. These techniques suffer from implementation and interoperability issues, as UML case tools need to be extended to support the newly specified meta-classes. The other technique, i.e., using standard UML extension mechanisms, is a better solution as it overcomes the limitations identified in the previous approaches.

In this setting, we have developed a UML profile for the specification of aspects at the design level. The proposed profile allows the specification of common aspect-oriented primitives, i.e., adding new elements *before/after/around* join points and removing existing elements. In addition, the proposed profile supports both structural and behavioral adaptations and covers the main diagrams that are used in UML design. Furthermore, we have defined a high-level and user-friendly pointcut language that can be used by security experts to designate UML elements. We have seen that the proposed pointcut language is expressive enough to designate the main elements that are used in a software design. In the next chapter, we will present our approach for systematically weaving the security aspects, specified using our AOM profile, into UML design models.

Chapter 7
Security Aspect Weaving

This chapter presents our aspect weaving framework for security hardening. The proposed framework allows software developers to systematically integrate security aspects, specified using our AOM profile, into UML design models. More precisely, we provide the design and the implementation of the weaving capabilities corresponding to the aspect adaptations that are supported by our AOM profile.

We start by providing a high-level overview that summarizes the main steps and the technologies that are followed to implement the weaving framework. Afterwards, we present the details of each weaving step. The proposed weaver is implemented as a model-to-model (M2M) transformation approach since the latter is defined following the OMG's standard recommendations. In addition, it provides many languages and tools that can help in automating the weaving process. As a transformation language, we adopt the OMG standard Query/View/Transformation (QVT) language [150] since it is compatible with UML and supports a large set of modifications on UML models. As for join points matching, we instrument the standard OCL language to query UML elements due to its expressiveness and conformance to UML. The proposed weaver covers all the diagrams that are supported by our approach, i.e., class diagrams, state machine diagrams, activity diagrams, and sequence diagrams. For each diagram, we provide algorithms that implement its corresponding weaving adaptations, i.e., *before* adaptation, *after* adaptation, and *around* adaptation. In addition, we present the transformation rules that implement aspect adaptation rules, i.e., *add* and *remove* adaptation rules.

The main advantages of our weaving framework are the portability and the expressiveness thanks to the use of OMG standards, namely, OCL and QVT. Using OCL, we were able to match a large and variant set of join points. Using QVT allowed us to support a wide variety of modifications on different UML diagrams. In addition, QVT extends portability of the designed weaver to all tools supporting QVT language.

The remainder of this chapter is organized as follows. Section 7.1 gives an overview of our security weaving approach. Section 7.2 presents the specialization of security aspects. The matching process is presented in Sect. 7.3. Afterwards, we

© Springer International Publishing Switzerland 2015

D. Mouheb et al., *Aspect-Oriented Security Hardening of UML Design Models*,

DOI 10.1007/978-3-319-16106-8_7

provide details about the actual weaving process in Sect. 7.4. Section 7.5 presents our weaving tool followed by case studies in Sect. 7.6. In Sect. 7.7, we discuss the related work on model weaving. Finally, we conclude this chapter in Sect. 7.8.

7.1 Approach Overview

In this section, we present an overview of our security weaving approach. The proposed approach allows software developers to systematically integrate security aspects, specified by a security expert using our AOM profile, into UML design models. As we mentioned previously, the weaving is based on model-to-model transformation technology. The main steps and the technologies that are followed to

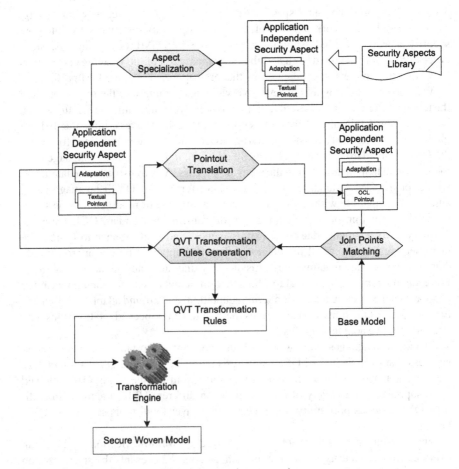

Fig. 7.1 Overview of the proposed security weaving approach

implement the weaving capabilities are presented in Fig. 7.1. In the following, we provide a brief description of each step:

- *Aspect Specialization*: The developer specializes the application-independent aspect, provided by the security expert in a security aspects library, to his/her application. An application-dependent aspect is automatically generated after this step. More details about this step are presented in Sect. 7.2.
- *Pointcut Translation*: The textual pointcut expressions specified in the aspect using our proposed pointcut language are automatically translated into equivalent OCL expressions. The aspect will then be updated with the new OCL expressions. This step and the previous one are preliminary steps before the actual weaving begins.
- *Join Point Matching*: The OCL expressions generated from the previous step are evaluated on the base model to identify the locations where the weaving should be performed. More details about pointcut translation and join point matching are presented in Sect. 7.3.
- *QVT Transformation Rules Generation*: Using the aspect adaptations and the locations identified from the previous step, we generate the equivalent QVT transformation rules. These rules, in turn, will be given as input to the transformation engine along with the base model, which will result in a secure woven model.

In the following sections, we explain each step of the weaving approach starting from specializing the application-independent aspects, to identifying the join point elements of the base model, where different kinds of adaptations need to be injected, all the way through the process of the actual weaving.

7.2 Security Aspect Specialization

For the purpose of reuse, security aspects can be designed, by security experts, as generic solutions that can be applied to any design model. More precisely, the pointcuts specified by security experts are chosen to match specific points of the design where security methods should be added. Since security solutions are provided in a library of aspects, pointcuts are specified as generic patterns that should match all possible join points that can be targeted by security solutions. Thus, before being able to weave aspects into base models, the developer needs to specialize the generic aspects to his/her application by choosing the elements of his/her model that are targeted by the security solutions.

To specialize the aspects, we provide a graphical weaving interface that hides the complexity of the security solutions and only exposes the generic pointcuts to the developers (Fig. 7.2). Indeed, the developer does not need to understand the inner working of the security solution. From this weaving interface and based on his/her understanding of the application, the developer has the possibility of mapping each generic element of the aspect to its corresponding element(s) in the base model. After mapping all the generic elements, the application-dependent aspect will be automatically generated.

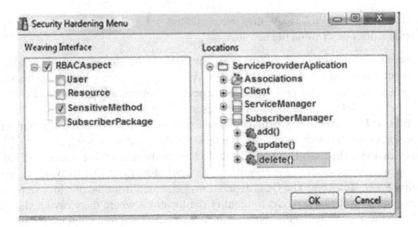

Fig. 7.2 Security aspects specialization

Notice here that this mapping operation has a *one-to-many* relationship. In other words, one generic element in the pointcut expression can be mapped to multiple elements in the base model. For example, consider the following pointcut expression that aims at capturing any call to a sensitive method: *Message_Call(sensitiveMethod)*. In order to specialize this expression, the developer maps the abstract element *sensitiveMethod* to the corresponding operation(s) in his/her application (e.g., *op1, op2*). This will result in an expanded expression, where all the selected elements are combined together with the logical operator *OR* (||) as follows: *Message_Call(op1) || Message_Call(op2)* (Fig. 7.2).

7.3 Join Point Matching

During this step, the actual join points where the aspect adaptations should be performed are selected from the base model. To select the targeted join points, the textual pointcuts, specified using our proposed pointcut language (Sect. 6.2.3), need to be translated to a language that can navigate the base model and query its elements. In our approach, we choose to translate the textual pointcut expressions into the standard OCL language [153]. This is due to the high expressiveness of the OCL language and its conformance to UML. In fact, OCL is defined as part of the UML standard and is typically used to write constraints on UML elements. However, since OCL 2.0 [149], it has been extended to include support for queries. Therefore, using OCL, we can match a large and variant set of join points using matching criteria that take into consideration different properties of UML elements such as names, types, arguments, and locations.

We translate textual pointcuts to OCL constraints, which serve as predicates to select the considered join points. This translation is done by producing a parser that is capable of parsing and translating any textual pointcut expression, that conforms to a defined grammar, to its equivalent OCL expression. Indeed, this process is executed automatically and in a total transparent way from the user. Once the OCL expression is generated, it will be evaluated on the base model to select the targeted join points. For example, the textual pointcut expression: "*Message_Call(SensitiveMethod) &&* *Message_Source(User) && Message_Target(Resource)*" will be tokenized into three tokens connected with the logical operator *&&* as follows: (1) *Message_Call* *(SensitiveMethod)*, (2) *Message_Source(User)*, and (3) *Message_Target(Resource)*. The parser will parse the textual expression and will translate it into the following OCL expression:

"self.oclIsTypeOf(Message) and self.name='*SensitiveMethod*' and
self.connector._end-> at(1).role.name='*User*' and
self.connector._end-> at(2).role.name='*Resource*'"

This expression will then be evaluated on the elements of the base model and the matched elements, which correspond to all message calls to *SensitiveMethod* from a *User* instance to a *Resource* instance, will be selected as join points.

7.4 Security Aspect Weaving

During this step, the aspect adaptations are automatically woven into the base model at the identified join points according to the specification of the security solution. In our framework, the process of weaving aspects into UML models is considered as a model-to-model transformation process, where the base model is being transformed into a new model that has been enhanced with some new features defined by the aspect. As a transformation language, we adopt QVT (Query/View/Transformation) language since it is an OMG standard compatible with UML and supports a large set of modifications on UML models. The proposed model weaver is implemented using well-known standards, which makes it a portable solution as it is independent of any specific UML tool. In the following subsections, we present the details of the weaver design and implementation, starting by a high-level description of the weaver architecture.

7.4.1 Weaver Architecture

The weaver is designed to manipulate both structural and behavioral UML diagrams. It is capable of weaving different types of UML diagrams that are used to model different views of a system. Figure 7.3 presents the general architecture of our model weaver. It consists of two main components: (1) Join point matching module and (2) Transformation module. The join point matching module is defined by extending the QVT engine through the QVT Black-Box mechanism [150]. On the other hand, the transformation module is composed of four different transformation definitions,

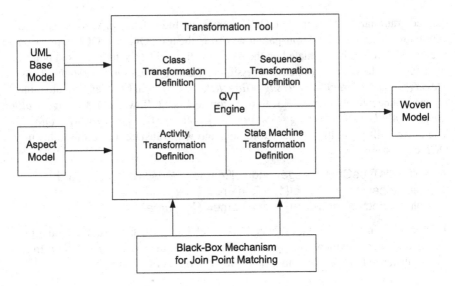

Fig. 7.3 General architecture of the weaver

each of which corresponds to a particular kind of UML diagram. In the sequel, we detail each component.

7.4.1.1 Join Point Matching Module

The join point matching module allows evaluating pointcut expressions, specified in OCL, on UML base model elements and identifying the appropriate join points that satisfy the given expressions. In our framework, this module is defined as an extension to the QVT main functionalities using the QVT Black-Box mechanism, which is an important feature of the QVT language. QVT Black-Box mechanism facilitates the integration of external programs, expressed in other transformation languages or programming languages, in order to perform a given task that is un-realizable by the QVT language. Algorithm 7.1 presents the pseudo-code of our join point matching algorithm. It takes as input an OCL expression along with the base model elements and returns as output a set of join point elements that satisfy the given expression.

This algorithm is executed for each pointcut expression specified in the aspect. However, when dealing with big models with a large set of elements, this process may become a significant overhead on the system. Therefore, some optimizations are needed. Since each pointcut expression belongs to a specific adaptation, we optimize this process by applying a filtering mechanism, such that we only evaluate the pointcut expression on those elements that conform to the given adaptation instead

---

Algorithm 7.1: Join Point Matching

Input: *OCLExp, BaseModelElements*
Output: *JoinPointElem-set*
  query = createQuery(*OCLExp*);
  for all *el* in *BaseModelElements* **do**
    result = validate(*query,el*);
    if *result* is **true then**
      JoinPointElem-set.update(*el*);
    end if
  end for
  return *JoinPointElem-set*;

---

of evaluating it on all base model elements. For example, in the case of a pointcut expression defined in a class adaptation, the filtering mechanism will select from the base model only class diagram elements, and then pass them to the join point matching module. This optimization increases the efficiency and the performance of the matching module.

7.4.1.2 Transformation Tool

The transformation tool consists of a set of transformation definitions, each of which targets a particular UML diagram. In addition, each transformation definition contains a set of mapping rules that define how each element in the corresponding diagram should be transformed. In our weaver, we classify the transformation definitions according to the supported UML diagrams. Thus, we provide four types of transformation definitions: class transformation definition, state machine transformation definition, activity transformation definition, and sequence transformation definition (Fig. 7.3). For instance, the class transformation definition consists of a set of mapping rules, which specify how each element of the class diagram can be transformed or woven into the base model. A detailed description of each transformation definition is provided in Sect. 7.4.2.

When the transformation tool receives the base model as input, each transformation definition applies some filtering operations on the input model to select the corresponding set of diagrams. Then, each transformation definition executes the appropriate mapping rules, using the underlying QVT engine, and produces the woven model as output. This architecture facilitates the extension of the transformation tool to support a wider range of UML diagrams since new components can be easily plugged-in without going through the hassle of modifying the existing architecture. Moreover, since the definition of the mapping rules is based on UML metamodel, the transformations can be used with any UML model and are not dependent on a particular specification or implementation.

7.4.2 *Transformation Definitions*

The transformation definitions describe how each element in the source model (the base model) is transformed in the target model (the woven model). This is achieved by using mapping rules that describe a certain behavior. For each aspect adaptation (e.g., class adaptation), we specify a corresponding transformation definition (e.g., class transformation definition). By analogy, the aspect adaptations are program source code and the transformation definitions are its execution semantics. In other words, a transformation definition defines how and when each construct in the aspect adaptation should produce a given behavior. In the following, the four kinds of transformation definitions are detailed.

7.4.2.1 Class Transformation Definition

The class transformation definition handles transformations of class diagrams. It contains a set of mapping rules that specify how each class diagram element should be transformed. To do so, the class transformation definition iterates through the different adaptations of an aspect and selects the adaptation difference between the

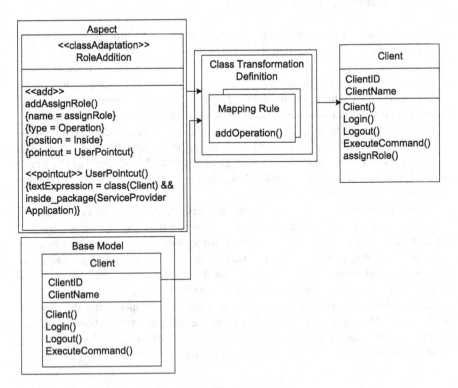

Fig. 7.4 Example of class transformation definition

class transformation definition and the other transformation definitions of behavioral diagrams. The class diagrams are structural in nature; they are considered as a static view. For example, the class transformation definition consists of adding/removing structural elements inside/between class diagram elements, such as adding an attribute/operation inside a given class or an association between two given classes. Whereas, the transformation definition of a behavioral diagram consists of adding/ removing elements *before/after/around* behavioral diagram elements, such as adding a new interaction fragment before sending a message in a sequence diagram.

Figure 7.4 shows an example of a class transformation definition. The aspect depicted in this figure contains a class adaptation named *RoleAddition*. This class adaptation specifies an add adaptation rule (*addAssignRole*) that adds an operation, named *assignRole*, to a class designated by the pointcut *UserPointcut*. Having a class adaptation and an adaptation rule that adds an element of type *Operation*, the class transformation definition is going to be selected and the mapping rule *addOperation* will be executed. The result of this transformation will be the addition of the new operation *assignRole()* to the class *Client* of the base model, i.e., the selected join point.

7.4.2.2 State Machine Transformation Definition

The state machine transformation definition handles transformations of state machine diagrams. It corresponds to an aspect adaptation that is stereotyped *StateMachineAdaptation*. In our approach, when handling transformations of state machine diagrams, we identify two kinds of pointcut designators: (1) *State-based pointcut* that designates a set of states without any consideration of the transitions/events that were triggered to reach them, and (2) *Path-based pointcut* that designates a set of states depending on the transitions that triggered them. For example, consider the state machine diagram, depicted in Fig. 7.5a, where we want to add a new state (*State4*) before the state *State3* when triggered by transition *Tr1*, as it is specified by the pointcut expression shown in Fig. 7.6.

During the matching process, the OCL expression is evaluated on the base model elements and the state *State3* is identified as a join point. Then, the weaving process will inject the new state (*State4*) before the identified join point. However, if the state *State3* has more than one incoming transition, which is the case in our example, the weaver will add the new state before all incoming transitions, which is not what we aim for. To solve this problem, the OCL expression is used not only as a query expression to identify the join points, but is also used to put further constraints on the identified join points during the weaving. Thus, our identified join point is the state *State3* under the constraint of being triggered by the transition *Tr1*. The result of the weaving is shown in Fig. 7.5b. In our approach, join points in state machine diagrams can be either *states* or *transitions*. Furthermore, three weaving adaptations: *before*, *after*, and *around* are supported. In the following, we provide the implementation details of each weaving adaptation.

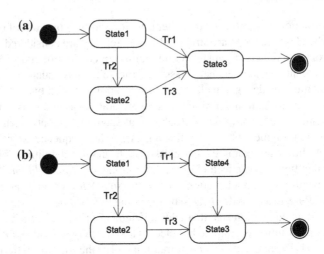

Fig. 7.5 Weaving example for path-based join point. **a** Before weaving. **b** After weaving

State(State3) && Incoming(Tr1)	(Textual pointcut)
self.oclIsTypeOf(State) and self.name='State3' and self.incoming ➤ exists(t:Transition | t.name='Tr1');	(OCL pointcut)

Fig. 7.6 Example of path-based pointcut

Weaving Before Adaptation

This adaptation adds a new node in a state machine diagram *before* an identified join point. Hence, it requires not only identifying the targeted join point, but also its direct predecessors. Algorithm 7.2 summarizes the steps needed to perform this adaptation. As shown in the algorithm, the two kinds of join points, *State* and *Transition*, are considered. In addition, both kinds of pointcuts, *State-based* and *Path-based* pointcuts, are matched. The algorithm takes as input a set of join points, an OCL expression, the new node to add, and a base model. It returns as output the woven model, where the new node has been added *before* each of the identified join points.

Weaving After Adaptation

This adaptation adds a new node in a state machine diagram *after* an identified join point. Hence, it requires not only identifying the targeted join point, but also its direct successors. Algorithm 7.3 summarizes the steps needed to perform this adaptation. The algorithm takes as input a set of join points, an OCL expression, the new node to add, and a base model. It returns as output the woven model, where the new node has been added *after* each of the identified join points. Similar to the *before* adaptation, we consider both kinds of join points and pointcuts.

Algorithm 7.2: State Machine Diagram: Weaving Before Adaptation

---

Input: *JoinPointElem-set, OCLExp, newNode, BaseModel*
  edgeSet: Edge-set;
  for *nextJoinPoint* in *JoinPointElem-set* **do**
    if *nextJoinPoint* is of type STATE **then**
      if isPathBased(*OCLExp*) **then**
        oclConstraint = extractConstraint(*OCLExp*);
        edgeSet = getInComingEdge(*nextJoinPoint, oclConstraint*);
      else
        edgeSet = getInComingEdges(*nextJoinPoint*);
      end if
      for all *edge* in *edgeSet* **do**
        edge.setTarget(newNode);
      end for
      BaseModel = CreateEdge(*newNode, nextJoinPoint*);
    else
      if *nextJoinPoint* is of type TRANSITION **then**
        temp = getSource(*nextJoinPoint*);
        nextJoinPoint.setSource(*newNode*);
        BaseModel = CreateEdge(*temp, newNode*);
      end if
    end if
  end for

Algorithm 7.3: State Machine Diagram: Weaving After Adaptation

---

Input: *JoinPointElem-set, OCLExp, newNode, BaseModel*
  edgeSet: Edge-set;
  for *nextJoinPoint* in *JoinPointElem-set* **do**
    if *nextJoinPoint* is of type STATE **then**
      if isPathBased(*OCLExp*) **then**
        oclConstraint = extractConstraint(*OCLExp*);
        edgeSet = getOutGoingEdge(*nextJoinPoint, oclConstraint*);
      else
        edgeSet = getOutGoingEdges(*nextJoinPoint*);
      end if
      for all *edge* in *edgeSet* **do**
        edge.setSource(newNode);
      end for
      BaseModel = CreateEdge(*nextJoinPoint, newNode*);
    else
      if *nextJoinPoint* is of type TRANSITION **then**
        temp = getTarget(*nextJoinPoint*);
        nextJoinPoint.setTarget(*newNode*);
        BaseModel = CreateEdge(*newNode, temp*);
      end if
    end if
  end for

Weaving Around Adaptation

Around adaptations are performed in place of the join points they operate over, rather than *before* or *after*. Additionally, inspired by AspectJ [113], the original join point can be invoked, within the behavior of the *around* adaptation, using a special element named `proceed`. *Around* adaptations can have one of two effects:

- In case there is no `proceed` element in the adaptation, then the join point is replaced by the adaptation behavior.
- In case the adaptation contains a `proceed` element, then all the elements that appear before the `proceed` element are injected before the join point, and similarly, all the elements appearing after the `proceed` element are injected after the join point.

Algorithm 7.4 summarizes the steps needed to perform an *around* adaptation in a state machine diagram. The algorithm takes as input a set of join points, an OCL expression, the new state machine element to add, and a base model. The algorithm then replaces the current join point with the new state machine element. In addition, it checks whether the new state machine element contains a `proceed` element or not. If the `proceed` element exists, then it will be identified and replaced with the current join point.

Algorithm 7.4: State Machine Diagram: Weaving Around Adaptation

---

Input: *JoinPointElem-set, OCLExp, newSMElem, BaseModel*
  for *nextJoinPoint* in *JoinPointElem-set* **do**
    replace(*nextJoinPoint, newSMElem*);
    if isProceed(*newSMElem*) **then**
      proceedElement = findProceed(*newSMElem*);
      replace(*proceedElement, nextJoinPoint*);
      delete(*proceedElement*);
    else
      delete(*nextJoinPoint*);
    end if
  end for
`Procedure replace:`
Input: *oldElement, newElement*
  edgeSet: Edge-set;
  edgeSet = inComingEdges(*oldElement*);
  for all *edge* in *edgeSet* **do**
    edge.setTarget(*newElement*);
  end for
  edgeSet = outGoingEdges(*oldElement*);
  for all *edge* in *edgeSet* **do**
    edge.setSource(*newElement*);
  end for

7.4.2.3 Activity Transformation Definition

The activity transformation definition handles transformations of activity diagrams. It corresponds to an aspect adaptation that is stereotyped *ActivityAdaptation*. In our approach, join points in activity diagrams can be either *nodes* or *edges*. A node can be either an action or a control node (e.g., fork, join, decision, merge). Since an activity diagram models the flow of actions in a business process, then ordering must be taken into consideration when weaving a new behavior into such a flow. Weaving adaptations in activity diagrams are very similar to those of state machine diagrams, as both diagrams are constructed from nodes and edges. In the following, we describe each weaving adaptation.

Weaving Before Adaptation
This adaptation adds a new node in an activity diagram *before* a join point. It requires identifying the join point kind, whether it is an action, a control node, or an edge, and its direct predecessor(s). In case of an action, all incoming edges are redirected to the new node. As such, a new edge is created between the new node and the join point. However, if the join point is a *join* or a *merge* node, where there is more than one incoming edge, then the new node is duplicated for each edge. Thus, each incoming edge to the join or the merge nodes is redirected to the new nodes. Moreover, two new edges are created between the new nodes and the join point (Fig. 7.7). Algorithm 7.5 summarizes the steps of the *before* weaving adaptation in activity diagrams. The algorithm takes as input a set of join points, the new node to add, and a base model. It returns as output the woven model together with the new node added *before* each of the identified join points.

Weaving After Adaptation
This adaptation adds a new node in an activity diagram *after* a join point. In case the join point is an action, all outgoing edges are redirected to the new node. Accordingly, a new edge is created between the join point and the new node. However, if the join point is a *fork* or a *decision* node, where there is more than one outgoing edge, then a new node is created for each edge. Moreover, two new edges are created between the new nodes and the original join point successors (Fig. 7.8). Algorithm 7.6 summarizes the steps of weaving an *after* adaptation in activity diagrams. It takes, as input, a set

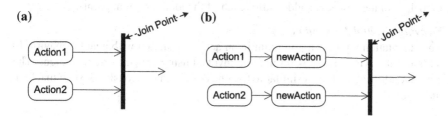

Fig. 7.7 Example of *Join* node as join point. **a** Before weaving. **b** After weaving

---

Algorithm 7.5: Activity Diagram: Weaving Before Adaptation

Input: *JoinPointElem-set*, *newNode*, *BaseModel*
  edgeSet: ActivityEdge-set;
  for *nextJoinPoint* in *JoinPointElem-set* **do**
    if *nextJoinPoint* is of type ActivityNode **then**
      edgeSet = getInComingEdges(*nextJoinPoint*);
      if *nextJoinPoint* is of type JoinNode or MergeNode **then**
        for all *edge* in *edgeSet* **do**
          copy *newNode*;
          edge.setTarget(*newNode*);
          BaseModel = CreateEdge(*newNode*, *nextJoinPoint*);
        end for
      else
        for all *edge* in *edgeSet* **do**
          edge.setTarget(*newNode*);
        end for
        BaseModel = CreateEdge(*newNode*, *nextJoinPoint*);
      end if
    else
      if *nextJoinPoint* is of type ActivityEdge **then**
        temp = getSource(*nextJoinPoint*);
        nextJoinPoint.setSource(*newNode*);
        BaseModel = CreateEdge(*temp*, *newNode*);
      end if
    end if
  end for

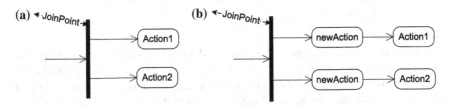

Fig. 7.8 Example of *Fork* node as join point. **a** Before weaving. **b** After weaving

of join points, the new node to add, and a base model. It returns, as output, the woven model, with the new node added after each of the identified join points.

Weaving Around Adaptation
This adaptation replaces a join point in an activity diagram with a new behavior. In addition, the original join point may be invoked using the `proceed` element. The corresponding algorithm is similar to the one described previously for state machine diagrams.

Algorithm 7.6: Activity Diagram: Weaving After Adaptation

Input: *JoinPointElem-set, newNode, BaseModel*
   edgeSet: ActivityEdge-set;
   for *nextJoinPoint* in *JoinPointElem-set* **do**
     if *nextJoinPoint* is of type ActivityNode **then**
       edgeSet = getOutgoingEdges(*nextJoinPoint*);
       if *nextJoinPoint* is of type ForkNode or DecisionNode **then**
         for all *edge* in *edgeSet* **do**
           copy *newNode*;
           edge.setSource(*newNode*);
           BaseModel = CreateEdge(*nextJoinPoint*, *newNode*);
         end for
       else
         for all *edge* in *edgeSet* **do**
           edge.setSource(*newNode*);
         end for
         BaseModel = CreateEdge(*nextJoinPoint*, *newNode*);
       end if
     else
       if *nextJoinPoint* is of type ActivityEdge **then**
         temp = getTarget(*nextJoinPoint*);
         nextJoinPoint.setTarget(*newNode*);
         BaseModel = CreateEdge(*newNode*, *temp*);
       end if
     end if
   end for

7.4.2.4 Sequence Transformation Definition

The sequence transformation definition handles transformations of sequence diagrams. It corresponds to an aspect adaptation that is stereotyped *SequenceAdaptation*. A sequence diagram is used to describe the interactions between different entities in a system. Ordering in sequence diagrams is realized by a trace of events (e.g., send and receive events), each of which is specified by an element called *Occurrence Specification* (Fig. 7.9). In our approach, we consider messages as join points, where a new behavior may be added *before*, *after*, or *around* the occurrence of send/receive message events. In the following, we describe each weaving adaptation in sequence diagrams.

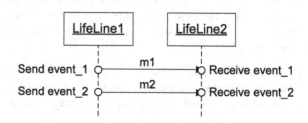

Fig. 7.9 Send/receive events in a sequence diagram

Weaving Before Adaptation

This adaptation adds a new element in a sequence diagram *before* a join point. As mentioned previously, the order in sequence diagrams is represented by a trace of events. Here, we are particularly interested in the send and the receive events of the exchanged messages. Weaving an adaptation *before* a join point message means that the adaptation should be performed before the "send event" of the message is fired. Algorithm 7.7 describes the steps needed to weave a new element before a join point message. The algorithm takes, as input, a set of join point messages, the new element to add, and a base model. It returns, as output, the woven model, where the new element has been added before each join point. The algorithm extracts the trace of events from the base model and identifies the send event of the join point message. Then, it inserts the send and the receive events of the new element before the identified send event of the message.

Algorithm 7.7: Sequence Diagram: Weaving Before Adaptation

Input: *JoinPointMessage-set, newElement, BaseModel*
  traceEvent: Event-list;
  traceEvent = getEventTrace(*BaseModel*);
  for all *nextJoinPointMessage* in *JoinPointMessage-set* **do**
    sndEvent = getSendEvent(*nextjoinPointMessage*);
    indx = *traceEvent*.getindexOf(*sndEvent*);
    newSendEvent = CreateSendEvent(*newElement*);
    newReceiveEvent = CreateReceiveEvent(*newElement*);
    if *indx* = 1 **then**
      traceEvent = *traceEvent*.prepend(*newReceiveEvent*);
      traceEvent = *traceEvent*.prepend(*newSendEvent*);
    else
      traceEvent.insertAt(*indx,newSendEvent*);
      traceEvent.insertAt(*indx* + 1,*newReceiveEvent*);
    end if
  end for

Weaving After Adaptation

This adaptation adds a new element in a sequence diagram *after* a join point. In contrast with a *before* weaving adaptation, here we are interested in the receive event of the join point message. In this case, the send/receive events of the new element are inserted after the receive event of the join point message. Algorithm 7.8 summarizes the steps needed to weave a new element after a join point message. The algorithm takes, as input, a set of join point messages, the new element to add, and a base model. It returns, as output, the woven model, where the new element has been added after each join point.

Weaving Around Adaptation

Weaving *around* adaptation in a sequence diagram is simply a replace operation. Both send and receive events of the join point message are replaced with the new element.

Algorithm 7.8: Sequence Diagram: Weaving After Adaptation

Input: *JoinPointMessage-set, newElement, BaseModel*
  traceEvent: Event-list;
  traceEvent = getEventTrace(*BaseModel*);
  for all *nextJoinPointMessage* in *JoinPointMessage-set* **do**
    rcvEvent = getReceiveEvent(*nextjoinPointMessage*);
    indx = *traceEvent*.getindexOf(*rcvEvent*);
    newSendEvent = CreateSendEvent(*newElement*);
    newReceiveEvent = CreateReceiveEvent(*newElement*);
    if *indx* = *traceEvent*.size() **then**
      traceEvent = *traceEvent*.append(*newSendEvent*);
      traceEvent = *traceEvent*.append(*newReceiveEvent*);
    else
      traceEvent.insertAt(*indx*+1,*newSendEvent*);
      traceEvent.insertAt(*indx*+2,*newReceiveEvent*);
    end if
  end for

Algorithm 7.9 presents the steps of weaving a new element around an identified join point message. The algorithm takes as input a set of join point elements, the new element to add, and a base model. It returns as output the woven model, where the new element has been added around each of the identified join points.

Algorithm 7.9: Sequence Diagram: Weaving Around Adaptation

Input: *JoinPointElem-set, newElem, BaseModel*
  for *nextJoinPoint* in *JoinPointElem-set* **do**
    replace(*nextJoinPoint, newElem*);
    if isProceed(*newElem*) **then**
      proceedElement = findProceed(*newElem*);
      replace(*proceedElement, nextJoinPoint*);
      delete(*proceedElement*);
    else
      delete(*nextJoinPoint*);
    end if
  end for
Procedure replace:
Input: *oldMsg, newMsg*
  traceEvent = getEventTrace(*BaseModel*);
  sndEvent = getSendEvent(*oldMsg*);
  rcvEvent = getReceiveEvent(*oldMsg*);
  snd_indx = *traceEvent*.getindexOf(*sndEvent*);
  rcv_indx = *traceEvent*.getindexOf(*rcvEvent*);
  traceEvent.insertAt(*snd_indx, newMsg*.sendEvent);
  traceEvent.insertAt(*rcv_indx, newMsg*.receiveEvent);

7.4.3 Transformation Rules

In this section, we present the transformation rules, also called *mapping rules*, that specify how elements of the base model should be transformed into the woven model. These mapping rules conform to the adaptation rules presented in Chap. 6. Two adaptation rules are supported in our approach: *add* and *remove*. We classify UML elements targeted by the adaptations into three main categories: (1) *Simple elements*, (2) *Composite elements*, and (3) *Two-end elements*. Simple elements are those that are compact, i.e., they are single atomic elements. Examples of simple elements are attributes, operations, simple states, and actions. Composite elements are those that are composed of other UML elements or contain references to other UML elements. Examples of composite elements are classes, sub-machine states, and structured activity nodes. Two-end elements are those that connect two UML elements together, such as associations, transitions, massages, and edges. Table 7.1 summarizes all the supported elements according to their categories.

Before describing the defined mapping rules, we first introduce the main operators that are defined by QVT language:

- *"map" operator*: It is used to apply a mapping rule to a single element or a set of elements.

Table 7.1 Classification of the supported UML elements

UML diagram	UML element	Category type
Class diagram	Package	Composite
	Class	Composite
	Operation	Simple
	Attribute	Simple
	Association	Two-end
State machine diagram	State machine	Composite
	State	Simple
	Sub-machine state	Composite
	Transition	Two-end
	Region	Composite
Sequence diagram	Interaction	Composite
	Interaction use	Composite
	Lifeline	Simple
	Message	Two-end
Activity diagram	Activity	Composite
	Action	Simple
	Structured activity node	Composite
	Edge	Two-end

- "→" *operator*: It is used to iterate on a collection of elements. When combined with the *map* operator, it facilitates the access to each element of a collection in order to apply the mapping rule to it.
- "." *operator*: It is used to access properties or operations of single elements.

For instance, the following expression shows how to apply a mapping rule *addAttribute*, which adds an attribute *attr* to a given set of Class elements *Set{classElem}*, using the *map* and → operators:

Set{*classElem*} → map *addAttribute(attr)*;

The → operator iterates through the set *classElem* and, for each element in that set, it applies the mapping rule *addAttribute* to it. The result of executing this expression is a new set of classes, where each class has the new attribute *attr* added to it. In the following, we detail the defined mapping rules.

7.4.3.1 Add Mapping Rule

Add mapping rule is called on all adaptation rules in the aspect that have the stereotype ≪*add*≫. It is important to mention here that the order of adaptation rules, as specified in the aspect, is preserved during the weaving. The following QVT expression illustrates how the add mapping rule is applied to each add adaptation rule extracted from the aspect.

OrderedSet{*addAdaptationRules*} → map *addMappingRule()*;

For each add adaptation rule, the associated tagged values determine the appropriate mapping rule to be invoked. In fact, the tagged value *type* determines the appropriate add sub-rule to be performed. In addition, the name of the new added element is identified by the tagged value *name*. The tagged value *position* of the add adaptation rule references the position where to add the new element in contrast with other existing elements in the base model. For instance, it indicates whether to add the new element *before*, *after*, or *around* the identified join point. In the case of a class adaptation, the value of the position property is set to its default value (*inside*) because of the nature of class diagrams, and therefore it is not taken into consideration during the weaving. Finally, the value of the tagged value *pointcut* is passed to the join point matching module to identify the set of join point elements. Depending on the type of the added element, one of the following add sub-rules is applied to the matched join points:

1. Add Simple Element(*elemName, position*)
   This mapping rule adds a simple element to the base model. It takes two parameters: the name of the element that should be added (*elemName*), and the position where to add the element (*position*). This mapping rule creates the appropriate meta-element object and sets its name to *elemName*. Depending on the position value, the newly created element is placed in the base model accordingly.
   object *simple-meta-element* {name := elemName};

2. Add Composite Element(*elemName, position*)

This mapping rule adds a composite element to the base model. It is similar to the add simple element rule. In addition, it adds a reference to the behavior of the composite element provided in the aspect. For example, in the case of an interaction use, a reference to the corresponding interaction is required. Thus, this mapping rule iterates through the elements of the aspect and selects the behavior that matches the element to add. Finally, the composite element is created.

behElem := Set{aspectElem} → Select(el *where* el.name = elemName);
object *composite-meta-element*{name:=elemName; refersTo:=behElem};

3. Add Two-End Element(*elemName, position, sourceExp, targetExp*)

Dealing with a two-end element is different from simple and composite elements because it requires the specification of the source and the target of that element. Therefore, two additional pointcuts are needed: one to select the source element, and one to select the target element. These two pointcuts are specified as parameters for the add adaptation, such that the first parameter represents the source pointcut whereas the second parameter represents the target pointcut.

Set{sourceElem}:=Set{baseModelElem}→joinPointMatching(sourceExp);
Set{targetElem}:=Set{baseModelElem}→joinPointMatching(targetExp);
object *two-end-meta-element*{name:=elemName; source:=sourceElem;
target := targetElem;}

7.4.3.2 Remove Mapping Rule

The remove mapping rule is applied to each adaptation rule in the aspect that has the stereotype ≪*remove*≫. It reads the value of the tagged value *pointcut* and passes it to the join point matching module to identify the set of elements to be removed. Unlike the additive rules, the type of the element to be removed is not important. Thus, there is only one general rule to remove any kind of UML element. Each identified join point element is removed using the destroy method provided by QVT.

Set{elemToRemove} := Set{baseModelElem} → joinPointMatching(pointcut);
Set{elemToRemove} → destroy();

Indeed, the remove operation is very sensitive and should be dealt with cautiously, otherwise it may result in an incorrect woven model. For instance, removing a state in a state machine diagram without reconnecting its predecessor with its successor may result in two disconnected state machines. Therefore, we assume that in case of any remove operation, it should be followed by an add operation that either replaces the removed element or corrects any arising problematic issues.

7.4.3.3 Tagging Mapping Rule

Tagging mapping rules are used to trace the modifications that are performed on the base model. Each element that has been added or modified by the transformation

Table 7.2 List of all mapping rules—part 1

Transformation definition	Mapping rule	Sub-rule
Class transformation definition	Add	addClass
		addAttribute
		addOperation
		addPackage
		addAssociation
	Remove	removeClass
		removeOperation
		removeAssociation
		removeAttribute
		removePackage
	Tag	tagElement
State machine transformation definition	Add	addState
		addTransition
		addSubMachineState
		addStateMachine
		addRegion
	Remove	removeState
		removeTransition
		removeSubMachineState
		removeStateMachine
		removeRegion
	Tag	tagElement
Activity transformation definition	Add	addAction
		addControlFlow
		addObjectFlow
		addStructuredActivityNode
		addActivity
	Remove	removeAction
		removeControlFlow
		removeObjectFlow
		removeStructuredActivityNode
		removeActivity
	Tag	tagElement

Table 7.3 List of all mapping rules—part 2

Transformation definition	Mapping rule	Sub-rule
Sequence transformation definition	Add	addMessage
		addInteractionUse
		addInteraction
		addLifeline
	Remove	removeMessage
		removeInteractionUse
		removeInteraction
		removeLifeline
	Tag	tagElement

needs to be easily identified in the woven model. To this end, we define special keywords, e.g., ≪AddedElement≫ and ≪ModifiedElement≫, and apply them to the affected elements. When the woven model is generated, the affected elements can be easily distinguished using these keywords. Note that keywords are properties of UML elements [152]. Some keywords are predefined in UML. Moreover, user-specific keywords can be defined as it is the case here. Tables 7.2 and 7.3 summarize all the supported mapping rules.

7.5 Tool Support

To demonstrate the feasibility of our security hardening approach, we have designed and implemented a prototype to support the specification and the systematic integration of security aspects into UML design models. The prototype is developed as a plug-in to IBM-Rational Software Architect (RSA) [103]. RSA is an advanced model-driven development tool. It contains a very powerful UML modeler that is compliant with UML 2 standard. In addition, it supports many important functionalities such as model manipulation, code generation, reverse engineering from Java and C++, etc. Moreover, as RSA is built on top of Eclipse,[1] our tool can be easily integrated with any IDE that is based on the Eclipse platform. In this section, we provide details about the authoring of our AOM profile and the weaving plug-in.

7.5.1 AOM Profile

This section provides details about the authoring of our AOM profile, presented in Chap. 6, in IBM-RSA tool. In RSA, UML Profiles are files with ".epx" extension. The modeling perspective of RSA provides creating and editing capabilities of UML

---

[1] http://www.eclipse.org.

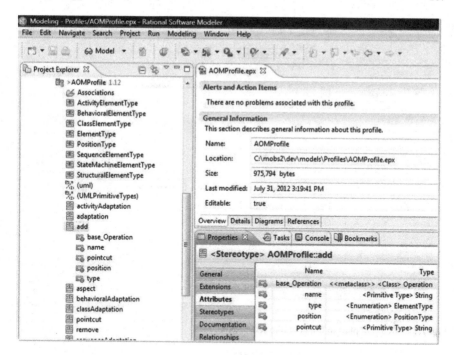

Fig. 7.10 AOM profile editor

profiles using the UML extensibility feature. Figure 7.10 depicts a screenshot of the AOM profile editor. The two main views that are used in profile authoring are the Model Explorer and the Properties View. The Model Explorer is used to create the stereotypes of the profile, e.g., *classAdaptation*, *pointcut*, *add*, and *remove*. The Properties View is used to create and set the tagged values that are associated with each stereotype, e.g., *name*, *type*, *position*, and *pointcut* that are associated with the stereotype *add*. In addition, the Properties View shows the profile properties, such as, the profile name, the file location and size, the time when the file was last modified, and whether or not the file is editable.

7.5.2 Weaving Framework

This section presents the design and the implementation details of our weaving tool. As mentioned previously, this tool has been implemented as a plug-in on top of IBM-RSA since it contains a very powerful UML modeler. In addition, RSA can be augmented with Eclipse plug-ins, which allows our weaving tool to be embedded into any Eclipse-based development environment. Figure 7.11 shows a screenshot of RSA tool with the weaving plug-in being deployed.

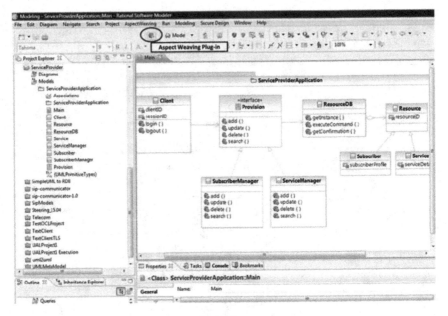

Fig. 7.11 Weaving plug-in integrated to IBM-RSA

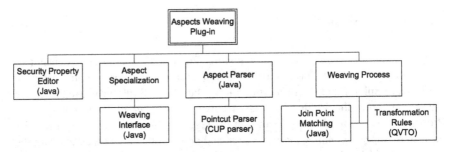

Fig. 7.12 Weaving plug-in

The weaving plug-in consists of 253 Java classes, 51 QVT mappings with a total of around 21,300 lines of code. This plug-in provides the weaving capabilities needed to weave the security aspects, specified using our AOM profile, into UML base models. Figure 7.12 highlights the different components that have been implemented as part of this plug-in. In the following, we detail each component.

7.5.2.1 Security Property Editor

The developer should be able to specify the security requirement that he/she wants to enforce on his/her design. To this end, we have implemented a security property editor, where the developer can select the model that he/she wants to harden, and on

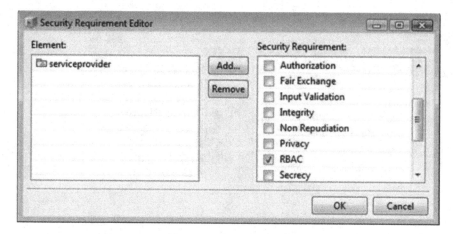

Fig. 7.13 Security property editor

the other hand the needed security requirement. Afterwards, the security aspect that provides the security solutions for the needed requirement is automatically selected from the security aspects library. The covered security requirements are those commonly specified and verified on software, and for which a security solution can be provided as an aspect. Examples of these security requirements are secrecy, authentication, authorization, etc. Figure 7.13 depicts a screenshot of the security property editor.

7.5.2.2 Aspect Specialization Through a Weaving Interface

Since security aspects are provided as generic solutions, the developer should be able to specialize those aspects to his/her application before weaving them into base models. To this end, we have implemented a graphical weaving interface to ease the specialization of aspects and their weaving in a systematic way. As shown in Fig. 7.14, the weaving interface presents, on the left hand side, all the generic elements of the aspect, and on the right hand side, all the elements of the base model. From this weaving interface and based on his/her understanding of the application, the developer maps each generic element of the aspect to its corresponding element(s) in the base model. Using this weaving interface, the developer does not need to understand how the security solution is specified. Indeed, all the details of the security solution are kept hidden from the developer and only the generic elements of the aspect are exposed to him/her. After mapping all the generic elements, the application-dependent aspect is automatically generated.

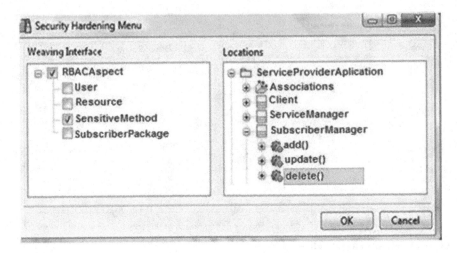

Fig. 7.14 Weaving interface

7.5.2.3 Aspect and Pointcut Parsers

The aspect parser is responsible for parsing the selected aspect, and identifying the different kinds of adaptations that are contained in the aspect. Then, for each adaptation kind, it will invoke the corresponding transformation definition. Furthermore, before executing the transformation rules, the textual pointcut expressions, specified in the aspect, should be translated into OCL expressions. This is done by another component, the *Pointcut Parser*, that is responsible of parsing and translating textual pointcut expressions into OCL. In this context, we use *CUP Parser Generator for Java*.[2] This parser generator takes as input: (1) The grammar of the pointcut language along with the actions required to translate each primitive pointcut designator to its corresponding OCL primitive, and (2) a scanner used to break the textual pointcut expression into meaningful tokens. It provides as output a Java parser that is capable of parsing and translating any textual pointcut expression into its equivalent OCL one. It is important to mention here that this process is executed automatically and in a total transparency to the developer.

7.5.2.4 Weaving Process

This component is responsible for performing the actual weaving of the aspect and the base model. It includes two main sub-components: *Join Point Matching Module* and *Transformation Rules*. The join point matching module is responsible for querying the base model elements using the generated OCL expressions, and returning those elements that satisfy the OCL expressions. This module is implemented as a Java pro-

---

[2] http://www2.cs.tum.edu/projects/cup/.

gram and integrated to the weaving framework by extending the QVT engine through the QVT/Black-Box mechanism [150]. This QVT feature allows the integration of external programs, expressed in other transformation languages or programming languages, to the QVT rules. The transformation rules implement the aspect adaptation rules. They are executed on the identified join points to produce the woven model. These rules are expressed using the Eclipse M2M QVT Operational [108], that we installed as a plug-in on top of IBM-RSA.

7.6 Case Studies

In this section, we detail the experiments that demonstrate the feasibility and the relevance of our security hardening framework. We conduct case studies to add security mechanisms and fix various security vulnerabilities in different applications. These conducted case studies can be summarized as follows:

- Adding input validation and access control to a service provider application.
- Adding authorization, blocking spam, and handling maximum size of instant messages in SIP-Communicator [2].
- Replacing deprecated functions in OpenSAF [15].

In the following, we detail these case studies to show how our defined approach can be applied to detect vulnerable points in UML design models, and afterwards inject the needed solutions at these points.

7.6.1 Service Provider Application

In this case study, we show how to automatically integrate different security mechanisms into a service provider application. The class diagram of the service provider application is depicted in Fig. 7.15. The class *Client* represents the application's users (e.g., administrator, subscribers, managers). Each type of users has specific privileges. A client can login to the database of subscribers (*ResourceDB*) through an interface *Provision*, which is implemented by the classes *SubscriberManager* and *ServiceManager* for manipulating subscribers and services respectively. Before clients can access a particular service, they must first authenticate by providing username and password as their credentials. The authentication process is modeled as an activity diagram (Fig. 7.16).

Furthermore, when a client issues a request to delete a subscriber, the method *delete()* of the *SubscriberManager* class is invoked. Then, this method executes the command to delete the subscriber from the database. Afterwards, the database destroys the respective instance of the subscriber by sending the destroy message. To guarantee the deletion of the subscriber instance, the *SubscriberManager* asks for the confirmation and sends the results to the client. The client's permissions

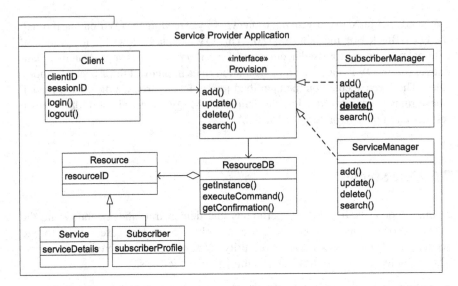

Fig. 7.15 Class diagram for a service provider application

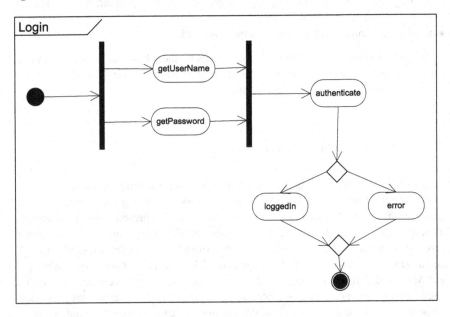

Fig. 7.16 Activity diagram specifying the authentication process

must be verified before deleting a subscriber (i.e., only the administrator can delete a subscriber). Figure 7.17 represents a sequence diagram specifying the behavior of the method *SubscriberManager.delete()*.

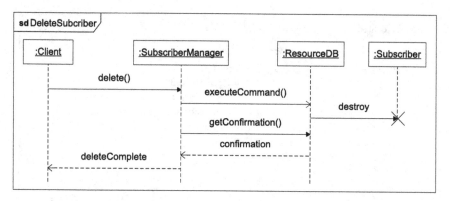

Fig. 7.17   Behavior of the method *SubscriberManager.delete()*

In the sequel, we show how our framework can be used to specify and integrate two security aspects to the service provider application: (1) *Input Validation* to check user input, and (2) *Role-Based Access Control* to check user permissions before deleting a subscriber.

7.6.1.1 Input Validation

The authentication process, as specified in Fig. 7.16, might be vulnerable to various security attacks such as SQL injection and Cross-site Scripting (XSS) [86] due to malicious inputs from the user. To fix such vulnerabilities, a security solution can be provided as an aspect that validates user input as shown in Fig. 7.18. The input validation aspect is specified using our proposed AOM profile presented in Chap. 6. The aspect contains an activity adaptation specifying the addition of an input vali-

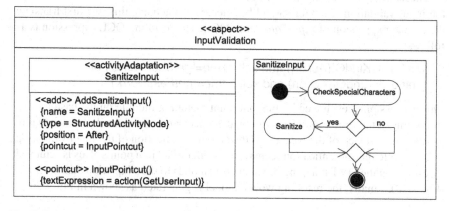

Fig. 7.18   Input validation aspect

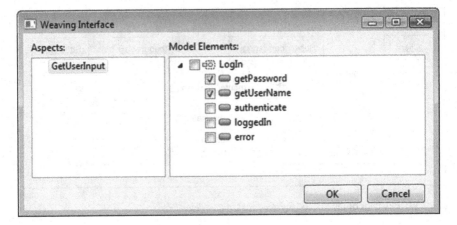

Fig. 7.19 Weaving interface: specializing the input validation aspect

dation behavior that sanitizes user input before being processed. In other words, it checks the user input for special characters. If any special character exists then the aspect sanitizes the input to remove its effect. This behavior will be injected as a structured activity node after any action that gets user input. In the following, we show how our framework can be used to weave this aspect into the authentication scenario presented in Fig. 7.16.

The first step of the weaving is to specialize the input validation aspect to the authentication scenario (Fig. 7.16). To this end, the developer uses the weaving interface, depicted in Fig. 7.19, where he/she maps the abstract action *GetUserInput* to the actions *getUserName* and *getPassword*. After this step, the application-dependent aspect is automatically generated. Its specification is similar to the application-independent one except for *InputPointcut* that will have the value: *action(getUserName) or action(getPassword)*.

The next step of the weaving is the automatic identification of the join points where the input validation behavior should be injected. To achieve this, we first translate the textual expression of *InputPointcut* to OCL. The resulting OCL expression is as follows:

"(self.oclIsKindOf(Action) and self.name='*getUserName*') or
(self.oclIsKindOf(Action) and self.name='*getPassword*')"

This expression is evaluated by the join point matching module on the base model. Accordingly, the actions *getUserName* and *getPassword* are selected as matched join points. The last step of the weaving is the automatic injection of the input validation behavior into the authentication scenario at the identified join points. This is achieved by executing the QVT mapping rule that corresponds to the adaptation *SanitizeInput* (Fig. 7.18). Finally, the resulting woven model is generated as shown in Fig. 7.20.

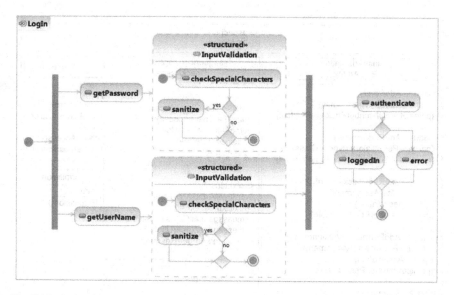

Fig. 7.20 Authentication scenario—woven model

7.6.1.2 Role-Based Access Control

Now, we show how a security expert can use the designed AOM profile to specify an RBAC aspect needed for enforcing access control into the design models of the service provider application (Figs. 7.15 and 7.17). Before illustrating the design of the RBAC aspect, first we give a short background on the different RBAC models. RBAC is organized into four models:

1. *Flat RBAC*: It is the core model that embodies the essential concepts of RBAC: users, roles, and permissions. It specifies the assignment of users to roles and the assignment of permissions to roles.
2. *Hierarchical RBAC*: It extends the Flat RBAC by supporting role hierarchies.
3. *Constrained RBAC*: It extends the Hierarchical RBAC by supporting separation of duty constraints.
4. *Symmetric RBAC*: It extends the Constrained RBAC by adding the ability to perform permission-role review.

In our case study, the Flat RBAC is used to enforce access control. The specification of the RBAC aspect is presented in Fig. 7.21. In order to enforce RBAC access control mechanisms on the different resources of the service provider application, we need to introduce the RBAC components into the application using aspect adaptations. The RBAC aspect contains two kinds of adaptations: *Class Adaptation* and *Sequence Adaptation*. The *Class Adaptation* specifies the necessary modifications that should be performed on the class diagram of the service provider application (Fig. 7.15). More precisely, it adds two classes, named *Role* and *Permission*, to

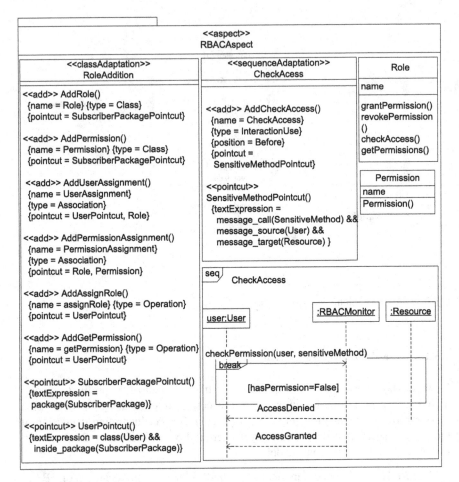

Fig. 7.21 Specification of the RBAC aspect

the service provider application by the add adaptations *AddRole* and *AddPermission* respectively. The location where to add these two classes is provided by the pointcut *SubscriberPackagePointcut*. In addition, it enforces the RBAC concepts, i.e., user-role assignment and role-permission assignment, by adding two associations: *UserAssignment* between the classes (User, Role) and *PermissionAssignment* between the classes (Role, Permission). Furthermore, the class adaptation adds two new operations, *assignRole* and *getPermission*, to assign different roles to users and get their permissions.

The *Sequence Adaptation* specifies the necessary modifications that should be performed on the sequence diagram of the service provider application (Fig. 7.17). More precisely, it adds a check access behavior, by the adaptation *AddCheckAccess*, before calling a sensitive method. This behavior is responsible for checking whether the user, trying to access a given resource, has the appropriate privileges or not. The location where to inject this behavior is specified by the pointcut *SensitiveMethod-Pointcut*, which selects all message calls to *SensitiveMethod()* from a *User* instance to a *Resource* instance.

In what follows, we show how the developer can use our framework to apply the RBAC aspect to the base model of the service provider application (Figs. 7.15 and 7.17). This RBAC aspect is though application-independent and must be specialized by the developer to the service provider application, as shown in Fig. 7.22. In this case, the developer maps *SensitiveMethod* to *SubscriberManager.delete()*. The same way, the developer maps *User* to *Client*, *Resource* to *Subscriber*, and *SubscriberPackage* to *ServiceProviderApplication*.

Having the RBAC aspect specialized to actual elements from the service provider application, each pointcut element is automatically translated into its equivalent OCL expression. For example, the pointcut *SensitiveMethodPointcut*, presented in Fig. 7.21 with the textual expression: *"Message_Call(delete) && Message_Source (Client) && Message_Target(SubscriberManager)"*, will be tokenized by the scanner into three tokens connected with the logical operator *&&* as follows: (1) *Message_Call(delete)*, (2) *Message_Source(Client)*, and (3) *Message_Target(Subscriber Manager)*. The pointcut parser will parse the textual expression and will translate it into the following OCL expression:

"self.oclIsTypeOf(Message) and self.name='*delete*' and
self.connector._end-> at(1).role.name='*Client*' and
self.connector._end-> at(2).role.name='*SubscriberManager*'"

This expression will then be evaluated on the elements of the service provider application and the matched elements will be selected as join points. Figure 7.23 shows the

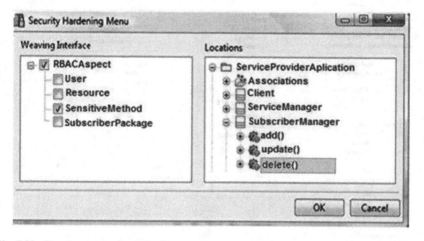

Fig. 7.22 Security aspects specialization

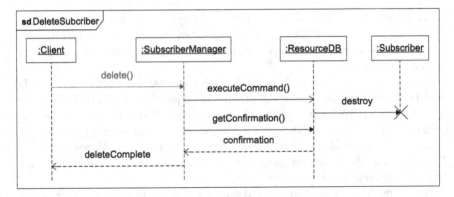

Fig. 7.23 Message *SubscriberManager.delete()* identified as join point

result of evaluating the previous OCL expression on the *DeleteSubscriber* sequence diagram.

After identifying all the existing join points, the next step is to inject the different adaptations of the RBAC aspect at the exact locations in the base model. This is done by executing the QVT mapping rules that correspond to the adaptation rules specified in the RBAC aspect. These mapping rules are then interpreted by the QVT transformation engine that transforms the base model into a woven model. Figures 7.24 and 7.25 show the final result after weaving the RBAC aspect into the base models of the service provider application. Note that the classes *Role* and *Permission* have been

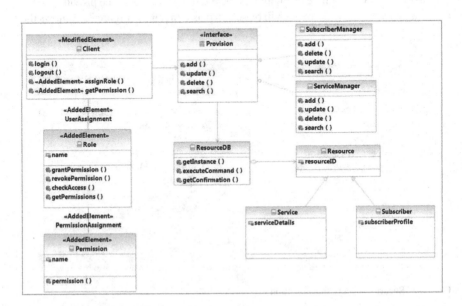

Fig. 7.24 Woven model of class diagram

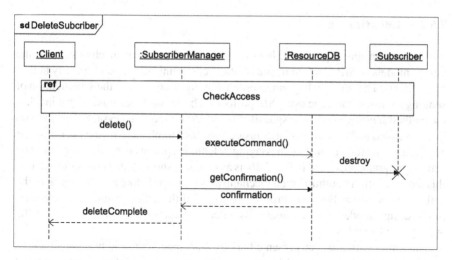

Fig. 7.25 Woven model of DeleteSubscriber

added to the class diagram as well as the associations *UserAssignment* and *PermissionAssignment* (Fig. 7.24). In addition, the methods *assignRole* and *getPermission* have been added to the class *Client*. As for the *DeleteSubscriber* sequence diagram, the *CheckAccess* fragment, in Fig. 7.21, has been added as an interaction use before sending the message *delete()* (Fig. 7.25).

7.6.2 SIP-Communicator

SIP-Communicator[3] is an open source software that provides internet-based audio/video telephony and instant messaging services. It supports some of the most popular instant messaging and telephony protocols, e.g., Session Initiation Protocol (SIP) [180], Extensible Messaging and Presence Protocol (XMPP) [181], and Internet Relay Chat (IRC) protocol [154]. It is composed of more than 1400 Java classes and 150 K lines of code based on version 1.0. In this sub-section, we use our framework to solve various issues that are reported in SIP-Communicator issue list.[4] The conducted experiments can be summarized as follows: (1) Adding authorization, (2) blocking spam in messaging accounts, and (3) handling maximum size of instant messages. In the following, we detail these experiments to show how our framework can be used to pick out specific points in UML design models of SIP-Communicator and afterwards inject the needed solutions at these points.

---

[3] https://jitsi.org/.

[4] http://java.net/jira/secure/IssueNavigator.jspa?mode=hide\&requestId=10290.

7.6.2.1 Authorization

We present, in this experiment, how to add an authorization mechanism into the design models of SIP-Communicator to allow communications between only authorized clients. The activity diagram, presented in Fig. 7.26, depicts the specification of sending an instant message using SIP protocol. The action *SendRequest*, that invokes the method *sendRequest( )*, is responsible for sending a request message. This method is being called in 32 different places inside functions implementing the operations of SIP communicator, i.e., instant messaging, telephony, presence, notification, etc. The activity diagram, presented in Fig. 7.26, is an example showing just one occurrence of this method call. An authorization mechanism is required before any execution of the action *SendRequest*. For this purpose, we catch all the actions named *SendRequest* in the design models and automatically inject the authorization mechanism at the appropriate locations.

The authorization aspect, presented in Fig. 7.27, specifies the addition of an access control behavior that checks client permissions based on the information contained in a message request. This is accomplished by defining the adaptation *AddCheckPermission* that injects the authorization behavior as a structured activity node before any sensitive method picked out by the pointcut *SensitiveMethod*. This aspect is application-independent and must be specialized by the developer.

The first step of the weaving is to specialize the authorization aspect to the base model depicted in Fig. 7.26. In this experiment, the developer maps the abstract

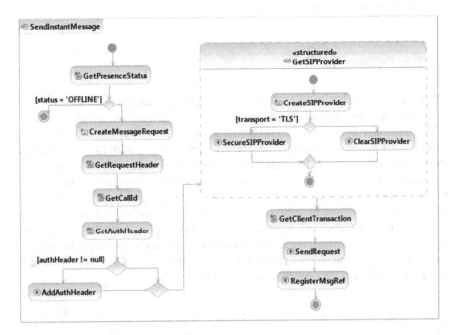

Fig. 7.26 Activity diagram for sending an instant message—base model

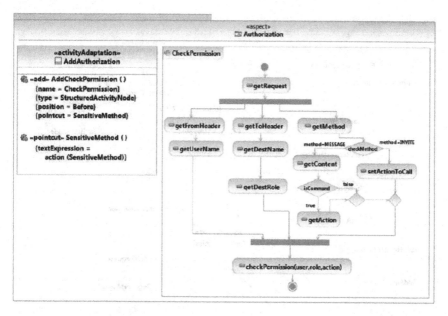

Fig. 7.27   Authorization aspect

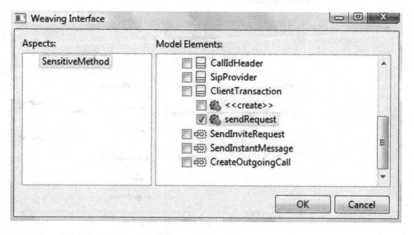

Fig. 7.28   Specialization of the authorization aspect

method *SensitiveMethod* to the method *sendRequest* as shown in Fig. 7.28. After this step, the application-dependent aspect is automatically generated and without the user intervention. Its specification is similar to the application-independent one except for the pointcut *SensitiveMethod* that will have the value *action(SendRequest)*.

The next step of the weaving is the automatic identification of the join points where the check permission behavior, shown in Fig. 7.27, should be injected. To achieve this, our framework first automatically translates the textual expression of

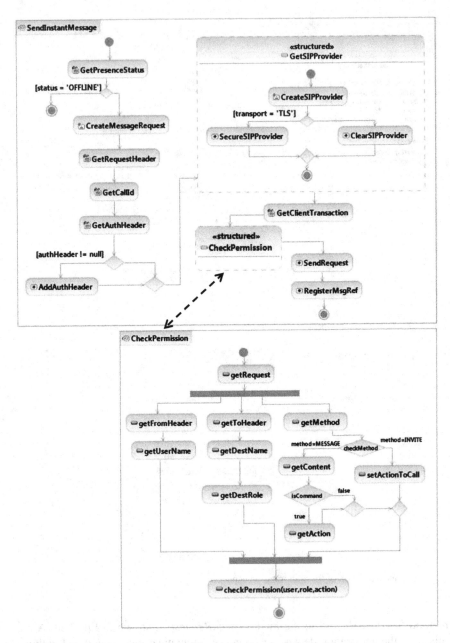

Fig. 7.29 Sending an instant message with authorization—woven model

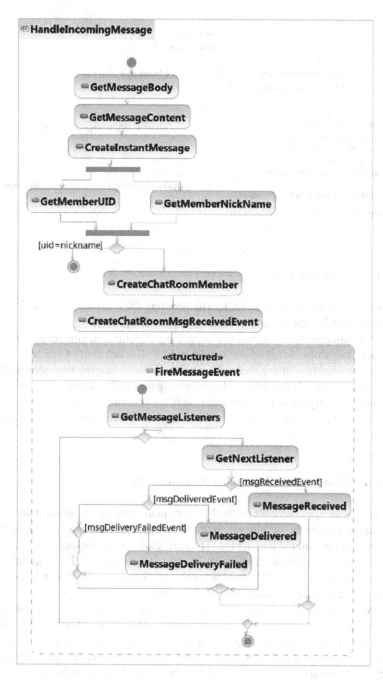

Fig. 7.30 Activity diagram for handling an incoming message—base model

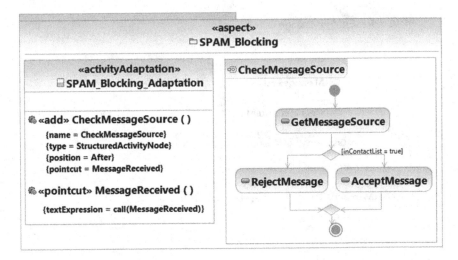

Fig. 7.31 Aspect for SPAM blocking

the pointcut *SensitiveMethod* to OCL. The resulting OCL expression is as follows: "self.oclIsTypeOf(Action) and self.name='*SendRequest*'".

The evaluation of this OCL expression by the join point matching module returns all the actions named *SendRequest* as join points. The last step of the weaving is the automatic injection of the check permission behavior into the base model at the identified join points. This is achieved by executing the QVT mapping rule that is generated automatically from the adaptation *AddCheckPermission* shown in Fig. 7.27. Finally, the resulting woven model for sending an instant message is generated as shown in Fig. 7.29.

7.6.2.2 Blocking Spam in Messaging Accounts

In this sub-section, we address the problem of spam in instant messaging accounts. To prevent this problem, we suggest, in this experiment, to reject any messages from people who are not on the contact list. The activity diagram, presented in Fig. 7.30, depicts the specification of handling an incoming message in SIP-Communicator. The action named *MessageReceived* is a call operation action that is invoked each time an instant message is received in a chat room.

To implement the aforementioned solution, we provide an aspect as depicted in Fig. 7.31. The aspect contains an add adaptation (*CheckMessageSource*) that adds a new behavior to reject any message whose sender is not in the contact list. This new behavior should be invoked after receiving any instant message, i.e., after any call to the method *MessageReceived*, picked out by the pointcut *MessageReceived*.

Since the aspect of Fig. 7.31 is application-dependent, there is no need to specialize it to SIP-Communicator application. To identify the join points where the aspect adaptation *CheckMessageSource* should be performed, our framework auto-

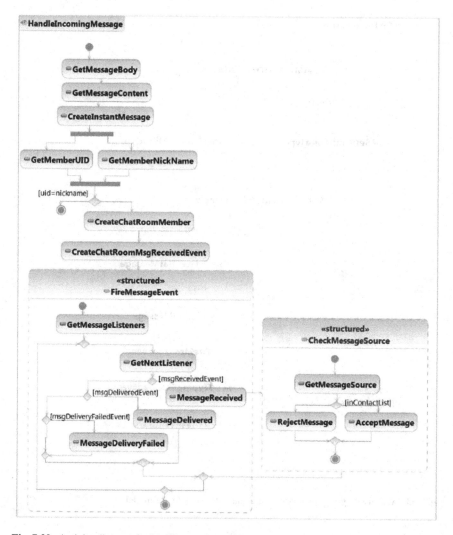

Fig. 7.32 Activity diagram for handling an incoming message—woven model

matically translates the textual expression of the pointcut *MessageReceived* to OCL. The resulting OCL expression is as follows:

    "self.oclIsTypeOf(CallOperationAction) and
     self.operation.name='MessageReceived'"

The evaluation of this OCL expression, by the join point matching module, returns as join points all the call operation actions that are invoking the method *MessageReceived()*. Finally, the last step of the weaving is the execution of the QVT mapping rule corresponding to the adaptation *CheckMessageSource*. As a result, the new

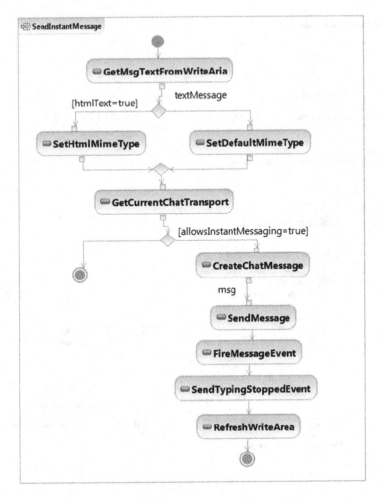

Fig. 7.33 Activity diagram for sending an instant message—base model

behavior *CheckMessageSource* is injected after the call action *MessageReceived* as shown in Fig. 7.32.

7.6.2.3 Handling Maximum Message Size

In SIP-Communicator, various protocols are able to send messages of various sizes. In this experiment, we handle the case where a user is trying to send messages that exceed the maximum length allowed by the protocol. After sending a long message to someone, we are never actually sure if it is received or not. One possible solution to this issue is to return an error indicating that the message exceeds the maximum size allowed. The detailed behavior of sending an instant message in SIP-Communicator

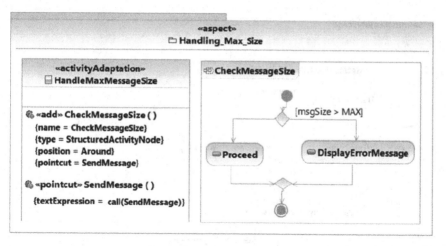

Fig. 7.34 Aspect for handling the size of instant messages

is depicted in the activity diagram of Fig. 7.33. Before weaving the aspect of Fig. 7.34 into the base model of Fig. 7.33, we first identify the join points where the aspect adaptation *CheckMessageSize* should be applied. For this purpose, our framework translates automatically the textual expression of the pointcut *SendMessage* to OCL. The resulting OCL expression is as follows:

"self.oclIsTypeOf(CallOperationAction) and
self.operation.name='*SendMessage*'"

The action named *SendMessage* is a call operation action that sends an instant message. An aspect is depicted in Fig. 7.34 to return an error indicating that the message exceeds the maximum size allowed. It contains an add adaptation (*CheckMessage-Size*) that adds a new behavior to check the size of the message to be sent. This new behavior should be invoked around sending any instant message, i.e., around any call to the method *SendMessage*, picked out by the pointcut *SendMessage*.

The evaluation of this OCL expression by the join point matching module returns as join points all the call operation actions that are invoking the method *SendMessage()*. Finally, the last step of the weaving is the execution of the QVT mapping rule corresponding to the adaptation *CheckMessageSize*. As a result, the new behavior *CheckMessageSize* is injected around the call action *SendMessage* as shown in Fig. 7.35. If the message size exceeds the maximum allowed, an error message is displayed to the user. Otherwise, the Proceed action in the aspect of Fig. 7.34 is replaced by the original join point, i.e., the action *SendMessage*.

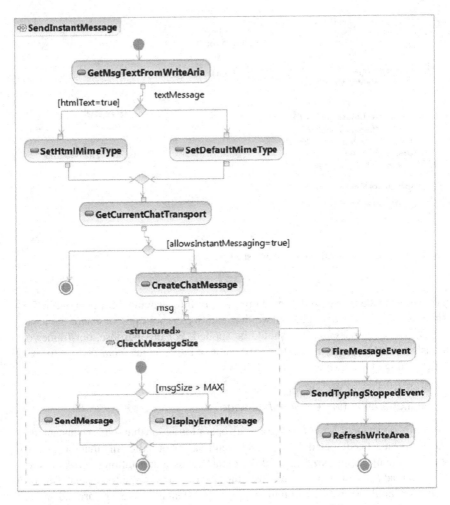

Fig. 7.35 Activity diagram for sending an instant message—woven model

7.6.3 Replacing Deprecated Functions in OpenSAF

OpenSAF [15] is an open source project established to develop high availability middleware that is consistent with the Service Availability Forum specifications [14]. The OpenSAF project consists of more than 4800 files and 1.7 M lines of code written in Java and C languages based on the release 4.0.M4. We have conducted an analysis of the C part of OpenSAF from a security point of view using a security verification tool [197]. The analysis tool has reported more than 100 potential errors of deprecated functions. These functions are quite abundant in the C library. In addition, they are vulnerable to attacks such as buffer overflows [13]. The usage of safe alternatives is

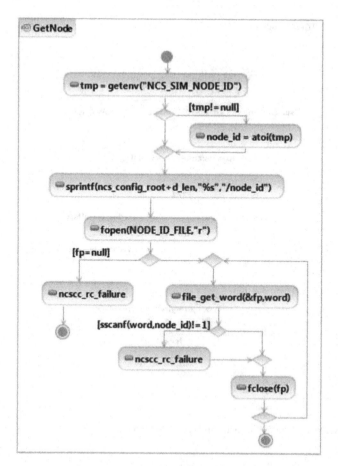

Fig. 7.36 Activity diagram of GetNode—base model

required as a preventive measure. We present next how to use our defined framework
to fix OpenSAF vulnerabilities that are related to the use of deprecated functions.

We illustrate our methods on two activity diagrams describing the behavior of the
functions *GetNode* and *GetChassisType* as shown in Figs. 7.36 and 7.37 respectively.
Both activity diagrams include call operation actions that invoke a vulnerable function *sprintf()*. This function uses a format string argument that enable programmers to
specify how strings should be formatted for output. This function is a deprecated function, which if not properly used, can be exploited to perform buffer overflows [12]. To
avoid this vulnerability, one possible solution is to use the secure function *sprintf_s()*
instead of *sprintf()*. Indeed, the function *sprintf_s()* allows checking the size of the
output buffer and the format string for valid formatting characters.

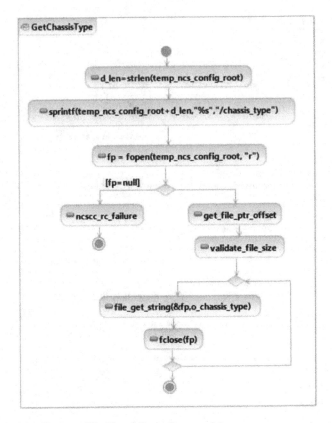

Fig. 7.37 Activity diagram of GetChassisType—base model

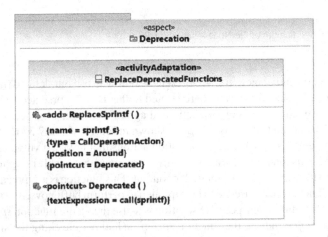

Fig. 7.38 Aspect for replacing deprecated functions

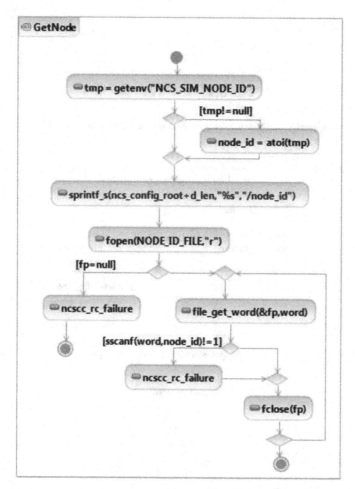

Fig. 7.39 Woven activity diagram of GetNode

An aspect is depicted in Fig. 7.38 to implement this solution. It contains the add adaptation *ReplaceSprintf* that replaces any call to the function *sprintf()*, picked out by the pointcut *Deprecated*, by a call to the secured function *sprintf_s()*.

Since the aspect of Fig. 7.38 is application-dependent, there is no need to specialize it to OpenSAF application. To identify the join points where the aspect adaptation should be performed, we first translate the textual expression of the pointcut *Deprecated* to OCL. The resulting OCL expression is as follows:

"self.oclIsTypeOf(CallOperationAction) and self.operation.name='*sprintf*'"

The evaluation of this OCL expression by the join point matching module returns, as join points, all the call operation actions that are invoking the function *sprintf()*. Finally, the last step of the weaving is the execution of the QVT mapping rule

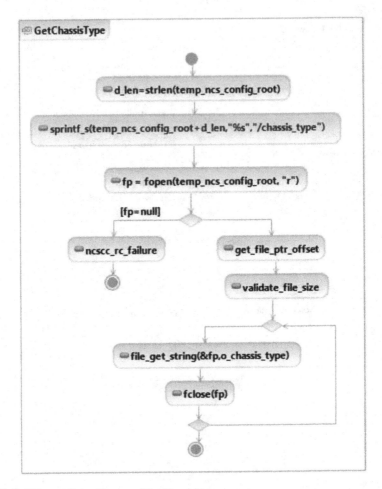

Fig. 7.40 Woven activity diagram of GetChassisType

corresponding to the adaptation *ReplaceSprintf*. As a result, all the calls to the function *sprintf()* are replaced by a call to the secured function *sprintf_s()* as shown in Figs. 7.39 and 7.40.

7.7 Related Work on Model Weaving

Various approaches have been proposed for weaving aspects into UML design models. Some of them adopt a symmetric approach [85, 100], where there is no distinction between aspects and base models, while others follow an asymmetric approach [62, 97, 118, 138, 175, 206], where there is a clear distinction between aspects and base models. In the following, we present a discussion of the main contributions.

Cui et al. [62] have presented an approach for modeling and integrating aspects into UML activity diagrams. Base models are modeled as activity diagrams while aspect models, consisting of pointcut and advice models, are depicted as activity diagrams extended by a set of stereotypes and tagged values. Compared to this contribution that supports only adding new elements *before* and *after* the matched join points, our framework considers also replacing existing elements by new ones and removing elements. In addition, control nodes are also considered as join points in our approach. Algorithms for matching and weaving are provided in [62]. However, the implementation strategies have not been detailed. Additionally, there is no formal semantics for these processes.

MATA [206] is a tool for weaving UML models based on graph transformations. It supports weaving aspects into class, sequence, and state machine diagrams. In contrast to our approach, in MATA there are no explicit join points; any model element can be a join point. The UML base model is transformed into an instance of type graph. Similarly, the aspect model is transformed into a graph rule that is automatically executed on the base graph. After the weaving, the result is transformed back to a UML model. Graph theory and tools allow MATA to perform some analysis such as aspect/feature interactions. MATA is one of the few tools that support both structural and behavioral composition. However, the weaving is not done on UML models directly, but rather is executed as a graph rule using graph transformation tools.

GeKo (Generic Composition with Kermeta) [138] is a generic AOM approach that can be applied to any well-defined meta-model. It supports both structural and behavioral composition. The weaving is implemented as model transformations using Kermeta [17], while the matching is performed using a Prolog-based pattern matching engine. GeKo is one of the few approaches that provide a clear semantics for the different operators used in the weaving. It supports adding, removing, and updating elements of the base model. The graphical representation of the woven model is supported. However, there is no support for traceability, meaning that the effect of an aspect on the base model is not visualized.

Fleurey et al. [85] have presented a generic tool, called Kompose, for model composition based on Kermeta [17]. Kompose focuses only on the structural composition of any modeling language described by a meta-model and does not support behavioral composition. In addition, it adopts a signature comparison mechanism for the matching of join points, which makes the specified aspects specific rather than generic.

Groher and Voelter [97] have presented XWeave; a weaver that supports the weaving of models and meta-models. This weaver is implemented following a model-to-model transformation approach using the openArchitectureWare framework.[5] The main limitation of XWeave is the fact that it only supports the addition of new

---

[5] http://www.itemis.com/itemis-ag/services-and-solutions/eclipse-modeling/language=en/35056/openarchitectureware-oaw.

elements to the base model. It does not support removing or replacing existing elements. In addition, there are no supported theoretical foundations for this weaver.

Hovsepyan et al. [100] have proposed an approach, called Generic Reusable Concern Compositions (GReCCo), for composing concern models. It supports composition of class and sequence diagrams. To support reusability, concerns are specified in a generic way. In order to compose two concerns, a *composition model* is specified, which provides directions to the transformation engine on how to compose the two models. The GReCCo tool is implemented using ATL language [1]. Since concerns are specified as generic models, their specialization to a particular context is needed in the composition model. However, this suggests that for each composition operation, a separate composition model needs to be specified, which may be a costly task in terms of effort and complexity.

Klein et al. [118] have proposed a semantic-based weaving algorithm for sequence diagrams. Similar to our approach, they support adding, replacing, and removing behaviors. The weaving algorithm is implemented as a set of transformations. The matching process consists of transforming the original model in such a way that pointcuts only match a finite number of paths, which is a limitation of this approach.

ATLAS Model Weaver (AMW) [80] has been developed for establishing links between models. These links are stored in the weaving model. The latter is created conforming to a specific weaving meta-model, which enables creating links between model elements and associations between links. AMW is based on ATL language, which supports automatic creation of traceability links between the source and the target models. However, AMW requires continuous interaction with the developer to build the weaving model. Additionally, AMW deals only with the XMI representation of the models.

Reddy et al. [175] have presented an approach for composing aspect-oriented class models. The authors have described a composition approach that utilizes a composition algorithm and composition directives. Composition directives are used when the default composition algorithm is known or expected to yield incorrect models. The prototype tool is based on Kermeta [17]. However, it supports only the default composition algorithm but not the composition directives. Other model weaving approaches [92, 105, 213] that handle executable UML (xUML) models are presented in the related work section of Chap. 10.

Table 7.4 summarizes the existing model weavers. It also compares the weavers according to the supported diagrams, formalization of the weaving, tool support, aspect reusability, weaver extensibility, and whether the approach adopts any standards for the implementation of the tool. The terms "CD", "SMD", "SD", and "AD" in the table refer respectively to class diagrams, state machine diagrams, sequence diagrams, and activity diagrams. The term "Generic" means that the approach supports any kind of models with a well-defined meta-model. From this table, we conclude that our approach is the only one that handles UML diagrams in a comprehensive way in terms of the defined criteria.

Table 7.4 Existing model weavers—summary and comparison

Research proposal	Diagrams	Formality	Tool	Aspect reuse	Extensibility	Standards
Cui et al. (Jasmine-AOI) [62]	AD	Algorithms	✓			
Fuentes and Sánchez [92]	AD					
Zhang et al. (Motorola WEAVR) [213]	SMD		✓	✓		✓
Groher and Voelter (XWeave) [97]	Generic		✓		✓	
Morin et al. (GeKo) [138]	Generic	✓	✓	✓	✓	
Whittle et al. (MATA) [206]	Generic	✓	Partially		✓	✓
Klein et al. [118]	SD	✓	✓	✓		
Kienzle et al. (RAM) [116]	CD, SMD, SD		Partially	✓		
Reddy et al. [175]	CD		Partially	✓		
Hovsepyan et al. [100]	CD, SD		✓	✓	✓	
Our approach	CD, SMD, SD, AD	✓	✓	✓	✓	✓

7.8 Conclusion

In this chapter, we have presented our weaving framework for integrating security aspects into UML design models. We have detailed the main steps of the proposed weaving approach. Additionally, we have presented the weaving algorithms that implement the weaving capabilities for each of the supported UML diagrams. The different transformation definitions and the mapping rules used to perform the weaving were also detailed. The main advantages of our weaving approach are the portability and the expressiveness thanks to the use of OMG standards, namely, OCL and QVT languages. By adopting OCL for evaluating the pointcuts, we were able to match a rich join point model with a large and variant set of join points. For instance, in activity diagrams, we consider not only executable nodes, i.e., action nodes, but also various control nodes, e.g., `fork`, `decision`. Some of these join points cannot be captured at the code level with existing pointcuts. Thus, capturing such control nodes, at the design level, allows modeling crosscutting concerns needed with alternatives, loops, exceptions, and multithreaded applications. Also, in state machine diagrams, we consider not only static states as join points, but also, we capture states that dynamically depend on the transitions that are triggered to reach them. The adoption of QVT for implementing the weaving allowed us to support a wide variety of modifications on different UML diagrams. In addition, QVT extends portability of the designed weaver to all tools supporting QVT language. Moreover, traceability of the performed weaving operations is also supported through the tagging rules for the added and the modified elements. After weaving the needed security aspects, the developer can validate the hardening of the models by making use of verification and validation tools [69, 126]. In our approach, these tools take, as inputs, the woven model and the corresponding security properties, and provide, as output, whether the security properties are satisfied or not. The weaver has been developed as a plug-in on top of IBM-RSA, which makes it portable to any IDE that is based on Eclipse. We have also explored the viability and the relevance of our framework by using it to inject security mechanisms into various mid-size open source projects, such as SIP communicator and OpenSAF. Using our framework, we successfully solved different security vulnerabilities in SIP communicator, replaced deprecated functions in OpenSAF, and added access control and input validation mechanisms into a service provider application.

Chapter 8
Static Matching and Weaving Semantics in Activity Diagrams

Aspect-Oriented Modeling (AOM) is an emerging solution for handling security concerns at the software modeling level. In this respect, we have proposed, in Chaps. 6 and 7, an AOM framework for specifying and systematically integrating security aspects into UML design models. In this chapter, we present formal specifications for aspect matching and weaving in UML activity diagrams. In fact, most of the existing work on weaving aspects into UML design models is presented from a practical perspective and lacks formal syntax and semantics. Accordingly, there is a desideratum to put more emphasis on the theoretical foundations that allow for rigorous definitions, establishment of theoretical results, and consequently a better understanding of AOM.

We focus on activity diagrams typically used to model business processes and operational workflows of systems [152]. Activity diagrams have a rich join point model, and accordingly, it will be very useful to formalize their matching and weaving processes. We formalize both types of adaptations, i.e., add adaptations, which add new elements to an activity diagram *before*, *after*, or *around* specific join points, and remove adaptations, which delete existing elements from activity diagrams. To the best of our knowledge, this is the first contribution in handling formal specifications of adaptation weaving specifically for *around* adaptation with or without `proceed`. Regarding the join point model, its novelty is that we consider not only executable nodes, i.e., action nodes, but also various control nodes, i.e., `initial`, `final`, `flow final`, `fork`, `join`, `decision`, and `merge` nodes. Actually, some of these join points cannot be captured at the code level, and thus, capturing such control nodes, at the design level, allows modeling crosscutting concerns with alternatives, loops, exceptions, and multithreaded applications.

The remainder of this chapter is structured as follows. Section 8.1 presents the syntax of UML activity diagrams and aspects. In Sect. 8.2, we define formal semantics for aspect matching and weaving. Afterwards, in Sect. 8.3, we formalize algorithms for matching and weaving. In addition, we prove the correctness and the completeness of these algorithms with respect to the proposed semantics. Finally, Sect. 8.4 concludes this chapter.

© Springer International Publishing Switzerland 2015
D. Mouheb et al., *Aspect-Oriented Security Hardening of UML Design Models*,
DOI 10.1007/978-3-319-16106-8_8

8.1 Syntax

This section presents the syntax of UML activity diagrams and aspects. The proposed syntax covers all the constructs that are required for the matching and the weaving semantics. We need first to introduce the notations that are used to express our semantics.

Notation

- Algorithms and notations are written with respect to OCaml [16].
- Given a record structure $D = \{f_1 : D_1; f_2 : D_2; \ldots; f_n : D_n\}$ and an element e of type D, the access to the field f_i of the element e is written as $e \cdot f_i$.
- Given a record structure $D = \{f_1 : D_1; f_2 : D_2; \ldots; f_n : D_n\}$ and an element e of type D, the update operation that produces a copy e' of the element e with a new value v for the field f_x, where $1 \le x \le n$, is written as $e' = \{e \; with \, f_x = v\}$.
- Given a type τ, we write τ-set to denote sets having elements of type τ.
- Given a type τ, we write τ-uset to denote sets having a unary element of type τ.
- Given a type τ, we write τ-list to denote lists having elements of type τ.
- The type Identifier classifies identifiers.

8.1.1 Activity Diagrams Syntax

An activity diagram, as shown in Fig. 8.1, consists of a set of nodes and a set of edges. An edge is a directed connection between two nodes represented by *source* and *target*. In addition, an edge may have a guard condition specifying if the edge can be traversed. A node can be either an executable node (e.g., action, structured activity) or a control node (e.g., initial, final). We consider the following nodes:

- Initial: represents an initial node, at which the activity starts executing. It has one outgoing edge and no incoming edges.
- Final: represents a final node that can be either: (1) an activity final, at which the activity execution terminates, or (2) a flow final, at which a flow terminates. It has one incoming edge and no outgoing edges.
- Fork/Decision: represents a fork or a decision node. It has one incoming edge and multiple outgoing edges.
- Join/Merge: represents a join or a merge node. It has one outgoing edge and multiple incoming edges.

Activity	$\ni \mathcal{A}$	::=	{*name*:	Identifier;	(Activity)
			nodes:	Node-set;	
			edges:	Edge-set}	
Node	$\ni n$	::=	Initial | Final | ForkDecision		(Node)
			|	JoinMerge | Action	
			|	StrActivity	
Initial	$\ni i$	::=	{*type*:	**initial**;	(Initial)
			name:	Identifier;	
			outgoing: Edge-uset}		
Final	$\ni f$	::=	{*type*:	**final** | **flowfinal**;	(Final)
			name:	Identifier;	
			incoming: Edge-uset}		
ForkDecision	$\ni fd$	::=	{*type*:	**fork** | **decision**;	(Fork/Decision)
			name:	Identifier;	
			incoming: Edge-uset;		
			outgoing: Edge-set}		
JoinMerge	$\ni jm$	::=	{*type*:	**join** | **merge**;	(Join/Merge)
			name:	Identifier;	
			incoming: Edge-set;		
			outgoing: Edge-uset}		
Action	$\ni a$	::=	OpaqueAction | SpecificAction		(Action)
OpaqueAction	$\ni oa$	::=	{*type*:	**action**;	
			name:	Identifier;	
			incoming: Edge-uset;		
			outgoing: Edge-uset;		
			inpin:	Type-list;	
			outpin:	Type-list}	
SpecificAction	$\ni sa$	::=	{*type*:	**call** | **read** | **write** | **create** | **destroy**	
			name:	Identifier;	
			operand: Identifier;		
			incoming: Edge-uset;		
			outgoing: Edge-uset;		
			inpin:	Type-list;	
			outpin:	Type-list}	
Type	$\ni \tau$	::=	Int | Nat | Bool | String | Enumeration		(Type)
Enumeration	$\ni enu$	::=	{*name*:	Identifier;	
			enuliteral: Identifier-list}		
StrActivity	$\ni sta$	::=	{*type*:	**structured_activity**;	(Structured Activity)
			name:	Identifier;	
			incoming: Edge-uset;		
			outgoing: Edge-uset;		
			nodes:	Node-set;	
			edges:	Edge-set}	
Edge	$\ni e$	::=	{*name*:	Identifier;	(Edge)
			source: Node;		
			target: Node;		
			guard:	**true** | **false**}	
PrNode	$\ni prn$	::=	Node | Proceed		(Proceed)
Proceed	$\ni pr$	::=	{*type*:	**proceed**;	
			incoming: Edge-uset;		
			outgoing: Edge-uset}		
PrStrActivity	$\ni prsa$	::=	{*type*:	**proceed_str_activity**;	(Proceed Structured Activity)
			name:	Identifier;	
			incoming: Edge-uset;		
			outgoing: Edge-uset;		
			nodes:	PrNode-set;	
			edges:	Edge-set}	

Fig. 8.1 Activity diagrams syntax—part 1

- **Action**: represents an action node. It has one incoming and one outgoing edge. Moreover it has input pins and output pins represented as a list of types. The type, as specified in [155], can be Int to classify integers, Nat to classify naturals, Bool to classify the usual truth values `true` or `false`, String to classify a sequence of characters, or enumeration to represent user-defined data types. There are various kinds of actions in UML 2. Among them, we consider the following:

  - Opaque action is represented by `action`.
  - Call operation action is represented by `call`. The operation to be invoked by the action execution is specified by the operand field.
  - Read structural feature action is represented by `read`. The structural feature to be read is specified by the operand field.
  - Write structural feature action is represented by `write`. The structural feature to be written is specified by the operand field.
  - Create object action is represented by `create`. The object to be created is specified by the operand field.
  - Destroy object action is represented by `destroy`. The object to be destroyed is specified by the operand field.

- **Proceed**: represents a node that can be any of the previously defined nodes or a `proceed` node. A `proceed` node is a special node that is used within the *around* adaptation to represent the original computation of the matched join point. A `proceed` node has one incoming and one outgoing edge.
- **Structured Activity**: represents a structured activity node, which may have in turn its own nodes and edges. It has one incoming and one outgoing edge.
- **Proceed Structured Activity**: represents a structured activity that may have `proceed` nodes. It has one incoming and one outgoing edge.

8.1.2 Aspect Syntax

An aspect, as depicted in Fig. 8.2, includes a list of adaptations. An adaptation can be of two kinds:

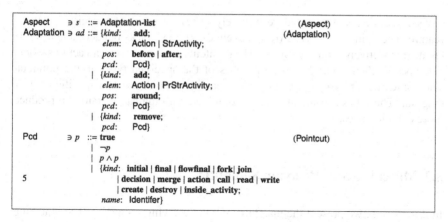

Fig. 8.2 Aspect syntax

- *Add adaptation*: It includes the following:
  - The activity element to be injected at specific locations picked out by pointcuts. It can be either a basic element (action) or a composed element (structured activity or proceed structured activity).
  - The insertion point that specifies where the activity element should be injected. It can have the following three values: *before*, *after*, and *around*. A *before-* (respectively *after-*) position means that the new element should be added *before* (respectively *after*) the identified location, while an *around-*position means that the existing element at the identified location should be replaced with a new one. In the case of *around*, the adaptation element may contain a proceed node that represents the computation of the matched join point.

- *Remove adaptation*: It includes a pointcut that picks out the elements that should be removed from the activity diagram.

A pointcut specifies a set of join points in the activity diagram where the aspect adaptations should be applied. We consider the following kinds of basic pointcuts: initial, final, flowfinal, fork, join, decision, merge, action, call, read, write, create, destroy, args, and inside_activity. The pointcuts initial, final, flowfinal, fork, join, decision, merge, and action pick out the nodes initial, final, flowfinal, fork, join, decision, merge, and action respectively. The pointcut call picks out action nodes that perform specific operation calls. The pointcut read (respectively write) picks out action nodes that read (respectively write) the values of a specific structural feature. The pointcut `create` (respectively `destroy`) picks out action nodes that create (respectively destroy) objects. The pointcut `args` picks out call actions where the types of their input pins are instances of the specified types in the pointcut. The pointcut `inside_activity` picks each join point inside a specific activity diagram. These basic pointcuts can be combined with logical operators to produce more complex ones.

8.2 Matching and Weaving Semantics

In this section, we present the matching and the weaving semantics. The matching semantics describes how to identify the join points targeted by the activity adaptations, whereas the weaving semantics describes how to apply the activity adaptations at the identified join points.

8.2.1 Matching Semantics

We define the judgment $A, n \vdash_{match} pcd$, which is used in the matching semantic rules, presented in Figs. 8.4 and 8.5, to describe that a node n belonging to the activity A matches the pointcut pcd. A node n can be an initial node i, an activity final node af, a flow final node ff, a fork node f, a join node j, a decision node d, a merge node m, an action node a, a call operation action node coa, a read structural feature action node ra, a write structural feature action node wa, a create object action node ca, a destroy object action node da, or either of these nodes sn. Before presenting the matching rules, we need to explain the notation of equality of type lists presented in Fig. 8.3, since it is used in the rule Args. Two lists of types are equal if the nth item in the first list is an instance of the nth item in the second list.

Fig. 8.3 Equality of type lists

$$\frac{L_1 = \tau_1 :: L_1' \quad L_2 = \tau_2 :: L_2' \quad \tau_1 \succeq \tau_2}{L_1' \equiv L_2'}$$
$$\frac{L_1' \equiv L_2'}{L_1 \equiv L_2}$$

$$\frac{L_1 = [] \quad L_2 = []}{L_1 \equiv L_2}$$

$$\frac{\tau_1 = \text{Int} \quad \tau_2 = \text{Nat}}{\tau_1 \succ \tau_2}$$

$$\frac{pcd.kind = \texttt{initial} \qquad pcd.name = i.name}{\mathcal{A}, i \vdash_{match} pcd} \qquad \text{(Initial)}$$

$$\frac{pcd.kind = \texttt{final} \qquad pcd.name = af.name}{\mathcal{A}, af \vdash_{match} pcd} \qquad \text{(Final)}$$

$$\frac{pcd.kind = \texttt{flowfinal} \qquad pcd.name = ff.name}{\mathcal{A}, ff \vdash_{match} pcd} \qquad \text{(FlowFinal)}$$

$$\frac{pcd.kind = \texttt{fork} \qquad pcd.name = f.name}{\mathcal{A}, f \vdash_{match} pcd} \qquad \text{(Fork)}$$

$$\frac{pcd.kind = \texttt{join} \qquad pcd.name = j.name}{\mathcal{A}, j \vdash_{match} pcd} \qquad \text{(Join)}$$

$$\frac{pcd.kind = \texttt{decision} \qquad pcd.name = d.name}{\mathcal{A}, d \vdash_{match} pcd} \qquad \text{(Decision)}$$

$$\frac{pcd.kind = \texttt{merge} \qquad pcd.name = m.name}{\mathcal{A}, m \vdash_{match} pcd} \qquad \text{(Merge)}$$

$$\frac{pcd.kind = \texttt{action} \qquad pcd.name = a.name}{\mathcal{A}, a \vdash_{match} pcd} \qquad \text{(Action)}$$

$$\frac{pcd.kind = \texttt{call} \qquad pcd.name = coa.operand}{\mathcal{A}, coa \vdash_{match} pcd} \qquad \text{(Call)}$$

$$\frac{pcd.kind = \texttt{read} \qquad pcd.name = ra.operand}{\mathcal{A}, ra \vdash_{match} pcd} \qquad \text{(Read)}$$

$$\frac{pcd.kind = \texttt{write} \qquad pcd.name = wa.operand}{\mathcal{A}, wa \vdash_{match} pcd} \qquad \text{(Write)}$$

$$\frac{pcd.kind = \texttt{create} \qquad pcd.name = ca.operand}{\mathcal{A}, ca \vdash_{match} pcd} \qquad \text{(Create)}$$

$$\frac{pcd.kind = \texttt{destroy} \qquad pcd.name = da.operand}{\mathcal{A}, da \vdash_{match} pcd} \qquad \text{(Destroy)}$$

$$\frac{pcd.kind = \texttt{inside\_activity} \qquad pcd.name = \mathcal{A}.name}{\mathcal{A}, sn \vdash_{match} pcd} \qquad \text{(InsideActivity)}$$

$$\frac{pcd.kind = \texttt{args} \qquad pcd.input \equiv coa.inpin}{\mathcal{A}, coa \vdash_{match} pcd} \qquad \text{(Args)}$$

$$\frac{\mathcal{A}, n \vdash_{match} pcd_1 \qquad \mathcal{A}, n \vdash_{match} pcd_2}{\mathcal{A}, n \vdash_{match} pcd_1 \wedge pcd_2} \qquad \text{(And)}$$

Fig. 8.4 Matching semantics—part 1

$$\frac{\mathcal{A}, n \vdash_{match} pcd_1}{\mathcal{A}, n \vdash_{match} pcd_1 \lor pcd_2} \qquad (\text{Or}_1)$$

$$\frac{\mathcal{A}, n \vdash_{match} pcd_2}{\mathcal{A}, n \vdash_{match} pcd_1 \lor pcd_2} \qquad (\text{Or}_2)$$

$$\frac{\mathcal{A}, n \nvdash_{match} pcd}{\mathcal{A}, n \vdash_{match} \neg pcd} \qquad (\text{Not})$$

Fig. 8.5 Matching semantics—part 2

In the following, we explain the matching semantic rules:

Initial
: Describes the case where the current node is an initial node, the current pointcut is an initial one, and the pointcut name equals the node name. In such a case, the initial node matches the pointcut.

Final
: Describes the case where the current node is an activity final node, the current pointcut is a final one, and the pointcut name equals the node name. In such a case, the activity final node matches the pointcut.

FlowFinal
: Describes the case where the current node is a flow final node, the current pointcut is a flow final one, and the pointcut name equals the node name. In such a case, the flow final node matches the pointcut.

Fork
: Describes the case where the current node is a fork node, the current pointcut is a fork one, and the pointcut name equals the node name. In such a case, the fork node matches the pointcut.

Join
: Describes the case where the current node is a join node, the current pointcut is a join one, and the pointcut name equals the node name. In such a case, the join node matches the pointcut.

Decision
: Describes the case where the current node is a decision node, the current pointcut is a decision one, and the pointcut name equals the node name. In such a case, the decision node matches the pointcut.

Merge
: Describes the case where the current node is a merge node, the current pointcut is a merge one, and the pointcut name equals the node name. In such a case, the merge node matches the pointcut.

Action

Describes the case where the current node is an action node that can be either an opaque action, a call operation action, a read structural feature action, a write structural feature action, a create object action, or a destroy object action, the current pointcut is an action one, and the pointcut name equals the node name. In such a case, the action node matches the pointcut.

Call

Describes the case where the current node is a call operation action node, the current pointcut is a call one, the pointcut name equals the name of the operation to be invoked. In such a case, the call operation action node matches the pointcut.

Read

Describes the case where the current node is a read structural feature action node, the current pointcut is a read one, the pointcut name equals the name of the structural feature to be read. In such a case, the read structural feature action node matches the pointcut.

Write

Describes the case where the current node is a write structural feature action node, the current pointcut is a write one, the pointcut name equals the name of the structural feature to be written. In such a case, the write structural feature action node matches the pointcut.

Create

Describes the case where the current node is a create object action node, the current pointcut is a create one, the pointcut name equals the name of the object to be created. In such a case, the create object action node matches the pointcut.

Destroy

Describes the case where the current node is a destroy object action node, the current pointcut is a destroy one, the pointcut name equals the name of the object to be destroyed. In such a case, the destroy object action node matches the pointcut.

InsideActivity

Describes the case where the current node is an *sn* node, i.e., initial, final, flow final, fork, join, decision, merge, or action node, the current pointcut is an inside_activity one, and the pointcut name equals the name of the activity containing the node. In such a case, the *sn* node matches the pointcut.

Args   Describes the case where the current node is a call oper-
                                ation action, the current pointcut is an args one, and the
                                types given in the pointcut are equal to the types given
                                in the input pins of the action. In such a case, the call
                                operation action matches the pointcut.

And, Or_1, Or_2, and Not   Describe the cases where pointcuts are combined using
                                logical operators to produce more complex ones.

8.2.2 Weaving Semantics

The weaving semantics, shown in Fig. 8.9, is represented by the weaving con-
figuration ⟨Activity, Aspect, Node, State⟩. The state State is a flag that represents the stage of the weaving process, which is either weaving or end. The
flag is equal to weaving when adaptations still have to be woven, whereas it
becomes end when the weaving is completed. Hence, the transformation
⟨A, s, n, weaving⟩ $\hookrightarrow$ ⟨A', [ ], n', end⟩ means that the activity diagram A' is the
result of weaving all the applicable adaptations in the adaptation list s into the node n.
A node whose type is proceed is denoted pr, whereas the set {action,
call, read, write, create, destroy} is called *actionSet*. Before presenting
the weaving rules, we need to explain the following notation:

- The axiom $\Vdash n$ defines that the node n is of type proceed or it is a structured
  activity node having, at least, one proceed node. Derivations of proceed nodes
  are shown in Fig. 8.6.
- The axiom $\Vvdash n$ defines that the node n is not of type proceed or it is a structured activity node that none of its nodes is of type proceed. Derivations of no
  proceed nodes are shown in Fig. 8.7.
- The representation $s' = s[n_1 \to n_2]$ describes that the set s' comes out as a result
  of substituting n_1 by n_2 wherever n_1 appears in the set s, as long as the nodes in the
  set s are not proceed structured activities. This is accompanied by modifying
  the incoming and the outgoing edges of the node n_2 together with modifying the
  corresponding edges' sources and targets. In the case that a node in the set s is a
  proceed structured activity, we substitute n_1 by n_2 wherever n_1 appears in the
  nodes of this proceed structured activity. The substitution rules are shown in
  Fig. 8.8.

$$\frac{n.type = \texttt{proceed}}{\Vdash n}$$

$$\frac{n.type = \texttt{proceed\_str\_activity} \quad \Vdash n' \quad n' \in n.nodes}{\Vdash n}$$

Fig. 8.6 Derivation of Proceed nodes

$$\frac{n.type \neq \texttt{proceed} \quad n.type \neq \texttt{proceed\_str\_activity}}{\Vdash n}$$

$$\Vdash \emptyset$$

$$\frac{s = \{n\} \cup s' \quad \Vdash n \quad \Vdash s'}{\Vdash s}$$

$$\frac{n.type = \texttt{proceed\_str\_activity} \quad \Vdash n.nodes}{\Vdash n}$$

Fig. 8.7 Derivation of no `Proceed` nodes

$$\frac{n_1.type \neq \texttt{proceed\_str\_activity} \quad e \in n_1.incoming \quad e' \in n_1.outgoing}{\{n'\} = \{n_1\}[n_1 \rightarrow n_2]}$$
$$n' = \{n_2 \text{ with } incoming = e, outgoing = e'\} \quad e.target = n' \quad e'.source = n'$$

$$\frac{n.type \neq \texttt{proceed\_str\_activity} \quad n \neq n_1}{\{n\} = \{n\}[n_1 \rightarrow n_2]}$$

$$\frac{s = \emptyset}{\emptyset = s[n_1 \rightarrow n_2]}$$

$$\frac{s = \{n\} \cup s' \quad s_1 = \{n\}[n_1 \rightarrow n_2] \quad s_2 = s'[n_1 \rightarrow n_2]}{s_1 \cup s_2 = s[n_1 \rightarrow n_2]}$$

$$\frac{n.type = \texttt{proceed\_str\_activity} \quad s = n.nodes[n_1 \rightarrow n_2] \quad n' = \{n \text{ with } nodes = s\}}{\{n'\} = \{n\}[n_1 \rightarrow n_2]}$$

Fig. 8.8 Substitution rules

In the following, we explain the weaving semantic rules:

Before	Describes the case where an *add before* adaptation matches a specific node. This adaptation can be applied before this matched node unless it is an initial node since this node starts the activity execution. The activity element of the adaptation is inserted before the matched node.
After	Describes the case where an *add after* adaptation matches a specific node. This adaptation can be applied after this matched node unless it is a final node or a flow final node since those nodes terminate the activity execution. The activity element of the adaptation is inserted after the matched node.
AroundWProceed	Describes the case where an *add around* adaptation matches an action node. Additionally, the adaptation

	element is a structured activity having, at least, one proceed node. The activity element of the adaptation replaces the matched node. Moreover, every occurrence of a proceed node in the nodes of the adaptation element is replaced by the corresponding matched node.
AroundWoutProceed	Describes the case where an *add around* adaptation matches an action node. Additionally, the adaptation element is an action node or a structured activity that none of its nodes is a proceed one. The activity element of the adaptation replaces the matched node.
Remove	Describes the case where a *remove* adaptation matches a specific node. This adaptation can be applied just on matched action nodes. The matched node is deleted from the activity diagram.
NoMatch	Describes the case where the current adaptation pointcut does not match a node n. In this case, the activity diagram remains the same and the weaving process continues with the rest of the adaptations.
End	Describes the case where there are no more adaptations to apply on the activity diagram. In this case, the activity diagram remains the same and the weaving process terminates.

8.3 Completeness and Correctness of the Weaving

In this section, we address the correctness and the completeness of the weaving in UML activity diagrams. We first present the algorithms that implement the matching and the weaving semantics reported in the rules in Figs. 8.4, 8.5, and 8.9. Then, we prove the correctness and the completeness of the matching and the weaving algorithms with respect to the semantics rules. By correctness (or soundness), we mean the output of the matching/weaving algorithm is predicted by its corresponding semantic rules. By completeness, we mean the behavior, derived from a semantic rule, corresponds to a particular execution of the corresponding algorithm.

8.3.1 Algorithms

In this sub-section, we present algorithms that implement the matching and the weaving processes. We have four algorithms: containProceed (Algorithm 8.1), substitute (Algorithm 8.2), $\mathcal{M}$ (Algorithm 8.3), and $\mathcal{W}$ (Algorithms 8.4 and 8.5). In the algorithms $\mathcal{M}$ and $\mathcal{W}$, *actionSet* is the set {action, call, read, write, create, destroy}. The algorithm containProceed takes a node n as input. It

Fig. 8.9 Weaving semantics

returns `true` if the node n is of type `proceed` or if it is a structured activity node that at least one of its nodes is of type `proceed`.

The algorithm **substitute** takes three arguments: a set s and two nodes n_1 and n_2. It returns a set that comes out as a result of substituting n_1 by n_2 wherever n_1 appears in the set s as long as the nodes in the set s are not `proceed` structured activities. This is accompanied by modifying the incoming and the outgoing edges of the node n_2 together with modifying the corresponding edges' sources and targets. In the case that a node in the set s is a `proceed` structured activity, we substitute n_1 by n_2 wherever n_1 appears in the nodes of this `proceed` structured activity.

Algorithm 8.1: Proceed Algorithm

---

containProceed(n) = **case** $n.type$ **of**

    proceed $\Rightarrow$ true
    proceed_str_activity $\Rightarrow$ containProceed(n') **and** $n' \in n.nodes$
    otherwise $\Rightarrow$ false

The matching algorithm $\mathcal{M}$ takes three arguments: A set of activity diagrams $\mathcal{AS}$, a node n, and a pointcut pcd. It returns true if the node n in the activity diagram $\mathcal{A}$, which belongs to the set $\mathcal{AS}$, matches the pointcut pcd, and returns false otherwise.

The weaving algorithm $\mathcal{W}$ takes three arguments: An activity diagram $\mathcal{A}$, an adaptation list s, and a node n. The outcome of the weaving algorithm is an activity diagram $\mathcal{A}'$ that represents the woven diagram. The function buildEdge, used in the weaving algorithm, takes two nodes, as inputs, and returns an edge between these two nodes as follows:

buildEdge : Node $\times$ Node $\rightarrow$ Edge
buildEdge(s, t) = e where $(e.source = s) \wedge (e.target = t)$

Algorithm 8.2: Substitute Algorithm

---

substitute(s, n_1, n_2) = **case** s **of**

  $\emptyset$ $\Rightarrow \emptyset$
  $\{n\}$ $\Rightarrow$ **if** $n.type \neq$ proceed_str_activity **and** $n \neq n_1$ **then** $\{n\}$ **else**
               if $n.type \neq$ proceed_str_activity **and** $e \in n.incoming$ **and** $e' \in n.outgoing$
               then
                   let $n' = \{n_2$ with incoming $= e$, outgoing $= e'\}$
                      $e.target = n'$
                      $e'.source = n'$
                 in $\{n'\}$
               else
                 if $n.type =$ proceed_str_activity **then**
                   let $s =$ substitute($n.nodes, n_1, n_2$)
                      $n' = \{n$ with nodes $= s\}$
                   in $\{n'\}$
  $\{n\} \cup s'$ $\Rightarrow$ **let** $s_1 =$ substitute($\{n\}, n_1, n_2$)
                    $s_2 =$ substitute(s', n_1, n_2)
                 in $s_1 \cup s_2$

Algorithm 8.3: Matching Algorithm

$\mathcal{M}(AS, n, pcd)$ = **if** $A \in AS$ **and** $n \in A.nodes$ **then case** $pcd.kind$ **of**

inside_activity	$\Rightarrow$ **if** $n.type \in \{$initial,final,flowfinal,fork,join, decision,merge,action,call,read,write,create, destroy$\}$ **then** $pcd.name = A.name$
initial|final| flowfinal|fork| join|decision|merge	$\Rightarrow$ **if** $n.type = pcd.kind$ **then** $n.name = pcd.name$
action	$\Rightarrow$ **if** $n.type \in actionSet$ **then** $pcd.name = n.name$
call|read|write| create|destroy	$\Rightarrow$ **if** $n.type = pcd.kind$ **then** $pcd.name = n.operand$
args	$\Rightarrow$ **if** $n.type = $ call **then**

  let rec $eq\ pcd.input\ n.inpin=$ **match** $pcd.input\ n.inpin$ **with**
  $\tau_1 :: l'_1, \tau_2 :: l'_2 \rightarrow$
  if $(\tau_1 = \tau_2)\ ||\ (\tau_1 = $ Int **and** $\tau_2=$Nat$)$ **then**
  $eq\ l'_1\ l'_2$
  else
  false
  $|\ [\ ], [\ ] \rightarrow$ **true**

8.3.2 Completeness and Correctness

In this sub-section, we state and prove results that establish the soundness and the completeness of the algorithms containProceed (Algorithm 8.1), substitute (Algorithm 8.2), $\mathcal{M}$ (Algorithm 8.3), and $\mathcal{W}$ (Algorithms 8.4 and 8.5) with respect to the semantics reported in Figs. 8.4, 8.5, 8.6, 8.8, and 8.9 respectively.

The following lemma states the soundness of the algorithm containProceed.

Lemma 8.1 (Soundness of containProceed) *Given a node n. If containProceed then* $\Vdash n$.

The following lemma states the completeness of the algorithm containProceed.

Lemma 8.2 (Completeness of containProceed) *Given a node n. If* $\Vdash n$ *then containProceed*.

The proofs of Lemmas 8.1 and 8.2 are straightforward since the algorithm containProceed results from the rules presented in Fig. 8.6.

The following lemma states the soundness of the algorithm substitute.

Lemma 8.3 (Soundness of substitute) *Given a set s and two nodes* n_1 *and* n_2. *If substitute*$(s, n_1, n_2) = s'$ *then* $s' = s[n_1 \rightarrow n_2]$.

The following lemma states the completeness of the algorithm substitute.

Lemma 8.4 (Completeness of substitute) *Given a set s and two nodes* n_1 *and* n_2. *If* $s' = s[n_1 \rightarrow n_2]$ *then substitute*$(s, n_1, n_2) = s'$.

The proofs of Lemmas 8.3 and 8.4 are straightforward since the algorithm substitute results from the rules presented in Fig. 8.8.

The following lemma states the soundness of the matching algorithm $\mathcal{M}$.

Algorithm 8.4: Weaving Algorithm - Part 1

$\mathcal{W}(\mathcal{A}, s, n)$ = **case** s **of**

$ad :: s' \Rightarrow$ **if** $\mathcal{M}(\{\mathcal{A}\}, n, ad.pcd)$ **then**

   case $ad.kind$ **of**

   add $\Rightarrow$ **case** $ad.pos$ **of**

       before $\Rightarrow$ **if** $n.type \neq$ initial **then**
           let $es = n.incoming$
               $e \in es$
               $e'' = \{e \text{ with } target = ad.elem\}$
               $e' = $ buildEdge$(ad.elem, n)$
               $n'' = \{ad.elem \text{ with } incoming = e'', outgoing = e'\}$
               $n' = \{n \text{ with } incoming = (es\backslash\{e\}) \cup \{e'\}\}$
               $no = \mathcal{A}.nodes$
               $ed = \mathcal{A}.edges$
               $\mathcal{A}' = \{\mathcal{A} \text{ with } nodes = (no\backslash\{n\}) \cup \{n', n''\},$
                          $edges = (ed\backslash\{e\}) \cup \{e', e''\}\}$
           in $\mathcal{W}(\mathcal{A}', s', n')$

       after $\Rightarrow$ **if** $n.type \neq$ final **and** $n.type \neq$ flowfinal **then**
           let $os = n.outgoing$
               $e \in os$
               $next = e.target$
               $e' = $ buildEdge$(ad.elem, next)$
               $e'' = \{e \text{ with } target = ad.elem\}$
               $n' = \{ad.elem \text{ with } incoming = e'', outgoing = e'\}$
               $es = next.incoming$
               $n'' = \{next \text{ with } incoming = (es\backslash\{e\}) \cup \{e'\}$
               $no = \mathcal{A}.nodes$
               $ed = \mathcal{A}.edges$
               $\mathcal{A}' = \{\mathcal{A} \text{ with } nodes = (no\backslash\{next\}) \cup \{n', n''\},$
                          $edges = (ed\backslash\{e\}) \cup \{e', e''\}\}$
           in $\mathcal{W}(\mathcal{A}', s', n)$

       around $\Rightarrow$ **if** $n.type \in actionSet$ **and** containProceed$(ad.elem)$ **then**
           let $e \in n.incoming$
               $e' \in n.outgoing$
               $e'' = \{e \text{ with } target = ad.elem\}$
               $e''' = \{e' \text{ with } source = ad.elem\}$
               $\{n''\} = $ substitute$(\{ad.elem\}, pr, n)$
               $n' = \{n'' \text{ with } incoming = e'', outgoing = e'''\}$
               $no = \mathcal{A}.nodes$
               $ed = \mathcal{A}.edges$
               $\mathcal{A}' = \{\mathcal{A} \text{ with } nodes = (no\backslash\{n\}) \cup \{n'\},$
                          $edges = (ed\backslash\{e, e'\}) \cup \{e'', e'''\}\}$
           in $\mathcal{W}(\mathcal{A}', s', n')$

       else
       if $n.type \in actionSet$ **and** $\neg$containProceed$(ad.elem)$ **then**
           let $\{n'\} = $ substitute$(\{n\}, n, ad.elem)$
               $no = \mathcal{A}.nodes$
               $\mathcal{A}' = \{\mathcal{A} \text{ with } nodes = (no\backslash\{n\}) \cup \{n'\}\}$
           in $\mathcal{W}(\mathcal{A}', s', n')$

Algorithm 8.5: Weaving Algorithm - Part 2

```
remove ⇒ if n.type ∈ actionSet then
              let e ∈ n.incoming
                  e' ∈ n.outgoing
                  next = e'.target
                  e'' = {e with target = next}
                  es = next.incoming
                  n' = {next with incoming = (es\{e'}) ∪ {e''}}
                  no = A.nodes
                  ed = A.edges
                  A' = {A with nodes = (no\{n, next}) ∪ {n'},
                        edges = (ed\{e, e'}) ∪ {e''}}
              in W(A', s', next)
           else W(A, s', n)
    [ ] ⇒ A
```

Lemma 8.5 (Soundness of $\mathcal{M}$) *Given a set of activity diagrams $\mathcal{AS}$, an activity node n, and a pointcut pcd. If $\mathcal{M}(\mathcal{AS}, n, pcd)$ where $A \in \mathcal{AS}$ and $n \in A.nodes$ then $A, n \vdash_{match} pcd$.*

Proof The proof of Lemma 8.5 is straightforward by case analysis. Let us take as example the following cases:

- **Case (initial)**:
  From the algorithm $\mathcal{M}$, we have:
  $pcd.kind = $ `initial`
  $n.type = $ `initial`
  $n.name = pcd.name$
  Since $n.type = $ `initial` then n is an initial node i.
  By the rule (Initial) of the matching rules presented in Fig. 8.4, we conclude:
  $A, i \vdash_{match} pcd$
- **Case (call)**:
  From the algorithm $\mathcal{M}$, we have:
  $pcd.kind = $ `call`
  $n.type = $ `call`
  $pcd.name = n.operand$
  Since $n.type = $ `call` then n is a call operation action node (*coa*).
  By the rule (Call) of the matching rules presented in Fig. 8.4, we conclude:
  $A, coa \vdash_{match} pcd$
- **Case (read)**:
  From the algorithm $\mathcal{M}$, we have:
  $pcd.kind = $ `read`
  $n.type = $ `read`
  $pcd.name = n.operand$
  Since $n.type = $ `read` then n is a read structural feature action node (*ra*).
  By the rule (Read) of the matching rules presented in Fig. 8.4, we conclude:
  $A, ra \vdash_{match} pcd$

- **Case (Write)**:
  From the algorithm $\mathcal{M}$, we have:
  $pcd.kind = \texttt{write}$
  $n.type = \texttt{write}$
  $pcd.name = n.operand$
  Since $n.type = \texttt{write}$ then n is a write structural feature action node (wa).
  By the rule (Write) of the matching rules presented in Fig. 8.4, we conclude:
  $\mathcal{A}, wa \vdash_{match} pcd$
- **Case (inside_activity)**:
  From the algorithm $\mathcal{M}$, we have:
  $pcd.kind = \texttt{inside\_activity}$
  $n.type = \texttt{action}$
  $pcd.name = \mathcal{A}.name$
  Since $n.type = \texttt{action}$ then n is a simple node (sn).
  By the rule (InsideActivity) of the matching rules presented in Fig. 8.4, we conclude:
  $\mathcal{A}, sn \vdash_{match} pcd$

The following lemma states the completeness of the matching algorithm $\mathcal{M}$.

Lemma 8.6 (Completeness of $\mathcal{M}$) *Given a set of activity diagrams $\mathcal{AS}$, an activity diagram $\mathcal{A}$ where $\mathcal{A} \in \mathcal{AS}$, an activity node n where $n \in \mathcal{A}.nodes$, and a pointcut pcd. If $\mathcal{A}, n \vdash_{match} pcd$ then $\mathcal{M}(\mathcal{AS}, n, pcd)$.*

Proof The proof of Lemma 8.6 is straightforward by propagating the matching rules presented in Figs. 8.4 and 8.5 from conclusion to premises. Let us take as example the following case:

- **Case (initial)**:
  From the rule (Initial), we have:
  $pcd.kind = \texttt{initial}$
  $pcd.name = i.name$
  Since n is an initial node i, then $n.type = \texttt{initial}$.
  Since $\mathcal{A} \in \mathcal{AS}$ and $n \in \mathcal{A}.nodes$, by the algorithm $\mathcal{M}$ presented (Algorithm 8.3), we conclude:
  $\mathcal{M}(\mathcal{AS}, n, pcd)$

The following theorem states the soundness of the weaving algorithm $\mathcal{W}$.

Theorem 8.1 (Soundness of $\mathcal{W}$) *Given an activity diagram $\mathcal{A}$, an adaptation list s, and a node n. If $\mathcal{W}(\mathcal{A}, s, n) = \mathcal{A}''$ then $\langle \mathcal{A}, s, n, \texttt{weaving} \rangle \hookrightarrow \langle \mathcal{A}'', [\,], n'', \texttt{end} \rangle$.*

Proof The proof is done by induction over the length of s.

1. Induction basis ($s = [\,]$):
   By the algorithm $\mathcal{W}$, we have:
   $\mathcal{W}(\mathcal{A}, [\,], n) = \mathcal{A}$
   From the algorithm $\mathcal{W}$, we conclude that $s = [\,]$.

From the rule (End) of the semantic weaving rules presented in Fig. 8.9, we conclude:

$\langle \mathcal{A}, s, n, \texttt{weaving} \rangle \hookrightarrow \langle \mathcal{A}, [\ ], n, \texttt{end} \rangle$

2. Induction step:

We assume as induction hypothesis:

If $\mathcal{W}(\mathcal{A}, s', n) = \mathcal{A}''$ then $\langle \mathcal{A}, s', n, \texttt{weaving} \rangle \hookrightarrow \langle \mathcal{A}'', [\ ], n'', \texttt{end} \rangle$.

Now, let us consider $(s = ad :: s')$. Since $ad.kind$ can be:

- **Case (add):**

  Since $ad.pos$ can be:

  - **Subcase (before):**

    From the algorithm $\mathcal{W}$, we have:

    $\mathcal{M}(\{\mathcal{A}\}, n, ad.pcd)$

    $ad.kind = \texttt{add}$

    $ad.pos = \texttt{before}$

    $n.type \neq \texttt{initial}$

    $es = n.incoming$

    $e \in es$

    $e'' = \{e \text{ with } target = ad.elem\}$

    $e' = \texttt{buildEdge}(ad.elem, n)$

    $n'' = \{ad.elem \text{ with } incoming = e'', outgoing = e'\}$

    $n' = \{n \text{ with } incoming = (es \backslash \{e\}) \cup \{e'\}\}$

    $no = \mathcal{A}.nodes$

    $ed = \mathcal{A}.edges$

    $\mathcal{A}' = \{\mathcal{A} \text{ with } nodes = (no \backslash \{n\}) \cup \{n', n''\},$
    $\qquad\qquad edges = (ed \backslash \{e\}) \cup \{e', e''\}\}$

    By the soundness of the algorithm $\mathcal{M}$, we conclude:

    $\mathcal{A}, n \vdash_{match} ad.pcd$

    From the rule (Before) of the semantic weaving rules presented in Fig. 8.9, we conclude:

    $\langle \mathcal{A}, s, n, \texttt{weaving} \rangle \hookrightarrow \langle \mathcal{A}', s', n', \texttt{weaving} \rangle$

    By the hypothesis, we conclude:

    $\langle \mathcal{A}', s', n', \texttt{weaving} \rangle \hookrightarrow \langle \mathcal{A}'', [\ ], n'', \texttt{end} \rangle$

    By the transitivity of $\hookrightarrow$, we conclude:

    $\langle \mathcal{A}, s, n, \texttt{weaving} \rangle \hookrightarrow \langle \mathcal{A}'', [\ ], n'', \texttt{end} \rangle$

  - **Subcase (after):**

    From the algorithm $\mathcal{W}$, we have:

    $\mathcal{M}(\{\mathcal{A}\}, n, ad.pcd)$

    $ad.kind = \texttt{add}$

    $ad.pos = \texttt{after}$

    $n.type \neq \texttt{final}$

    $n.type \neq \texttt{flowfinal}$

    $os = n.outgoing$

    $e \in os$

    $next = e.target$

$e' = \mathsf{buildEdge}(ad.elem, next)$

$e'' = \{e \text{ with } target = ad.elem\}$

$n' = \{ad.elem \text{ with } incoming = e'', outgoing = e'\}$

$es = next.incoming$

$n'' = \{next \text{ with } incoming = (es \backslash \{e\}) \cup \{e'\}$

$no = \mathcal{A}.nodes$

$ed = \mathcal{A}.edges$

$\mathcal{A}' = \{\mathcal{A} \text{ with } nodes = (no \backslash \{next\}) \cup \{n', n''\},$
$\qquad edges = (ed \backslash \{e\}) \cup \{e', e''\}\}$

By the soundness of the algorithm $\mathcal{M}$, we conclude:

$\mathcal{A}, n \vdash_{match} ad.pcd$

From the rule (**After**) of the semantic weaving rules presented in Fig. 8.9, we conclude:

$\langle \mathcal{A}, s, n, \mathsf{weaving} \rangle \hookrightarrow \langle \mathcal{A}', s', n, \mathsf{weaving} \rangle$

By the hypothesis, we conclude:

$\langle \mathcal{A}', s', n, \mathsf{weaving} \rangle \hookrightarrow \langle \mathcal{A}'', [\,], n'', \mathsf{end} \rangle$

By the transitivity of $\hookrightarrow$, we conclude:

$\langle \mathcal{A}, s, n, \mathsf{weaving} \rangle \hookrightarrow \langle \mathcal{A}'', [\,], n'', \mathsf{end} \rangle$

- **Subcase (around with proceed)**:

From the algorithm $\mathcal{W}$, we have:

$\mathcal{M}(\{\mathcal{A}\}, n, ad.pcd)$

$ad.kind = \mathsf{add}$

$ad.pos = \mathsf{around}$

$n.type \in actionSet$

$\mathsf{containProceed}(ad.elem)$

$e \in n.incoming$

$e' \in n.outgoing$

$e'' = \{e \text{ with } target = ad.elem\}$

$e''' = \{e' \text{ with } source = ad.elem\}$

$\{n''\} = \mathsf{substitute}(\{ad.elem\}, pr, n)$

$n' = \{n'' \text{ with } incoming = e'', outgoing = e'''\}$

$no = \mathcal{A}.nodes$

$ed = \mathcal{A}.edges$

$\mathcal{A}' = \{\mathcal{A} \text{ with } nodes = (no \backslash \{n\}) \cup \{n'\},$
$\qquad edges = (ed \backslash \{e, e'\}) \cup \{e'', e'''\}\}$

By the soundness of the algorithm $\mathcal{M}$, we conclude:

$\mathcal{A}, n \vdash_{match} ad.pcd$

By the soundness of the algorithm $\mathsf{containProceed}$, we conclude:

$\Vdash ad.elem$

By the soundness of the algorithm $\mathsf{substitute}$, we conclude:

$\{n''\} = \{ad.elem\}[pr \to n]$

From the rule (**AroundWProceed**) of the semantic weaving rules presented in Fig. 8.9, we conclude:

$\langle \mathcal{A}, s, n, \mathsf{weaving} \rangle \hookrightarrow \langle \mathcal{A}', s', n', \mathsf{weaving} \rangle$

By the hypothesis, we conclude:

$\langle \mathcal{A}', s', n', \text{weaving} \rangle \hookrightarrow \langle \mathcal{A}'', [\,], n'', \text{end} \rangle$

By the transitivity of $\hookrightarrow$, we conclude:

$\langle \mathcal{A}, s, n, \text{weaving} \rangle \hookrightarrow \langle \mathcal{A}'', [\,], n'', \text{end} \rangle$

- **Subcase (around without proceed)**:

From the algorithm $\mathcal{W}$, we have:

$\mathcal{M}(\{\mathcal{A}\}, n, ad.pcd)$

$ad.kind = \text{add}$

$ad.pos = \text{around}$

$n.type \in actionSet$

$\{n'\} = \text{substitute}(\{n\}, n, ad.elem)$

$no = \mathcal{A}.nodes$

$\mathcal{A}' = \{\mathcal{A} \text{ with nodes} = (no \backslash \{n\}) \cup \{n'\}\}$

By the soundness of the algorithm $\mathcal{M}$, we conclude:

$\mathcal{A}, n \vdash_{match} ad.pcd$

By the soundness of the algorithm containProceed and the rules presented in Figs. 8.6 and 8.7, we conclude:

$\Vdash ad.elem$

By the soundness of the algorithm substitute, we conclude:

$\{n'\} = \{n\}[n \rightarrow ad.elem]$

From the rule (AroundWoutProceed) of the semantic weaving rules presented in Fig. 8.9, we conclude:

$\langle \mathcal{A}, s, n, \text{weaving} \rangle \hookrightarrow \langle \mathcal{A}', s', n', \text{weaving} \rangle$

By the hypothesis, we conclude:

$\langle \mathcal{A}', s', n', \text{weaving} \rangle \hookrightarrow \langle \mathcal{A}'', [\,], n'', \text{end} \rangle$

By the transitivity of $\hookrightarrow$, we conclude:

$\langle \mathcal{A}, s, n, \text{weaving} \rangle \hookrightarrow \langle \mathcal{A}'', [\,], n'', \text{end} \rangle$

- **Case (remove)**:

From the algorithm $\mathcal{W}$, we have:

$\mathcal{M}(\{\mathcal{A}\}, n, ad.pcd)$

$ad.kind = \text{remove}$

$n.type \in actionSet$

$e \in n.incoming$

$e' \in n.outgoing$

$next = e'.target$

$e'' = \{e \text{ with target} = next\}$

$es = next.incoming$

$n' = \{next \text{ with incoming} = (es \backslash \{e'\}) \cup \{e''\}$

$no = \mathcal{A}.nodes$

$ed = \mathcal{A}.edges$

$\mathcal{A}' = \{\mathcal{A} \text{ with nodes} = (no \backslash \{n, next\}) \cup \{n'\}, edges = (ed \backslash \{e, e'\}) \cup \{e''\}\}$

By the soundness of the algorithm $\mathcal{M}$, we conclude:

$\mathcal{A}, n \vdash_{match} ad.pcd$

From the rule (Remove) of the semantic weaving rules presented in Fig. 8.9, we conclude:

$\langle \mathcal{A}, s, n, \texttt{weaving} \rangle \hookrightarrow \langle \mathcal{A}', s', next, \texttt{weaving} \rangle$

By the hypothesis, we conclude:

$\langle \mathcal{A}', s', next, \texttt{weaving} \rangle \hookrightarrow \langle \mathcal{A}'', [\,], n'', \texttt{end} \rangle$

By the transitivity of $\hookrightarrow$, we conclude:

$\langle \mathcal{A}, s, n, \texttt{weaving} \rangle \hookrightarrow \langle \mathcal{A}'', [\,], n'', \texttt{end} \rangle$

- **Case (no match):**

  By the soundness and the completeness of the algorithm $\mathcal{M}$, we conclude:

  $\mathcal{A}, n \vdash_{match} \neg\, ad.pcd$

  From the rule (NoMatch) of the semantic weaving rules presented in Fig. 8.9, we conclude:

  $\langle \mathcal{A}, s, n, \texttt{weaving} \rangle \hookrightarrow \langle \mathcal{A}, s', n, \texttt{weaving} \rangle$

  By the hypothesis, we conclude:

  $\langle \mathcal{A}, s', n, \texttt{weaving} \rangle \hookrightarrow \langle \mathcal{A}'', [\,], n'', \texttt{end} \rangle$

  By the transitivity of $\hookrightarrow$, we conclude:

  $\langle \mathcal{A}, s, n, \texttt{weaving} \rangle \hookrightarrow \langle \mathcal{A}'', [\,], n'', \texttt{end} \rangle$

The following theorem states the completeness of the weaving algorithm $\mathcal{W}$.

Theorem 8.2 (Completeness of $\mathcal{W}$) *Given an activity diagram $\mathcal{A}$, an adaptation list s, and a node n.*
If $\langle \mathcal{A}, s, n, \texttt{weaving} \rangle \hookrightarrow \langle \mathcal{A}'', [\,], n'', \texttt{end} \rangle$ then $\mathcal{W}(\mathcal{A}, s, n) = \mathcal{A}''$.

Proof The proof is done by induction over the length of s.

1. Induction basis ($s = [\,]$):

   By the rule (End) of the semantic weaving rules presented in Fig. 8.9, we have:

   $\langle \mathcal{A}, s, n, \texttt{weaving} \rangle \hookrightarrow \langle \mathcal{A}, [\,], n, \texttt{end} \rangle$

   From the rule (End) of the semantic weaving rules presented in Fig. 8.9, we conclude that $s = [\,]$.

   From the algorithm $\mathcal{W}$, we conclude:

   $\mathcal{W}(\mathcal{A}, [\,], n) = \mathcal{A}$.

2. Induction step:

   We assume as induction hypothesis:

   If $\langle \mathcal{A}, s', n, \texttt{weaving} \rangle \hookrightarrow \langle \mathcal{A}'', [\,], n'', \texttt{end} \rangle$ then $\mathcal{W}(\mathcal{A}, s', n) = \mathcal{A}''$.

   Now, let us consider ($s = ad :: s'$). Since $ad.kind$ can be:

   - **Case (add):**

     Since $ad.pos$ can be:

     - **Subcase (before):**

       From the rule (Before) of the semantic weaving rules presented in Fig. 8.9, we conclude:

       $ad.kind = \texttt{add}$

       $ad.pos = \texttt{before}$

       $n.type \neq \texttt{initial}$

       $\mathcal{A}, n \vdash_{match} ad.pcd$

       $es = n.incoming$

$e \in es$

$e'' = \{e \text{ with } target = ad.elem\}$

$e' = \mathsf{buildEdge}(ad.elem, n)$

$n'' = \{ad.elem \text{ with } incoming = e'', outgoing = e'\}$

$n' = \{n \text{ with } incoming = (es \backslash \{e\}) \cup \{e'\}\}$

$no = \mathcal{A}.nodes$

$ed = \mathcal{A}.edges$

$\mathcal{A}' = \{\mathcal{A} \text{ with } nodes = (no \backslash \{n\}) \cup \{n', n''\},$
$\qquad edges = (ed \backslash \{e\}) \cup \{e', e''\}\}$

By the completeness of the algorithm $\mathcal{M}$, we conclude:

$\mathcal{M}(\{\mathcal{A}\}, n, ad.pcd)$

From the algorithm $\mathcal{W}$, we conclude:

$\mathcal{W}(\mathcal{A}, s, n) = \mathcal{W}(\mathcal{A}', s', n')$

By the hypothesis, we conclude:

$\mathcal{W}(\mathcal{A}', s', n') = \mathcal{A}''$

– **Subcase (after)**:

From the rule (After) of the semantic weaving rules presented in Fig. 8.9, we conclude:

$ad.kind = \mathsf{add}$

$ad.pos = \mathsf{after}$

$n.type \neq \mathsf{final}$

$n.type \neq \mathsf{flowfinal}$

$\mathcal{A}, n \vdash_{match} ad.pcd$

$os = n.outgoing$

$e \in os$

$next = e.target$

$e' = \mathsf{buildEdge}(ad.elem, next)$

$e'' = \{e \text{ with } target = ad.elem\}$

$n' = \{ad.elem \text{ with } incoming = e'', outgoing = e'\}$

$es = next.incoming$

$n'' = \{next \text{ with } incoming = (es \backslash \{e\}) \cup \{e'\}$

$no = \mathcal{A}.nodes$

$ed = \mathcal{A}.edges$

$\mathcal{A}' = \{\mathcal{A} \text{ with } nodes = (no \backslash \{next\}) \cup \{n', n''\},$
$\qquad edges = (ed \backslash \{e\}) \cup \{e', e''\}\}$

By the completeness of the algorithm $\mathcal{M}$, we conclude:

$\mathcal{M}(\{\mathcal{A}\}, n, ad.pcd)$

From the algorithm $\mathcal{W}$, we conclude:

$\mathcal{W}(\mathcal{A}, s, n) = \mathcal{W}(\mathcal{A}', s', n)$

By the hypothesis, we conclude:

$\mathcal{W}(\mathcal{A}', s', n) = \mathcal{A}''$

– **Subcase (around with proceed)**:

From the rule (AroundWProceed) of the semantic weaving rules presented in Fig. 8.9, we conclude:

$ad.kind = \mathsf{add}$

$ad.pos = \text{around}$

$\vDash ad.elem$

$n.type \in actionSet$

$\mathcal{A}, n \vdash_{match} ad.pcd$

$e \in n.incoming$

$e' \in n.outgoing$

$e'' = \{e \text{ with target} = ad.elem\}$

$e''' = \{e' \text{ with source} = ad.elem\}$

$\{n''\} = \{ad.elem\}[pr \rightarrow n]$

$n' = \{n'' \text{ with incoming} = e'', outgoing = e'''\}$

$no = \mathcal{A}.nodes$

$ed = \mathcal{A}.edges$

$\mathcal{A}' = \{\mathcal{A} \text{ with nodes} = (no\backslash\{n\}) \cup \{n'\},$
$\qquad edges = (ed\backslash\{e, e'\}) \cup \{e'', e'''\}\}$

By the completeness of the algorithm $\mathcal{M}$, we conclude:

$\mathcal{M}(\{\mathcal{A}\}, n, ad.pcd)$

By the completeness of the algorithm containProceed, we conclude:

containProceed($ad.elem$)

By the completeness of the algorithm substitute, we conclude:

$\{n''\} = \text{substitute}(\{ad.elem\}, pr, n)$

From the algorithm $\mathcal{W}$, we conclude:

$\mathcal{W}(\mathcal{A}, s, n) = \mathcal{W}(\mathcal{A}', s', n')$

By the hypothesis, we conclude:

$\mathcal{W}(\mathcal{A}', s', n') = \mathcal{A}''$

- **Subcase (around without proceed):**
  From the rule (AroundWouProceed) of the semantic weaving rules presented
  in Fig. 8.9, we conclude:

  $ad.kind = \text{add}$

  $ad.pos = \text{around}$

  $\Vdash ad.elem$

  $n.type \in actionSet$

  $\mathcal{A}, n \vdash_{match} ad.pcd$

  $\{n'\} = \{n\}[n \rightarrow ad.elem]$

  $no = \mathcal{A}.nodes$

  $\mathcal{A}' = \{\mathcal{A} \text{ with nodes} = (no\backslash\{n\}) \cup \{n'\}\}$

  By the completeness of the algorithm $\mathcal{M}$, we conclude:

  $\mathcal{M}(\{\mathcal{A}\}, n, ad.pcd)$

  By the completeness of the algorithm containProceed, we conclude:

  $\neg$containProceed($ad.elem$)

  By the completeness of the algorithm substitute, we conclude:

  $\{n'\} = \text{substitute}(\{n\}, n, ad.elem)$

  From the algorithm $\mathcal{W}$, we conclude:

  $\mathcal{W}(\mathcal{A}, s, n) = \mathcal{W}(\mathcal{A}', s', n')$

By the hypothesis, we conclude:

$\mathcal{W}(\mathcal{A}', s', n') = \mathcal{A}''$

- **Case (remove)**:

From the rule (Remove) of the semantic weaving rules presented in Fig. 8.9, we conclude:

$ad.kind = \texttt{remove}$

$n.type \in actionSet$

$\mathcal{A}, n \vdash_{match} ad.pcd$

$e \in n.incoming$

$e' \in n.outgoing$

$next = e'.target$

$e'' = \{e \ with \ target = next\}$

$es = next.incoming$

$n' = \{next \ with \ incoming = (es \backslash \{e'\}) \cup \{e''\}$

$no = \mathcal{A}.nodes$

$ed = \mathcal{A}.edges$

$\mathcal{A}' = \{\mathcal{A} \ with \ nodes = (no \backslash \{n, next\}) \cup \{n'\},$
$\quad edges = (ed \backslash \{e, e'\}) \cup \{e''\}\}$

By the completeness of the algorithm $\mathcal{M}$, we conclude:

$\mathcal{M}(\{\mathcal{A}\}, n, ad.pcd)$

From the algorithm $\mathcal{W}$, we conclude:

$\mathcal{W}(\mathcal{A}, s, n) = \mathcal{W}(\mathcal{A}', s', next)$

By the hypothesis, we conclude:

$\mathcal{W}(\mathcal{A}', s', next) = \mathcal{A}''$

- **Case (no match)**:

From the rule (NoMatch) of the semantic weaving rules presented in Fig. 8.9, we conclude:

$\mathcal{A}, n \vdash_{match} \neg ad.pcd$

By the soundness and the completeness of the algorithm $\mathcal{M}$, we conclude:

$\texttt{not } \mathcal{M}(\{\mathcal{A}\}, n, ad.pcd)$

From the algorithm $\mathcal{W}$, we conclude:

$\mathcal{W}(\mathcal{A}, s, n) = \mathcal{W}(\mathcal{A}, s', n)$

By the hypothesis, we conclude:

$\mathcal{W}(\mathcal{A}, s', n) = \mathcal{A}''$

8.4 Conclusion

We have presented in this chapter our contribution towards ascribing a formal semantics for the proposed weaving framework. We have focused on UML activity diagrams since they offer a rich join point model that includes various kinds of actions and control nodes. However, a formal semantics for matching and weaving for the other diagrams, i.e., class diagrams, state machine diagrams, and sequence diagrams, can be provided in the same vein as for activity diagrams. In this respect, a syntax of activity diagrams together with their corresponding adaptations has been defined to express the matching and the weaving semantics. Then, we have elaborated formal specifications for the matching and the weaving processes. We have addressed all kinds of adaptations that are supported in our framework, namely, add *before/after/around* (with and without `proceed`), and remove adaptations. Afterwards, we have provided algorithms that implement the matching and the weaving processes and proved the correctness and the completeness of these algorithms with respect to the defined semantics. It is important to mention here that our implementation of the weaving rules, presented in Chap. 7, is derived from these semantic descriptions. This work on formalizing the matching and the weaving processes in UML activity diagrams constitutes a first contribution towards elaborating robust theoretical foundations for AOM. In the next chapters, we will extend this framework with executable specifications to allow matching and weaving in the presence of more complex pointcut primitives.

Chapter 9
Dynamic Matching and Weaving Semantics in λ-Calculus

In Chap. 8, we have presented a formal semantics for aspect matching and weaving in UML activity diagrams. To get the full advantages of our AOM framework for security hardening, we have decided to enrich it with more security-related pointcuts together with their semantic foundations. An example of such pointcuts is the dataflow pointcut (dflow) [130]. This pointcut analyzes information flow in a system to detect input validation vulnerabilities, such as SQL injection and Cross-site Scripting (XSS) [86]. These vulnerabilities, if exploited by attackers, may lead to serious security problems, such as breaking the confidentiality and the integrity of sensitive information.

In order to match this kind of pointcut, UML models should be detailed enough to include behaviors that manipulate variables and their data values that are useful to be analyzed in terms of dataflow. In addition, runtime values should be available at the time of matching in order to track dependencies between these values. To this end, we extend our semantic framework to support executable UML (xUML) [134] specifications and capture the semantics of matching and weaving dynamically during the execution of the models. For clarity and to facilitate the understanding of the semantics, we proceed in two steps: First, we elaborate the dynamic semantics for matching and weaving on λ-calculus [57], since it serves as a base for many programming languages and contains constructs that are similar to the ones of action languages. In addition, it offers a powerful mathematical tool based on solid theoretical foundations. Afterwards, in Chap. 10, we present the dynamic semantics for matching and weaving on xUML models.

Various research proposals have investigated formal semantics of aspect-oriented languages [34, 53, 60, 66, 76, 88, 106, 129, 132, 201, 202]. However, the proposed semantic models mainly define join points in an intuitive and ad-hoc manner. In many cases, auxiliary structures need to be maintained for representing join points and executing pieces of advice. As a result, the semantics for the matching and the weaving processes become difficult to express, especially in the case of complex pointcut primitives. Accordingly, there is a desideratum to put more emphasis on the theoretical foundations that capture the definitions of aspect-oriented mechanisms in a precise and rigorous way. Such theoretical foundations can serve both as a reference

© Springer International Publishing Switzerland 2015
D. Mouheb et al., *Aspect-Oriented Security Hardening of UML Design Models*,
DOI 10.1007/978-3-319-16106-8_9

for an implementation and as a foundation to establish theoretical properties and mathematical proofs.

The goal of this chapter is to provide a formal semantics for aspect matching and weaving based on Continuation-Passing Style (CPS) [193]. As a first step, we consider a core language based on λ-calculus. More precisely, we perform advice matching and weaving during the evaluation of λ-expressions. We choose CPS as the basis of our semantics because, as previously demonstrated in [74], modeling aspect-oriented constructs, i.e., join points, pointcuts, and pieces of advice, in a frame-based continuation-passing style provides a concise, accurate, and elegant description of these mechanisms. Indeed, in CPS join points arise naturally as continuation frames during the evaluation of the language expressions. In this setting, pointcuts are expressions that designate a set of continuation frames. An advice specifies actions to be performed when continuation frames satisfying a particular pointcut are activated. In addition, by modeling join points as continuation frames, matching and weaving can be described in a simplified and unified way for different kinds of primitives. Furthermore, CPS simplifies matching flow-based pointcuts (e.g., cflow [113] and dflow [130] pointcuts), that are usually complex to express and require additional structures to maintain the order of join points.

We start by formalizing matching and weaving semantics for basic pointcuts, such as get, set, call, and exec pointcuts. These pointcuts are useful for injecting security at specific points, such as, adding authorization before calling a sensitive method, adding encryption before sending a secret message and decryption after receiving the message, etc. In addition, we extend our semantic framework with flow-based pointcuts, namely, cflow and Dflow pointcuts. These pointcuts are important from a security perspective since they can detect and fix a considerable number of vulnerabilities related to information flow, such as Cross-site Scripting (XSS) and SQL injection attacks [86].

The remainder of this chapter is organized as follows. We start in Sect. 9.1 by presenting the necessary background needed to understand the semantics. Section 9.2 presents the syntax of a core language based on λ-calculus and its denotational semantics. We transform the semantics into a frame-based CPS style in Sect. 9.3. Section 9.4 explores the semantics for matching and weaving based on CPS. In Sect. 9.5, we extend our work by considering flow-based pointcuts and present an example to illustrate the proposed framework. We discuss related work in Sect. 9.6. Finally, concluding remarks are presented in Sect. 9.7.

9.1 Background

This section provides the background knowledge that is needed to understand the semantics presented in this chapter. We start by an overview of λ-calculus, more specifically, the untyped λ-calculus since it is the language targeted in this chapter. Then, we introduce the denotational semantics. Afterwards, we review the concepts of continuation-passing style and defunctionalization.

9.1.1 λ-Calculus

λ-calculus is a theory of functions introduced by Alonzo Church in the 1930s as a foundation for functional computing [57]. It provides a simple notation for defining functions. The notation consists of a set of λ-expressions, each of which denotes a function. A key characteristic of λ-calculus is that functions are values, just like booleans and integers. In other words, functions in λ-calculus can be passed as arguments to other functions or returned as values from other functions. In the following, we provide details about the syntax and the semantics of λ-expressions based on the work done in [96].

9.1.1.1 Syntax

The pure λ-calculus contains three kinds of λ-expressions, as shown in Fig. 9.1:

1. *Variables*: represented by x, y, z, etc.
2. *Function abstractions (or function definitions)*: represented by the expression $\lambda x.\ e$, where x is a variable that represents the argument and e is a λ-expression that represents the body of the function. For example, the expression $\lambda x.\ \mathbf{square}\ x$ is a function abstraction that takes a variable x and returns the square of x.
3. *Function applications*: represented by the expression $e\ e'$, where e and e' are λ-expressions. The expression e should evaluate to a function that is then applied to the expression e'. For example, the expression $(\lambda x.\ \mathbf{square}\ x)\ 3$ evaluates, intuitively, to 9, which is the result of applying the squaring function to 3.

9.1.1.2 Free and Bound Variables

An occurrence of a variable in a λ-expression is either bound or free. An occurrence of a variable x in a λ-expression is bound if there is an enclosing $\lambda x.\ e$, otherwise, it is free.

Example Let us consider the following λ-expression:
$e = \lambda x.\ (x\ (\lambda y.\ y\ z)\ x)\ y$

Fig. 9.1 Syntax of λ-Calculus

In this expression:

- Both occurrences of the variable x are bound since they are within the scope of λx.
- The first occurrence of the variable y is bound since it is within the scope of λy.
- The last occurrence of the variable y is free since it is outside the scope of λy.
- The variable z is free since there is no enclosing λz.

9.1.1.3 Semantics of λ-Expressions

The meaning of a λ-expression is obtained after all its function applications are carried out. The process of evaluating a λ-expression is called *conversion* (or *Reduction*). There are three kinds of λ-conversion: α-conversion, β-conversion, and η-conversion. In the following, we provide a brief description of them. The notation $e[e'/x]$ used hereafter means substituting e' for each free occurrence of x in e. The substitution is called *valid* if no free variable in e' becomes bound after the substitution.

α-conversion

It deals with the manipulation of bound variables by allowing their names to be changed. More precisely, it states that any abstraction $\lambda x.\ e$ can be converted to $\lambda y.\ e[y/x]$ provided that the substitution of y for x in e is valid. For example, the expression $\lambda x.\ x$ can be α-converted to $\lambda y.\ y$. However, the expression $\lambda x.\ \lambda y.\ x$ cannot be α-converted to $\lambda y.\ \lambda y.\ y$ because the substitution $(\lambda y.\ x)[y/x]$ is not valid since y that substitutes x becomes bound in $\lambda y.\ y$.

β-conversion

It is the most important conversion in evaluating λ-expressions. It states that any application $(\lambda x.\ e_1)\ e_2$ can be converted to $e_1[e_2/x]$ provided that the substitution of e_2 for x in e_1 is valid. This conversion is similar to the evaluation of a function call, i.e., the body e_1 of the function $\lambda x.\ e_1$ is evaluated in an environment, in which the formal parameter x is bound to the actual parameter e_2. For example, the expression $(\lambda x.\ (\lambda y.\ x))\ 2$ can be β-converted to $\lambda y.\ 2$. However, the expression $(\lambda x.\ (\lambda y.\ x))\ y$ cannot be β-converted to $\lambda y.\ y$ because the substitution $(\lambda y.\ x)[y/x]$ is not valid since y that substitutes x becomes bound in $\lambda y.\ y$.

There are different ways by which a β-reduction can be performed. For example, the expression $(\lambda x.\ \textbf{square}\ x)\ ((\lambda y.\ y)\ 3)$ may be β-reduced to either $(\lambda x.\ \textbf{square}\ x)$ 3 or $\textbf{square}\ ((\lambda y.\ y)\ 3)$. The order in which β-reductions are performed results in different semantics, such as, call-by-value and call-by-name semantics:

- *Call-by-value*: ensures that functions are only called on values, i.e., given an application $(\lambda x.\ e)\ e'$, call-by-value semantics makes sure that e' is first reduced to a value before applying the function.
- *Call-by-name*: applies the function as soon as possible, i.e., given an application $(\lambda x.\ e)\ e'$, call-by-name semantics does not need to ensure that e' is a value before applying the function.

η-conversion

It expresses the property that two functions are equal if they always give the same results when applied to the same arguments. More precisely, it states that an abstraction $\lambda x.\ (e\ x)$ can be converted to e provided that x is not free in e. As we have seen, the function $\lambda x.\ (e\ x)$ when applied to an argument e' returns $(e\ x)[e'/x]$. If x is not free in e then $(e\ x)[e'/x] = e\ e'$. Thus $\lambda x.\ (e\ x)$ and e denote the same function since both return the same result, namely $e\ e'$, when applied to the same argument e'. For example, the expression $\lambda y.\ (f\ x\ y)$ can be η-converted to $f\ x$. However, the expression $\lambda x.\ (f\ x\ x)$ cannot be converted to $f\ x$ because x is free in $f\ x$.

9.1.2 Denotational Semantics

Denotational semantics is an approach proposed by Christopher Strachey and Dana Scott in the late 1960s to provide a formal semantics of programming languages [183]. Concisely, it gives programs a meaning (or denotation) by mapping the syntactic constructs of a language to mathematical objects [183]. The important characteristic of this approach is that it is generally compositional, i.e., the denotation of a program is built out of the denotations of its sub-expressions. Denotational semantics is mostly used to illustrate the essence of a language feature, without specifying how these features are actually realized. Hence, the semantics is abstract and does not provide full implementation details. In this semantics, each syntactic construct is mapped directly into its meaning by defining a semantic function $[\![\ \_\ ]\!]$ and a semantic domain D, such that every syntactic construct is mapped by $[\![\ \_\ ]\!]$ to elements of D, which are abstract values such as integers, booleans, tuples of values, and functions [136]. Therefore, for each syntactic construct, a semantic equation is defined to describe how the semantic function acts on the construct.

In denotational semantics, the context in which expressions are evaluated is called an *environment*. The latter maps variables to values. Given two sets A and B, we will write $A \xrightarrow{m} B$ to denote the set of all mappings from A to B. A mapping $m \in A \xrightarrow{m} B$ could be defined by extension as $[a_1 \mapsto b_1, \ldots, a_n \mapsto b_n]$ to denote the association of the elements b_i's to a_i's. Given two mappings m and m', we will write $m \dagger m'$ to denote the overwriting of the mapping m by the associations of the mapping m'. Figure 9.2 presents the denotational semantics of the λ-expressions presented in Fig. 9.1. Given an expression e and an environment ε, the semantic function $[\![\ \_\ ]\!]$ yields the computed value v. In the case of:

- *Variables*: The denotation (computed value) is the value that the variable is bound to in the environment.
- *Function abstractions*: The denotation is a closure $\langle x, e, \varepsilon' \rangle$ capturing the function parameter x, the function body e, and the evaluation environment ε', which maps each free variable of e into its value at the time of the declaration of the function.

$$[\![x]\!] \varepsilon \quad = \varepsilon(x)$$

$$[\![\lambda x.\, e]\!] \varepsilon = \langle x, e, \varepsilon' \rangle$$

$$[\![e\ e']\!] \varepsilon \ = \textbf{let } v = [\![e']\!] \varepsilon \textbf{ in}$$
$$\textbf{let } \langle x, e'', \varepsilon' \rangle = [\![e]\!] \varepsilon \textbf{ in}$$
$$[\![e'']\!] \varepsilon' \dagger [x \mapsto v]$$
$$\textbf{end}$$
$$\textbf{end}$$

Fig. 9.2 Denotational semantics of λ-Calculus

- *Function applications*: The denotation is computed in three steps: (1) The expression e', which is the argument, is evaluated to a value v, (2) the expression e, which is an abstraction, is evaluated to a closure $\langle x, e'', \varepsilon' \rangle$, (3) the expression e'' is evaluated in the environment ε' where the variable x is bound to the value v.

9.1.3 Continuation-Passing Style

Continuation-Passing Style (CPS) is a style of programming, in which every aspect of control flow and data flow is passed explicitly in the form of a continuation [193]. Continuations were first discovered in 1964 by Van Wijngaarden [177]. Later in the 1970s, many researchers [121, 176, 194] have applied them in a wide variety of settings [177]. In the following, we start by explaining the concept of a continuation then we provide the main steps of a CPS transformation.

9.1.3.1 Continuations

A continuation is a function that describes the semantics of the rest of a computation. Instead of returning a value, as in the familiar direct style, a function in CPS style takes another function as an additional argument, to which it will pass the current computational result. This additional function argument is the continuation. To better illustrate the idea of continuations, let us consider the example presented in Fig. 9.3, which is taken from [39].

The function prodprimes computes the product of all prime numbers that are less than or equal to a given number n. There are several points in the control flow of this program where control is returned. For example, the call to the function isprime returns to a point κ_1 with a boolean value b. The first call to the function prodprimes (in the **then** clause of the second **if**) returns to a point κ_2 with an integer i, and the second call to prodprimes returns to a point κ_3 with an integer j. Similarly, the call to the main function prodprimes returns to a point κ with a result r.

```
let prodprimes n =

    if (n = 1) then 1

    else if (isprime(n)) then n * prodprimes(n − 1)

        else prodprimes(n − 1)
```

Fig. 9.3 Example of an OCaml function in direct style

```
let prodprimes n κ =

    if (n = 1) then κ (1)

    else let κ₁ b =
            if (b) then
                let κ₂ i = κ(n * i) in prodprimes(n − 1, κ₂) end
            else
                let κ₃ j = κ(j) in prodprimes(n − 1, κ₃) end
        in
            isprime(n, κ₁)
        end
```

Fig. 9.4 Example of an OCaml function in CPS style

These return points represent continuations that express "what to do next". In addition, each of these points can be considered as an additional argument to the corresponding function. When the function call terminates, this additional argument will tell us where to continue the computation. For example, the function prodprimes can be given as additional argument the return point (the continuation) κ, and when it has computed its result r, it will continue by applying κ to r. Similarly, the function isprime can be given as additional argument the return point κ_1, and when it has computed its result b, it will continue by applying κ_1 to b. The same treatment can be done to the other function calls. Figure 9.4 shows another version of the example presented above using continuations. Notice that all the return points mentioned above, κ, κ_1, κ_2, and κ_3 are continuation functions. Thus, as we can see, returning from a function in CPS style is just like a function call.

9.1.3.2 CPS Transformation

Given a λ-expression e, it is possible to translate it into CPS. This translation is known as *CPS conversion*. In the following, we provide the main steps of this conversion.

An expression e is in a tail position if it is a sub-expression of an expression e' and when it is evaluated, it will be returned as the result of the evaluation of e'. The keyword **return** is used hereafter just to indicate that e is in a tail position.

1. Each function definition should be augmented with an additional argument; the continuation function to which it will pass the current computational result.
   let f *args* $= e$ $\Rightarrow$ **let** f *args* $\kappa = e$
2. A variable or a constant in a tail position should be passed as an argument to the continuation function instead of being returned.
   return e $\Rightarrow$ $\kappa\ e$
3. Each function call in a tail position should be augmented with the current continuation. This is because in CPS, each function passes the result forward instead of returning it.
   return f *args* $\Rightarrow$ f *args* κ
4. Each function call that is not in a tail position needs to be converted into a new continuation, containing the old continuation and the rest of the computation. Here, *op* represents a primitive operation, which could include an application.
   op $(f\ args)$ $\Rightarrow$ f *args* $(\lambda r.\ \kappa\ op\ r)$

9.1.4 Defunctionalization

Defunctionalization is a technique by which higher-order programs, i.e., programs where functions can represent values, are transformed into semantically equivalent first-order programs [176]. In a defunctionalized program, a first-class function is represented with a constructor, holding the values of the free variables of a function abstraction, and it is eliminated with a case expression dispatching over the corresponding constructors [68]. More precisely, the defunctionalization process consists of two main steps:

1. Transform each function abstraction into a data structure holding the free variables of the function abstraction and replace all function abstractions with their corresponding data structures.
2. Define a second-class *apply* function that takes a data structure, which represent the original function, and a value as its arguments. Basically, the *apply* function is a collection of the bodies of all original functions with a case expression dispatching over the corresponding data structures. Afterwards, replace all function applications with a call to the *apply* function.

Therefore, the result of the transformation is a program that contains only first-order functions. However, the original higher-order structure is implicit in the program. For a better understanding of the defunctionalization process, let us consider the example, shown in Fig. 9.5, which was initially provided in [68]. The function

```
aux   : (Int → Int) → Int
main : Int × Int × Bool → Int
let aux f      = f 1 + f 10
let main x y b = aux(λz. z + x) * aux(λz. if (b) then y + z else y − z)
```

Fig. 9.5 Example of a higher-order program

```
type Lam   = Lam1 | Lam2

type Lam1 = {id : Int}

type Lam2 = {id : Int; cond : Bool}
```

Fig. 9.6 New data structures

```
apply : Lam × Int → Int

let apply l z = match l with

   Lam1 l ⇒ z + l.id

   | Lam2 l ⇒ if (l.cond) then l.id + z else l.id − z
```

Fig. 9.7 Apply function

aux takes a first-class function f as an argument, applies it to 1 and 10, and outputs the summation of the two applications. The function main calls aux twice and outputs the multiplication of the results.

There are two function abstractions in the main function. To defunctionalize the program, we should define data structures for these function abstractions and their corresponding apply function. The first function abstraction ($\lambda z.\ z + x$) contains one free variable (x, of type integer), and therefore the first data structure requires an integer. The second function abstraction ($\lambda z.$ **if** (b) **then** $y + z$ **else** $y - z$) contains two free variables (y, of type integer, and b, of type boolean), and therefore the second data structure requires an integer and a boolean. The newly defined data structures are shown in Fig. 9.6 and their corresponding apply function is presented in Fig. 9.7.

Lastly, we rewrite the program by replacing the function abstractions with their corresponding data structures and their applications with the newly defined apply function. The defunctionalized program is presented in Fig. 9.8.

```
aux_def   : Lam → Int
main_def : Int × Int × Bool → Int

let aux_def f      = apply(f, 1) + apply(f, 10)
let main_def x y b = aux_def(Lam1(x)) * aux_def(Lam2(y, b))
```

Fig. 9.8 Defunctionalized program

9.2 Syntax and Denotational Semantics

In this section, we present the syntax of our core language and its denotational semantics. The language is based on untyped λ-calculus. The syntax is presented in Fig. 9.9. We consider the following expressions:

- Constants and variables
- Functional constructs (function abstraction and function application)
- Local definitions
- Conditional expressions
- Sequential expressions
- Imperative features (referencing, dereferencing, and assignment expressions). The expression ref e allocates a new reference and initializes it with the value of e. The expression $!\, e$ reads the value stored at the location referenced by the value of e. The expression $e := e'$ writes the value of e' to the location referenced by the value of e.

The denotational semantics of the core language is presented in Fig. 9.10. It associates a value to each expression of the language. First, we define the function and the types that are used in the semantics:

```
[[ _ ]]_ _ : Exp → Env → Store → Result
Result  : Value × Store
Value   : Int | Bool | Unit | Location | Closure
Closure : Identifier × Exp × Env
Env     : Identifier → Value
Store   : Location → Value
```

Given an expression e, a dynamic environment ε, and a store σ, the dynamic evaluation function $[[\_]]$ yields a pair (v, σ'), where v is the computed value and σ' is the updated store. The environment ε maps identifiers to values. The store σ maps locations to values. A value can be either a constant, a location, or a closure. In the case of an abstraction expression $\lambda x.\ e$, the computed value is a closure $\langle x, e, \varepsilon' \rangle$ capturing the function parameter x, the function body e, and the evaluation

$$
\begin{array}{llr}
e & ::=\ c & \textbf{constant} \\
 & |\quad x & \textbf{variable} \\
 & |\quad \lambda x.\,e & \textbf{abstraction} \\
 & |\quad e\ e' & \textbf{application} \\
 & |\quad \texttt{let } x = e \texttt{ in } e' & \textbf{local definition} \\
 & |\quad \texttt{if } e_1 \texttt{ then } e_2 \texttt{ else } e_3 & \textbf{conditional} \\
 & |\quad e_1;\,e_2 & \textbf{sequence} \\
 & |\quad \texttt{ref } e & \textbf{referencing} \\
 & |\quad !\,e & \textbf{dereferencing} \\
 & |\quad e := e' & \textbf{assignment}
\end{array}
$$

Fig. 9.9 Core syntax

$[\![\,c\,]\!]\varepsilon\,\sigma = (c,\sigma)$

$[\![\,x\,]\!]\varepsilon\,\sigma = (\varepsilon(x),\sigma)$

$[\![\,\lambda x.\,e\,]\!]\varepsilon\,\sigma = (\langle x,e,\varepsilon'\rangle,\sigma)$

$[\![\,e\ e'\,]\!]\varepsilon\,\sigma = \textbf{let } (v,\sigma') = [\![\,e'\,]\!]\varepsilon\,\sigma \textbf{ in}$
$\qquad\qquad \textbf{let } (\langle x,e'',\varepsilon'\rangle,\sigma'') = [\![\,e\,]\!]\varepsilon\,\sigma' \textbf{ in } [\![\,e''\,]\!]\varepsilon' \dagger [x \mapsto v]\ \sigma'' \textbf{ end}$
$\qquad \textbf{end}$

$[\![\,\texttt{let } x = e \texttt{ in } e'\,]\!]\varepsilon\,\sigma = \textbf{let } (v,\sigma') = [\![\,e\,]\!]\varepsilon\,\sigma \textbf{ in } [\![\,e'\,]\!]\varepsilon \dagger [x \mapsto v]\ \sigma' \textbf{ end}$

$[\![\,\texttt{if } e_1 \texttt{ then } e_2 \texttt{ else } e_3\,]\!]\varepsilon\,\sigma = \textbf{let } (v,\sigma') = [\![\,e_1\,]\!]\varepsilon\,\sigma \textbf{ in}$
$\qquad\qquad\qquad\qquad\qquad \textbf{if } (v) \textbf{ then } [\![\,e_2\,]\!]\varepsilon\,\sigma' \textbf{ else } [\![\,e_3\,]\!]\varepsilon\,\sigma'$
$\qquad\qquad\qquad \textbf{end}$

$[\![\,e_1;\,e_2\,]\!]\varepsilon\,\sigma = \textbf{let } (v,\sigma') = [\![\,e_1\,]\!]\varepsilon\,\sigma \textbf{ in } [\![\,e_2\,]\!]\varepsilon\,\sigma' \textbf{ end}$

$[\![\,\texttt{ref } e\,]\!]\varepsilon\,\sigma = \textbf{let } (v,\sigma') = [\![\,e\,]\!]\varepsilon\,\sigma \textbf{ in}$
$\qquad\qquad \textbf{let } \ell = \mathsf{alloc}(\sigma') \textbf{ in } (\ell,\sigma' \dagger [\ell \mapsto v]) \textbf{ end}$
$\qquad \textbf{end}$

$[\![\,!\,e\,]\!]\varepsilon\,\sigma = \textbf{let } (\ell,\sigma') = [\![\,e\,]\!]\varepsilon\,\sigma \textbf{ in } (\sigma'(\ell),\sigma') \textbf{ end}$

$[\![\,e := e'\,]\!]\varepsilon\,\sigma = \textbf{let } (\ell,\sigma') = [\![\,e\,]\!]\varepsilon\,\sigma \textbf{ in}$
$\qquad\qquad \textbf{let } (v,\sigma'') = [\![\,e'\,]\!]\varepsilon\,\sigma' \textbf{ in } ((),\sigma'' \dagger [\ell \mapsto v]) \textbf{ end}$
$\qquad \textbf{end}$

Fig. 9.10 Denotational semantics

environment ε', which maps each free variable of e to its value at the time of the declaration of the function. The function alloc used in the semantics allocates a new cell in the store and returns a reference to it.

9.3   Continuation-Passing Style Semantics

In this section, we transform the previously defined denotational semantics into CPS style. As we mentioned earlier, frame-based semantics allows describing AOP semantics in a precise and unified way. To help understanding this transformation, we proceed in two steps. First, we elaborate CPS semantics by representing continuations as functions. Then, we provide CPS semantics by representing continuations as frames.

9.3.1 Representation of Continuations as Functions

The CPS semantics is presented in Fig. 9.11. We translate the denotational semantics into CPS following the original formulation of the CPS transformation [84]. In essence, we modify the evaluation function to take a continuation as an additional argument as follows:

$$[\![\_]\!]\_\_\_ : \text{Exp} \rightarrow \text{Env} \rightarrow \text{Store} \rightarrow \text{Cont} \rightarrow \text{Result}$$
$$\text{Cont} \quad = \text{Result} \rightarrow \text{Result}$$

The continuation, represented as a λ-expression, receives the result of the current evaluation and provides the semantics of the rest of the computation.

9.3.2 Representation of Continuations as Frames

Continuations, which are λ-expressions, are often represented as closures. Ager et al. [26] have provided a systematic conversion of these closures into data structures (or frames) and an apply function interpreting the operations of these closures. This conversion is based on the concept of defunctionalization [176]. Each frame stores the value(s) of the free variable(s) of the original continuation function and awaits the value(s) of the previous computation. Following this technique, we transform the continuation functions, obtained from the previous step, into frames as shown in Fig. 9.12.

$$[\![c]\!] \varepsilon \ \sigma \ \kappa = \kappa(c, \sigma)$$

$$[\![x]\!] \varepsilon \ \sigma \ \kappa = \kappa(\varepsilon(x), \sigma)$$

$$[\![\lambda x. e]\!] \varepsilon \ \sigma \ \kappa = \kappa(\lambda(v, \kappa'). \ [\![e]\!] \varepsilon \dagger [x \mapsto v] \ \sigma \ \kappa')$$

$$[\![e \ e']\!] \varepsilon \ \sigma \ \kappa = [\![e']\!] \varepsilon \ \sigma \ (\lambda(v, \sigma'). \ [\![e]\!] \varepsilon \ \sigma' \ (\lambda f. f \ v \ \kappa))$$

$$[\![\text{let } x = e \text{ in } e']\!] \varepsilon \ \sigma \ \kappa = [\![e]\!] \varepsilon \ \sigma \ (\lambda(v, \sigma'). \ [\![e']\!] \varepsilon \dagger [x \mapsto v] \ \sigma' \ \kappa)$$

$$[\![\text{if } e_1 \text{ then } e_2 \text{ else } e_3]\!] \varepsilon \ \sigma \ \kappa = [\![e_1]\!] \varepsilon \ (\lambda(v, \sigma'). \ \textbf{if } (v) \ \textbf{then } [\![e_2]\!] \varepsilon \ \sigma' \ \kappa$$
$$\textbf{else } [\![e_3]\!] \varepsilon \ \sigma' \ \kappa)$$

$$[\![e_1; e_2]\!] \varepsilon \ \sigma \ \kappa = [\![e_1]\!] \varepsilon \ \sigma \ (\lambda(v, \sigma'). \ [\![e_2]\!] \varepsilon \ \sigma' \ \kappa)$$

$$[\![\text{ref } e]\!] \varepsilon \ \sigma \ \kappa = [\![e]\!] \varepsilon \ \sigma \ (\lambda(v, \sigma'). \ \textbf{let } \ell = \mathsf{alloc}(\sigma') \ \textbf{in } \kappa(\ell, \sigma' \dagger [\ell \mapsto v]) \ \textbf{end})$$

$$[\![! e]\!] \varepsilon \ \sigma \ \kappa = [\![e]\!] \varepsilon \ \sigma \ (\lambda(\ell, \sigma'). \ \kappa(\sigma'(\ell), \sigma'))$$

$$[\![e := e']\!] \varepsilon \ \sigma \ \kappa = [\![e]\!] \varepsilon \ \sigma \ (\lambda(\ell, \sigma'). \ [\![e']\!] \varepsilon \ \sigma' \ (\lambda(v, \sigma''). \ \kappa((), (\sigma'' \dagger [\ell \mapsto v]))))$$

Fig. 9.11 CPS semantics: continuations as functions

Using frame-based semantics, the continuation κ consists of a list of frames. Before presenting the semantics, we first define the primitive functions that will be used. The primitive push extends a continuation list with another frame.

push : Frame $\rightarrow$ Cont $\rightarrow$ Cont

let push $f \ \kappa = f :: \kappa$

The primitive apply, defined in Fig. 9.13, extracts the top frame from the continuation list and evaluates it based on its corresponding continuation function. When the list becomes empty, the primitive apply returns the current value and store as a result.

In this style, the semantics is defined in two parts: (1) The expression side, shown in Fig. 9.14, provides the evaluation of the language expressions, and (2) the frame side, shown in Fig. 9.15, provides the evaluation of the frames.

Example To illustrate this transformation, let us consider the following very simple expression: $e = (\lambda x. \ x)(1)$. By applying the CPS semantics presented in Fig. 9.11, the evaluation of this expression is as follows:

$$[\![e]\!] \varepsilon \ \sigma \ \kappa = [\![1]\!] \varepsilon \ \sigma \ (\lambda(v, \sigma'). \ [\![\lambda x. \ x]\!] \varepsilon \ \sigma' \ (\lambda f. \ f \ v \ \kappa))$$

The GetF frame does not store any value.
It awaits a location and a store.
type GetF = {}

The SetF frame stores a location.
It awaits a value and a store.
type SetF = {*loc* : Value}

The CallF frame stores a function abstraction and an environment.
It awaits the value of the function argument.
type CallF = {*fun* : Exp; *env* : Env}

The ExecF frame stores the value of the argument.
It awaits a closure, which is the result of the evaluation of the function
abstraction, and a store.
type ExecF = {*arg* : Value}

The LetF frame stores an identifier, a body of a let expression,
and an environment.
It awaits the value of the identifier and a store.
type LetF = {*id* : Identifier; *exp* : Exp; *env* : Env}

The IfF frame stores then and else expressions and an environment.
It awaits the value of the condition and a store.
type IfF = {*thenExp* : Exp; *elseExp* : Exp; *env* : Env}

The SeqF frame stores the next expression and an environment.
It awaits the value of the first expression and a store.
type SeqF = {*nextExp* : Exp; *env* : Env}

The AllocF frame does not store any value.
It awaits the value to be stored in the newly allocated cell and a store.
type AllocF = {}

The RhsF frame stores the right-hand side expression of an assignment
and an environment.
It awaits a location and a store.
type RhsF = {*exp* : Exp; *env* : Env}

Fig. 9.12 Frames

$$\boxed{\begin{array}{l} \mathsf{apply} \ : \ \mathsf{Cont} \to (\mathsf{Value} \times \mathsf{Store}) \to (\mathsf{Value} \times \mathsf{Store}) \\[2mm] \textbf{let } \mathsf{apply}\ \kappa\ (v, \sigma) = \textbf{match } \kappa \textbf{ with} \\ \qquad [\,] \ \Rightarrow \ (v, \sigma) \\ \qquad | f :: \kappa' \ \Rightarrow \ \mathcal{F}[\![f]\!] \sigma\ v\ \kappa' \end{array}}$$

Fig. 9.13 Apply function

$$\boxed{\begin{array}{l} [\![\,c\,]\!]\varepsilon\ \sigma\ \kappa = \mathsf{apply}(\kappa, (c, \sigma)) \\[2mm] [\![\,x\,]\!]\varepsilon\ \sigma\ \kappa = \mathsf{apply}(\kappa, (\varepsilon(x), \sigma)) \\[2mm] [\![\,\lambda x.\,e\,]\!]\varepsilon\ \sigma\ \kappa = \mathsf{apply}(\kappa, (\langle x, e, \varepsilon' \rangle, \sigma)) \\[2mm] [\![\,e\,e'\,]\!]\varepsilon\ \sigma\ \kappa = [\![\,e'\,]\!]\varepsilon\ \sigma\ (\mathsf{push}(\mathsf{CallF}(e, \varepsilon),\ \kappa)) \\[2mm] [\![\,\mathtt{let}\ x = e\ \mathtt{in}\ e'\,]\!]\varepsilon\ \sigma\ \kappa = [\![\,e\,]\!]\varepsilon\ \sigma\ (\mathsf{push}(\mathsf{LetF}(x, e', \varepsilon), \kappa)) \\[2mm] [\![\,\mathtt{if}\ e_1\ \mathtt{then}\ e_2\ \mathtt{else}\ e_3\,]\!]\varepsilon\ \sigma\ \kappa = [\![\,e_1\,]\!]\varepsilon\ \sigma\ (\mathsf{push}(\mathsf{IfF}(e_2, e_3, \varepsilon), \kappa)) \\[2mm] [\![\,e_1; e_2\,]\!]\varepsilon\ \sigma\ \kappa = [\![\,e_1\,]\!]\varepsilon\ \sigma\ (\mathsf{push}(\mathsf{SeqF}(e_2, \varepsilon), \kappa)) \\[2mm] [\![\,\mathtt{ref}\ e\,]\!]\varepsilon\ \sigma\ \kappa = [\![\,e\,]\!]\varepsilon\ \sigma\ (\mathsf{push}(\mathsf{AllocF}(), \kappa)) \\[2mm] [\![\,!\,e\,]\!]\varepsilon\ \sigma\ \kappa = [\![\,e\,]\!]\varepsilon\ \sigma\ (\mathsf{push}(\mathsf{GetF}(), \kappa)) \\[2mm] [\![\,e := e'\,]\!]\varepsilon\ \sigma\ \kappa = [\![\,e\,]\!]\varepsilon\ \sigma\ (\mathsf{push}(\mathsf{RhsF}(e', \varepsilon), \kappa)) \end{array}}$$

Fig. 9.14 Frame-based CPS semantics: expression side

The defunctionalization process consists of transforming the following λ-expressions into frames as shown below:

$\lambda(v, \sigma').\ [\![\,\lambda x.\,x\,]\!]\varepsilon\ \sigma'\ (\lambda f.\ f\ v\ \kappa)$ transformed into $\mathsf{CallF}(\lambda x.\,x, \varepsilon)$
$\lambda f.\ f\ v\ \kappa$ transformed into $\mathsf{ExecF}(1)$

Using these frames, the evaluation of the expression e is provided as follows, by applying the frame semantics presented in Figs. 9.14 and 9.15:

$$\begin{array}{rl} [\![\,e\,]\!]\varepsilon\ \sigma\ \kappa = & [\![\,1\,]\!]\varepsilon\ \sigma\ (\mathsf{push}(\mathsf{CallF}(\lambda x.\,x, \varepsilon), \kappa)) \\ = & \mathsf{apply}(\kappa, (1, \sigma)) \\ = & [\![\,\lambda x.\,x\,]\!]\varepsilon\ \sigma\ (\mathsf{push}(\mathsf{ExecF}(1), \kappa)) \\ = & \mathsf{apply}(\kappa, (\langle x, x, \varepsilon \rangle, \sigma)) \\ = & [\![\,x\,]\!]\varepsilon \dagger [x \mapsto 1]\ \sigma\ \kappa \end{array}$$

$$\mathcal{F}[\![\,\_\,]\!]\_\_\_ \;:\; \mathsf{Frame} \to \mathsf{Store} \to \mathsf{Value} \to \mathsf{Cont} \to \mathsf{Result}$$

$$\mathcal{F}[\![\, \mathsf{GetF}\; f \,]\!]\sigma\, v\, \kappa = \mathsf{apply}(\kappa,(\sigma(v),\sigma))$$

$$\mathcal{F}[\![\, \mathsf{SetF}\; f \,]\!]\sigma\, v\, \kappa = \mathsf{apply}(\kappa,((),\sigma \dagger [f.loc \mapsto v]))$$

$$\mathcal{F}[\![\, \mathsf{CallF}\; f \,]\!]\sigma\, v\, \kappa = [\![\, f.fun \,]\!](f.env)\; \sigma\; (\mathsf{push}(\mathsf{ExecF}(v),\kappa))$$

$$\mathcal{F}[\![\, \mathsf{ExecF}\; f \,]\!]\sigma\, v\, \kappa = [\![\, e \,]\!]\varepsilon' \dagger [x \mapsto f.arg]\; \sigma\; \kappa \quad \text{where } v = \langle x,e,\varepsilon'\rangle$$

$$\mathcal{F}[\![\, \mathsf{LetF}\; f \,]\!]\sigma\, v\, \kappa = [\![\, f.exp \,]\!](f.env) \dagger [f.id \mapsto v]\; \sigma\; \kappa$$

$$\mathcal{F}[\![\, \mathsf{IfF}\; f \,]\!]\sigma\, v\, \kappa = \mathbf{if}\,(v)\; \mathbf{then}\; [\![\, f.thenExp \,]\!](f.env)\; \sigma\; \kappa\; \mathbf{else}\; [\![\, f.elseExp \,]\!](f.env)\; \sigma\; \kappa$$

$$\mathcal{F}[\![\, \mathsf{SeqF}\; f \,]\!]\sigma\, v\, \kappa = [\![\, f.nextExp \,]\!](f.env)\; \sigma\; \kappa$$

$$\mathcal{F}[\![\, \mathsf{AllocF}\; f \,]\!]\sigma\, v\, \kappa = \mathbf{let}\; \ell = \mathsf{alloc}(\sigma)\; \mathbf{in}\; \mathsf{apply}(\kappa,(\ell,\sigma \dagger [\ell \mapsto v]))\; \mathbf{end}$$

$$\mathcal{F}[\![\, \mathsf{RhsF}\; f \,]\!]\sigma\, v\, \kappa = [\![\, f.exp \,]\!](f.env)\; \sigma\; (\mathsf{push}(\mathsf{SetF}(v),\kappa))$$

Fig. 9.15 Frame-based CPS semantics: frame side

$$= \mathsf{apply}(\kappa, (\varepsilon(x), \sigma))$$
$$= (\varepsilon(x), \sigma)$$
$$= (1, \sigma)$$

The frames CallF and ExecF correspond respectively to the states where the function $\lambda x.\, x$ is being called and executed with an argument equal to 1. In AOP, these states are join points where a certain advice can be applied. Thus, by transforming the denotational semantics into a frame-based style, the join points automatically arise within the semantics, which makes it an appropriate approach for defining the semantics of AOP.

9.4 Aspect Syntax and Semantics

In this section, we present our aspect extension to the core language and elaborate its semantics. Our methodology of using CPS is based on a previous effort describing the semantics of a first-order procedural language (PROC) [74]. In the following, we start by presenting the aspect syntax. Then, we elaborate the matching and the weaving semantics.

9.4.1 Aspect Syntax

An aspect, depicted in Fig. 9.17, includes a list of advice. An advice specifies actions to be performed when join points satisfying a particular pointcut are reached. As in AspectJ [113], an advice may also compute the original join point through a special expression named `proceed`. Hence, as shown in Fig. 9.16, we extend the core syntax with an additional expression, `proceed` (*e*), to denote the computation of the original join point with possibly a new argument *e*.

Syntactically, an advice contains two parts: (1) A body, which is an expression, and (2) a pointcut, which designates a set of join points. An advice can be applied *before*, *after*, or *around* a join point. However, *before* and *after* advice can be expressed as *around* advice using the `proceed` expression [74]. Hence, we consider all kinds of advice as *around* advice as this does not restrict the generality of the approach.

A pointcut is an expression that designates a set of join points. We first consider the following basic pointcuts: `GetPC`, `SetPC`, `CallPC`, and `ExecPC`. The pointcut `GetPC` (resp. `SetPC`) picks out join points where the value of a variable is got from (resp. set to) the store. The pointcut `CallPC` (resp. `ExecPC`) picks out join points where a function is called (resp. executed).

9.4.2 Matching Semantics

Matching is a mechanism for identifying the join points targeted by an advice. In a defunctionalized continuation-passing style, join points correspond to continuation frames and arise naturally when a particular continuation frame receives the value that it awaits. The matching semantics is shown in Fig. 9.18.

Given a pointcut *p*, the current frame *f*, the current value *v*, an environment *ε*, a store *σ*, and a continuation *κ*, the matching semantics examines whether *f* matches *p*. Matching depends on three factors: the kind and the content of the frame *f* and the current value *v* that *f* receives. In the case of:

- **GetPC** pointcut, there is a match if *f* is a **GetF** frame and the location of the identifier given in *p* is equal to the location that *f* receives.
- **SetPC** pointcut, there is a match if *f* is a **SetF** frame and the location of the identifier given in *p* is equal to the location that is stored in *f*.
- **CallPC** pointcut, there is a match if *f* is a **CallF** frame and it holds a function equal to the one given in *p*. Notice that the pointcut *p* contains only the function identifier *id* and *ε*(*id*) gives its abstraction, assuming that in the environment identifiers map to values in case of variables and function abstractions in case of functions.
- **ExecPC** pointcut, there is a match if *f* is an **ExecF** frame and the evaluation of the function given in *p* is equal to the closure that *f* receives.
- **NotPC** pointcut, there is a match if *f* does not match the sub-pointcut of *p*.
- **AndPC** pointcut, there is a match if *f* matches both its sub-pointcuts.

$$
\begin{array}{lll}
e & ::= & ... \\
  & \mid & \texttt{proceed}\,(e) \qquad\qquad\qquad\qquad \textbf{proceed}
\end{array}
$$

Fig. 9.16 `Proceed` expression

type Aspect   = Advice list

type Advice   = {*body* : Exp; *pc* : Pointcut}

type Pointcut = GetPC | SetPC | CallPC | ExecPC | NotPC | AndPC

type GetPC   = {*id* : Identifier}

type SetPC   = {*id* : Identifier; *val* : Value}

type CallPC   = {*id* : Identifier; *arg* : Identifier}

type ExecPC = {*id* : Identifier; *arg* : Identifier}

type NotPC   = {*pc* : Pointcut}

type AndPC   = {*pc*$_1$: Pointcut; *pc*$_2$: Pointcut}

Fig. 9.17 Aspect syntax

Example Let us consider the previous expression (slightly changed to define a function f):

$$e = (\textbf{let}\, f = \lambda x.\ x\ \textbf{in}\ f(1)\ \textbf{end})$$

and a pointcut p that captures any call to the function f with an argument x:

$$\text{CallPC}\ p = \{id = f;\ arg = x\}$$

As shown in the previous section, the frame-based semantics of the expression e use the frames CallF($\lambda x.\ x, \varepsilon$) and ExecF(1), which correspond to the states where the function $\lambda x.\ x$ is called and executed respectively. By applying the matching semantics presented in Fig. 9.18, it is clear that the pointcut p matches the CallF frame.

---

match_pc : Pointcut → Frame → Value → Store → Env → Cont → Bool

let match_pc $p f v \sigma \varepsilon \kappa$ = **match** (p, f) **with**

  $(\text{GetPC } p, \text{GetF } f)$ $\Rightarrow \varepsilon(p.id) = v$

  | $(\text{SetPC } p, \text{SetF } f)$ $\Rightarrow \varepsilon(p.id) = f.loc$

  | $(\text{CallPC } p, \text{CallF } f)$ $\Rightarrow$ **let** $(v', \sigma') = [\![f.fun]\!] \varepsilon \sigma \kappa$ **in**
                               let $(v'', \sigma'') = [\![\varepsilon(p.id)]\!] \varepsilon \sigma \kappa$ **in** $v' = v''$ **end**
                               end

  | $(\text{ExecPC } p, \text{ExecF } f)$ $\Rightarrow$ **let** $(v', \sigma') = [\![\varepsilon(p.id)]\!] \varepsilon \sigma \kappa$ **in** $v = v'$ **end**

  | $(\text{NotPC } p, \text{Frame } f)$ $\Rightarrow$ **not** match_pc$(p.pc, f, v, \sigma, \varepsilon, \kappa)$

  | $(\text{AndPC } p, \text{Frame } f)$ $\Rightarrow$ match_pc$(p.pc_1, f, v, \sigma, \varepsilon, \kappa)$ **and**
                               match_pc$(p.pc_2, f, v, \sigma, \varepsilon, \kappa)$

  | **otherwise** $\Rightarrow$ **false**

Fig. 9.18 Matching semantics

9.4.3 Weaving Semantics

The weaving semantics describes how to apply the matching advice at the identified join points. Since join points correspond to continuation frames, advice body provides a means to modify the behavior of those continuation frames. The weaving is performed directly in the evaluation function. To do so, we redefine the apply function, as shown in Fig. 9.19, to take an aspect α and an environment ε into account. Accordingly, the signatures of the evaluation functions as well as the matching ones are also modified to take the aspect and the environment as additional arguments.

The weaving is done in two steps. When a continuation frame is activated, we first check for a matching advice by calling the **get_matches** function. If there is any applicable advice, the function **execute_advice** is called. Otherwise, the original computation is performed. In the following, we explain these two steps.

9.4.3.1 Advice Matching

Advice matching is shown in Fig. 9.20. To get an applicable advice, we go through the aspect and check whether its enclosed pointcuts match the current frame. This is done by using the function **match_pc** defined previously in Fig. 9.18. In case there

---

apply : Cont $\rightarrow$ (Value $\times$ Store) $\rightarrow$ Env $\rightarrow$ Aspect $\rightarrow$ (Value $\times$ Store)

let apply κ (v, σ) ε α = **match** κ **with**

$$[\,] \Rightarrow (v, \sigma)$$

$$| f :: \kappa' \Rightarrow \textbf{let } ms = \text{get\_matches}(f, v, \sigma, \varepsilon, \alpha, \kappa') \textbf{ in}$$

        if ms = $[\,]$ **then** $\mathcal{F}[\![f]\!]\varepsilon\ \sigma\ v\ \alpha\ \kappa'$
        else
                let $argV$ = **match** f **with**
                    SetF f $\Rightarrow$ v
                    | CallF f $\Rightarrow$ v
                    | ExecF f $\Rightarrow$ $f.arg$
                    | **otherwise** $\Rightarrow$ $(\,)$
                in execute_advice$(ms, f, argV, \sigma, \varepsilon, \alpha, \kappa')$
                end
        end

Fig. 9.19 Redefined apply function

---

type MatchedAD = $\{arg : \text{Identifier}; ad : \text{Advice}\}$
get_matches   :   Frame $\rightarrow$ Value $\rightarrow$ Store $\rightarrow$ Env $\rightarrow$ Aspect $\rightarrow$ Cont
                           $\rightarrow$ MatchedAD list

let get_matches f v σ ε α κ = **match** α **with**

$$[\,] \Rightarrow [\,]$$

$$| ad :: \alpha' \Rightarrow \textbf{let } p = ad.pc \textbf{ in}$$

                if match_pc$(p, f, v, \sigma, \varepsilon, \alpha, \kappa)$ **then**
                    let arg = **match** p **with**
                    SetPC p $\Rightarrow$ $p.id$
                    | CallPC p | ExecPC p $\Rightarrow$ $p.arg$
                    | **otherwise** $\Rightarrow$ $(\,)$
                in
                    MatchedAD(arg, ad) :: get_matches$(f, v, \sigma, \varepsilon, \alpha', \kappa)$
                end
                else
                  get_matches$(f, v, \sigma, \varepsilon, \alpha', \kappa)$
              end

Fig. 9.20 Advice matching

---

execute_advice : MatchedAD list → Frame → Value → Store → Env
→ Aspect → Cont → Result

let execute_advice $ms\, f\, v\, \sigma\, \varepsilon\, \alpha\, \kappa$ = **match** ms **with**

$\quad [\,] \Rightarrow$ apply(push(MarkerF(), (push(f, κ))), $(v, \sigma), \varepsilon, \alpha$)
$\mid m :: ms' \Rightarrow$ **let** $ad = m.ad$ **in**
$\qquad [\![\, ad.body\,]\!] \varepsilon \,\dagger\, [\&proceed \mapsto ms', \&jp \mapsto f, m.arg \mapsto v]\, \sigma\, \alpha\, \kappa$
$\quad$ **end**

Fig. 9.21 Advice execution

is a match, we return a structure MatchedAD containing the advice itself and the pointcut arguments that will pass values to the advice execution.

9.4.3.2 Advice Execution

Advice execution is shown in Fig. 9.21. It starts by evaluating the body of the first applicable advice. The remaining applicable pieces of advice as well as the current frame are stored in the environment by binding them to auxiliary variables, &*proceed* and &*jp* respectively. To evaluate the advice body, we define a new continuation frame, AdvExecF, as follows:

type AdvExecF = {*matches* : MatchedAD list; *jp* : Frame}
$\mathcal{F}[\![$ AdvExecF $f\,]\!] \varepsilon\, \sigma\, v\, \alpha\, \kappa =$ execute_advice($f.matches, f.jp, v, \sigma, \varepsilon, \alpha, \kappa$)

The evaluation of the proceed expression is provided below. The value of its argument is passed to the next advice or to the current join point if there is no further advice. To execute the remaining pieces of advice, the AdvExecF frame is added to the list of frames.

$[\![$ proceed $(e)\,]\!] \varepsilon\, \sigma\, \alpha\, \kappa = [\![\, e\,]\!] \varepsilon\, \sigma\, \alpha\, ($push(AdvExecF($\varepsilon(\&proceed), \varepsilon(\&jp)), \kappa$))

When all applicable pieces of advice are executed, the original computation, i.e., the current join point, is invoked. To avoid matching the currently matched frame repeatedly, we introduce a new frame, MarkerF, which invokes the primary apply function, renamed here as apply_prim.

type MarkerF = { }
$\mathcal{F}[\![$ MarkerF $f\,]\!] \varepsilon\, \sigma\, v\, \alpha\, \kappa =$ apply_prim($\kappa, (v, \sigma)$)

Example If we consider the previous example:
Expression: $e = ($**let** $f = \lambda x.\, x$ **in** $f(1)$ **end**$)$

Pointcut: CallPC $p = \{id = f; \; arg = x\}$

and we define advice a as:

Advice $a = \{body = \texttt{proceed}\,(2); \; pc = p\}$

As we have seen in the matching semantics, the frame CallF$(\lambda x. \, x, \varepsilon)$ is matched as a join point. The advice a is then executed at the state when this frame is extracted from the continuation list, i.e., when it receives the value of the argument. Since the advice body is $\texttt{proceed}$ (2), the frame CallF$(\lambda x. \, x, \varepsilon)$ will be evaluated with an argument equal to 2 instead of 1.

9.5 Semantics of Flow-Based Pointcuts

In this section, we extend our framework to flow-based pointcuts, namely, control flow (cflow) [113] and dataflow (dflow) [130] pointcuts. These pointcuts are useful from a security perspective since they can detect a considerable number of vulnerabilities related to information flow, such as Cross-site Scripting (XSS) and SQL injection attacks [86]. First, we extend the aspect syntax with these two pointcuts, as shown in Fig. 9.22, and then we provide their semantics in the following subsections.

9.5.1 Control Flow Pointcut

The control flow pointcut, cflow(p), picks out each join point in the control flow of the join points picked out by the pointcut p [113]. One of the techniques that are used to implement cflow is the stack-based approach [71, 132]. The latter maintains a stack of join points. The algorithm for matching cflow pointcut starts from the top of the stack and matches each join point against p. If there is a match then the current join point satisfies the cflow pointcut [132]. Implementing the cflow pointcut by adopting this approach in our framework is straightforward as the stack of join points

---

type Pointcut $= ... \mid$ CFlowPC $\mid$ DFlowPC

type CFlowPC $= \{pc : \text{Pointcut}\}$

type DFlowPC $= \{pc : \text{Pointcut}; \; tag : \text{Identifier}\}$

Fig. 9.22 Syntax of cflow and dflow pointcuts

---

type JpF = GetF | SetF | CallF | ExecF

let match_pc $p f$ v σ ε α κ = **match** (p,f) **with**

...

| (CFlowPC p, JpF f) $\Rightarrow$ **let** b_1 = match_pc$(p.pc, f, v, \sigma, \varepsilon, \alpha, \kappa)$ **in**
       if (b_1) **then**
          let κ' = push(CFlowF$(p.pc)$, κ) **in** b_1 **end**
       else
          exists(CFlowF$(p.pc)$, κ)
       end

Fig. 9.23 Matching semantics of the `cflow` pointcut

corresponds to the list of continuation frames in our model. Figure 9.23 shows the `cflow` matching semantics.

When a frame matches the sub-pointcut p of a `cflow` pointcut, a special marker frame, CFlowF, is pushed into the continuation list. The purpose of using this marker frame is to detect exit points of join points that match p. For example, if p is a `call` pointcut, the marker frame is pushed into the continuation list if the top frame matches p. Then, the marker frame will be extracted from the continuation list when the evaluation of the function call terminates. The CFlowF is defined as follows:

type CFlowF = $\{pc$: Pointcut$\}$
$\mathcal{F}[\![$ CFlowF f $]\!]\varepsilon$ σ v α κ = apply$(\kappa, (v, \sigma), \varepsilon, \alpha)$

In summary, a join point frame f matches a `cflow` pointcut that contains a pointcut p if: (1) The frame f matches the sub-pointcut p, or (2) a CFlowF marker frame that contains p exists in the continuation list. The primitive function exists used in the matching semantics is defined in Fig. 9.24. This function takes a frame f and a continuation list κ and checks whether f exists in the list or not.

9.5.2 Dataflow Pointcut

The dataflow pointcut, as defined in [130], picks out join points based on the origins of values, i.e., `dflow`[x, x'](p) matches a join point if the value of x originates from the value of x'. Variable x should be bound to a value in the current join point whereas variable x' should be bound to a value in a past join point matched by p. Therefore, `dflow` must be used in conjunction with some other pointcut that binds x to a value in the current join point [130]. To match a `dflow` pointcut, tags are used to discriminate `dflow` pointcuts and track dependencies between values [130]. This pointcut is useful where information flow is important, such as to detect input validation vulnerabilities in Web applications.

exists : Frame → Cont → Bool

let exists f κ = **match** κ **with**

$\qquad$ [] $\qquad$ ⇒ `false`

$\qquad$ $| f' :: \kappa'$ ⇒ **let** b = **match** f' **with**
$\qquad\qquad\qquad\qquad\qquad$ CflowF f' $\qquad$ ⇒ $f'.pc = f.pc$
$\qquad\qquad\qquad\qquad\qquad$ | **otherwise** $\quad$ ⇒ `false`
$\qquad\qquad\qquad$ **in**
$\qquad\qquad\qquad\qquad$ b **or** exists(f, κ')
$\qquad\qquad\qquad$ **end**

Fig. 9.24 Exists function

As defined in Fig. 9.22, the `dflow` pointcut has a sub-pointcut pc and a unique tag that discriminates this `dflow` pointcut from other `dflow` pointcuts. In order to track dependencies between values, we use a tagging environment γ that maps values to tags. As shown in Figs. 9.25 and 9.26, tag propagation is performed dynamically at the same time we evaluate each expression. Thus, we augment the signatures of the evaluation functions as well as the apply function with the tagging environment as follows:

$[\![\_]\!]_{\_ \_ \_ \_ \_}$ $\qquad$: Exp → Env → Tag_Env → Store → Aspect → Cont
$\qquad\qquad\qquad\qquad$ → Result

$\mathcal{F}[\![\_]\!]_{\_ \_ \_ \_ \_ \_}$ $\qquad$: Frame → Env → Tag_Env → Store → Value → Aspect
$\qquad\qquad\qquad\qquad$ → Cont → Result

apply $\qquad\qquad$: Cont → (Value × Store) → Env → Tag_Env → Aspect
$\qquad\qquad\qquad\qquad$ → (Value × Store)

Notice that the definition of the apply function does not change, only the tagging environment is passed to the matching function. Notice also that in the case of an abstraction expression, the closure $\langle x, e, \varepsilon' \rangle$ is extended with a tagging environment γ' to capture the tags generated during the function execution. In addition, we define a marker frame DflowF that is used for tag propagation in the case of an application expression. This frame stores a tagging environment before entering a function call and awaits the result of the call.

type DflowF = {tag_env : Env}

In the following, we explain the tag propagation rules for the affected expressions:

- The value of a constant is associated with an empty set.
- In the case of an application expression $(\lambda x.\ e)\ e'$, the tags of the value of the argument e' propagate to the value of the variable x. This is performed during the

evaluation of the ExecF frame as shown in Fig. 9.26. In addition, the tags of the argument as well as the tags that are generated during the execution of the function body propagate to the result of the function call. For this reason, we use a DflowF frame to access the result of the function call and restore the tagging environment after returning from the call. The function getTags(γ) is used to retrieve all the tags stored in the tagging environment γ.

- In the case of a let expression (let $x = e$ in e'), the tags of the value of the expression e propagate to the value of x. This is performed during the evaluation of the LetF frame as shown in Fig. 9.26.
- In the case of a referencing expression ref e, the tags of the value of the expression e propagate to the value of the expression ref e. This is performed during the evaluation of the AllocF frame as shown in Fig. 9.26.
- In the case of a dereferencing expression ! e, the tags of the value of the reference e propagate to the value stored at that reference. This is performed during the evaluation of the GetF frame as shown in Fig. 9.26.
- In the case of an assignment expression $e := e'$, the tags of the value of the expression e' propagate to the value of the expression e. This is performed during the evaluation of the SetF frame as shown in Fig. 9.26.

$$[\, c \,] \varepsilon \, \gamma \, \sigma \, \alpha \, \kappa = \mathsf{apply}(\kappa, (c, \sigma), \varepsilon, \gamma \dagger [c \mapsto \{\,\}], \alpha)$$

$$[\, x \,] \varepsilon \, \gamma \, \sigma \, \alpha \, \kappa = \mathsf{apply}(\kappa, (\varepsilon(x), \sigma), \varepsilon, \gamma, \alpha)$$

$$[\, \lambda x. \, e \,] \varepsilon \, \gamma \, \sigma \, \alpha \, \kappa = \mathsf{apply}(\kappa, (\langle x, e, \varepsilon', \gamma' \rangle, \sigma), \varepsilon, \gamma, \alpha)$$

$$[\, e \, e' \,] \varepsilon \, \gamma \, \sigma \, \alpha \, \kappa = [\, e' \,] \varepsilon \, \gamma \, \sigma \, \alpha \, (\mathsf{push}(\mathsf{CallF}(e, \varepsilon), \, \kappa))$$

$$[\, \mathtt{let}\, x = e \,\mathtt{in}\, e' \,] \varepsilon \, \gamma \, \sigma \, \alpha \, \kappa = [\, e \,] \varepsilon \, \gamma \, \sigma \, \alpha \, (\mathsf{push}(\mathsf{LetF}(x, e', \varepsilon), \kappa))$$

$$[\, \mathtt{if}\, e_1 \,\mathtt{then}\, e_2 \,\mathtt{else}\, e_3 \,] \varepsilon \, \gamma \, \sigma \, \alpha \, \kappa = [\, e_1 \,] \varepsilon \, \gamma \, \sigma \, \alpha \, (\mathsf{push}(\mathsf{IfF}(e_2, e_3, \varepsilon), \kappa))$$

$$[\, e_1; e_2 \,] \varepsilon \, \gamma \, \sigma \, \alpha \, \kappa = [\, e_1 \,] \varepsilon \, \gamma \, \sigma \, \alpha \, (\mathsf{push}(\mathsf{SeqF}(e_2, \varepsilon), \kappa))$$

$$[\, \mathtt{ref}\, e \,] \varepsilon \, \gamma \, \sigma \, \alpha \, \kappa = [\, e \,] \varepsilon \, \gamma \, \sigma \, \alpha \, (\mathsf{push}(\mathsf{AllocF}(), \kappa))$$

$$[\, !\, e \,] \varepsilon \, \gamma \, \sigma \, \alpha \, \kappa = [\, e \,] \varepsilon \, \gamma \, \sigma \, \alpha \, (\mathsf{push}(\mathsf{GetF}(), \kappa))$$

$$[\, e := e' \,] \varepsilon \, \gamma \, \sigma \, \alpha \, \kappa = [\, e \,] \varepsilon \, \gamma \, \sigma \, \alpha \, (\mathsf{push}(\mathsf{RhsF}(e', \varepsilon), \kappa))$$

$$[\, \mathtt{proceed}\,(e) \,] \varepsilon \, \gamma \, \sigma \, \alpha \, \kappa = [\, e \,] \varepsilon \, \gamma \, \sigma \, \alpha \, (\mathsf{push}(\mathsf{AdvExecF}(\varepsilon(\&proceed), \varepsilon(\&jp)), \kappa))$$

Fig. 9.25 Frame-based CPS semantics with the dflow pointcut: expression side

$\mathcal{F}[\![\,\text{GetF}\ f\,]\!]\,\varepsilon\ \gamma\ \sigma\ v\ \alpha\ \kappa = \text{apply}(\kappa,(\sigma(v),\sigma),\varepsilon,\gamma\dagger[\sigma(v)\mapsto\gamma(v)],\alpha)$

$\mathcal{F}[\![\,\text{SetF}\ f\,]\!]\,\varepsilon\ \gamma\ \sigma\ v\ \alpha\ \kappa = \text{apply}(\kappa,((),\sigma\dagger[f.loc\mapsto v]),\varepsilon,\gamma\dagger[f.loc\mapsto\gamma(v)],\alpha)$

$\mathcal{F}[\![\,\text{CallF}\ f\,]\!]\,\varepsilon\ \gamma\ \sigma\ v\ \alpha\ \kappa = [\![\,f.fun\,]\!]\,(f.env)\ \gamma\ \sigma\ \alpha\ (\text{push}(\text{ExecF}(v),\kappa))$

$\mathcal{F}[\![\,\text{ExecF}\ f\,]\!]\,\varepsilon\ \gamma\ \sigma\ v\ \alpha\ \kappa =$
$[\![\,e\,]\!](\varepsilon'\dagger[x\mapsto f.arg])(\gamma'\dagger[\varepsilon(x)\mapsto\gamma(f.arg)])\ \sigma\ \alpha\ (\text{push}(\text{DflowF}(\gamma),\kappa))$
where $v=\langle x,e,\varepsilon',\gamma'\rangle$

$\mathcal{F}[\![\,\text{LetF}\ f\,]\!]\,\varepsilon\ \gamma\ \sigma\ v\ \alpha\ \kappa = [\![\,f.exp\,]\!](f.env\dagger[f.id\mapsto v])(\gamma\dagger[\varepsilon(f.id)\mapsto\gamma(v)])\ \sigma\ \kappa$

$\mathcal{F}[\![\,\text{IfF}\ f\,]\!]\,\varepsilon\ \gamma\ \sigma\ v\ \alpha\ \kappa = \textbf{if}\ (v)\ \textbf{then}\ [\![\,f.thenExp\,]\!](f.env)\ \gamma\ \sigma\ \alpha\ \kappa$
$\textbf{else}\ [\![\,f.elseExp\,]\!](f.env)\ \gamma\ \sigma\ \alpha\ \kappa$

$\mathcal{F}[\![\,\text{SeqF}\ f\,]\!]\,\varepsilon\ \gamma\ \sigma\ v\ \alpha\ \kappa = [\![\,f.nextExp\,]\!](f.env)\ \gamma\ \sigma\ \alpha\ \kappa$

$\mathcal{F}[\![\,\text{AllocF}\ f\,]\!]\,\varepsilon\ \gamma\ \sigma\ v\ \alpha\ \kappa =$
$\textbf{let}\ \ell = \text{alloc}(\sigma)\ \textbf{in}\ \text{apply}(\kappa,(\ell,\sigma\dagger[\ell\mapsto v]),\varepsilon,\gamma\dagger[\ell\mapsto\gamma(v)],\alpha)\ \textbf{end}$

$\mathcal{F}[\![\,\text{RhsF}\ f\,]\!]\,\varepsilon\ \gamma\ \sigma\ v\ \alpha\ \kappa = [\![\,f.exp\,]\!](f.env)\ \gamma\ \sigma\ \alpha\ (\text{push}(\text{SetF}(v),\kappa))$

$\mathcal{F}[\![\,\text{AdvExecF}\ f\,]\!]\,\varepsilon\ \gamma\ \sigma\ v\ \alpha\ \kappa = \text{execute\_advice}(f.matches,f.jp,v,\sigma,\varepsilon,\gamma,\alpha,\kappa)$

$\mathcal{F}[\![\,\text{MarkerF}\ f\,]\!]\,\varepsilon\ \gamma\ \sigma\ v\ \alpha\ \kappa = \text{apply\_prim}(\kappa,(v,\sigma))$

$\mathcal{F}[\![\,\text{CFlowF}\ f\,]\!]\,\varepsilon\ \gamma\ \sigma\ v\ \alpha\ \kappa = \text{apply}(\kappa,(v,\sigma),\varepsilon,\gamma,\alpha)$

$\mathcal{F}[\![\,\text{DFlowF}\ f\,]\!]\,\varepsilon\ \gamma\ \sigma\ v\ \alpha\ \kappa = \text{apply}(\kappa,(v,\sigma),\varepsilon,f.tag\_env\dagger[v\mapsto\text{getTags}(\gamma)],\alpha)$

Fig. 9.26 Frame-based CPS semantics with the dflow pointcut: frame side

The matching semantics of the dflow pointcut is presented in Fig. 9.27. A join point frame f matches a dflow pointcut that contains a pointcut pc and a tag t if: (1) The frame f matches the pointcut pc of the dflow pointcut, or (2) the set of tags of the value that the frame f awaits (captured by the variable val') contains the tag t. In case a frame f matches the pointcut pc of the dflow pointcut, the tag t propagates to the value associated with the frame f (captured by the variable val).

---

let match_pc $p f v \sigma \varepsilon \gamma \alpha \kappa =$ **match** (p,f) **with**

...

$\mid$ (DFlowPC p, JpFf) $\Rightarrow$ **let** $(b,\gamma') =$ match_pc$(p.pc, f, v, \sigma, \varepsilon, \gamma, \alpha, \kappa)$ **in**
       let $val =$ **match** f **with**
        GetFf $\Rightarrow$ v
        SetFf $\Rightarrow$ v
        CallFf $\Rightarrow$ **let** $p = p.pc$ **in**
            let $(v',\sigma') = [\![\varepsilon(p.id)]\!] \varepsilon \gamma \sigma \alpha \kappa$
            in
             v'
            end
          end
        ExecFf $\Rightarrow$ v
       in
        if (b) **then** $(\mathtt{true}, \gamma' \dagger [val \mapsto \gamma'(val) \cup \{p.tag\}])$
        else let $val' =$ **match** f **with**
          CallFf $\Rightarrow$ v
          otherwise $\Rightarrow$ val
        in
         $(p.tag \in \gamma'(val'), \gamma')$
        end
       end
      end

Fig. 9.27 Matching semantics of the `dflow` pointcut

9.5.3 Example

To illustrate the semantics of the `dflow` pointcut, let us consider this example:

let $userId = 1$ **in**
 let $getInput = \lambda x.\, e_1$ **in** # $getInput$: gets a user input
  let $write = \lambda x'.\, e_2$ **in** # $write$: writes a string on a web page
   $z = getInput(userId);\ w = write(z)$
  end
 end
end

The presented example is vulnerable to Cross-Site Scripting (XSS) attacks [86] since an untrusted input received from a user has not been sanitized before being placed into the contents of a web page. Therefore, it enables an attacker to inject malicious scripts into a web page and reveal confidential information. The `dflow` pointcut can be remarkably used to address XSS flaws as shown in [130]. Below, we provide a sanitizing aspect to fix the discussed vulnerability.

Aspect (Pointcuts and Advice):

$$\text{CallPC } p_1 \quad = \{id = getInput;\ arg = x\}$$
$$\text{DFlowPC } p_2 = \{pc = p_1;\ tag = t\}$$
$$\text{CallPC } p_3 \quad = \{id = write;\ arg = y\}$$
$$\text{AndPC } p \quad = \{pc_1 = p_2;\ pc_2 = p_3\}$$
$$\text{Advice } a \quad = \{body = \textbf{let } sanitize = \lambda r.\ e_3 \textbf{ in } \texttt{proceed } (sanitize(y));\ pc = p\}$$

The pointcut p_1 is a $\texttt{call}$ pointcut that captures all calls to the *getInput* function. Likewise, the pointcut p_3 captures all calls to the *write* function. The pointcut p_2 is a $\texttt{dflow}$ pointcut that captures all join points that depend on the join points captured by the pointcut p_1. Finally, the pointcut p picks out all calls to the *write* function that are dependent on the results of invoking the function *getInput*. The advice a first sanitizes the arguments of the join points captured by p, and then invokes the original join points with the sanitized arguments. More precisely, advice a picks out all calls to *write*(z) that depend on the result of *getInput* and replaces them with *write*$(sanitize(z))$ by the following justification:

- The call to *getInput*$(userId)$ matches the pointcut p_2, and consequently, the tag t is added to the tagging environment of the function and is given to the result of the function evaluation.
- According to the tag propagation rule for assignment expressions, the value of the variable z gets the tag t.
- Subsequently, the call to *write*(z) matches the pointcut p since it matches both sub-pointcuts of p. More precisely, it matches the pointcut p_3 as it is a call to the *write* function, and matches the pointcut p_2 as the value of the argument z has the tag t.

Therefore, the advice a will be woven at this point and the function *write* will be called with the sanitized input, which is the result of calling *sanitize*(z).

9.6 Related Work on AOP Semantics

There are many research contributions that have addressed AOP semantics [34, 35, 53, 60, 66, 74, 76, 88, 106, 129, 132, 201, 202]. Among these contributions, we explore those that are more relevant to our work, mainly contributions that are based on CPS or those handling flow-based pointcuts. Dutchyn [74] has presented a formal model of dynamic join points, pointcuts, and advice using a first-order procedural language called PROC [74]. The proposed semantic model is based on defunctionalization and continuation-passing style. The author has demonstrated that modeling AOP concepts in this style provides a natural and precise way of describing these mechanisms. The proposed model supports $\texttt{get}$, $\texttt{set}$, $\texttt{call}$, and $\texttt{exec}$ pointcuts. The author has also provided some hints for implementing the $\texttt{cflow}$ pointcut but did not provide the matching algorithm. Compared to [74], our contribution provides a clear presentation allowing a better view of this style of semantics. In addition, we extend the aspect layer with flow-based pointcuts.

Masuhara et al. [129] have proposed the point-in-time join point model, where they redefine join points as the states at the beginning and the end of certain events. Based on this new model, the authors have designed a small AOP language and defined its formal semantics in CPS. Moreover, they have demonstrated that this approach is useful to model advanced pointcuts, such as exception handling and control flow. The idea of this work is similar to ours in using continuations to model matching and weaving semantics. However, the main difference is that our semantics is based on frames, while in [129] the semantics follows the style of Danvy and Filinski [67] that represent continuations as λ-functions. As we have seen, presenting continuations as frames is a better approach since join points arise naturally within this semantics.

Wand et al. [202] have proposed semantics for AOP that handles dynamic join points and recursive procedures. They have provided a denotational semantics for a mini-language that embodies the key features of dynamic join points, pointcuts, and advice. Three kinds of join points were supported, namely pcall, pexecution, and aexecution. The proposed model is implemented as part of Aspect Sandbox (ASB)[75], which is a framework for modeling AOP systems. This model is based on a direct denotational semantics. Consequently, separate data-structures are required for maintaining the dynamic join points, while in our semantics the join points arise from the continuation list.

Djoko et al. [71] have defined an operational semantics for the main features of AspectJ including cflow. The semantics of the cflow pointcut presented in this approach is slightly different from AspectJ as they restricted the sub-pointcut to the call pointcut. Comparing to this approach, our semantics of the cflow pointcut is more general as we support all kinds of pointcuts. In addition, this approach requires additional structures to maintain the join points. By adopting operational semantics and partial evaluation approaches, Masuhara et al. [132] have provided a compilation framework for a simple AOP language named AJD. They have also provided two methods for implementing the cflow pointcut, namely, stack-based and state-based implementations. However, no formal semantics is given for the defined pointcut.

The dflow pointcut was initially proposed by Masuhara and Kawauchi [130]. The authors have argued about the usefulness of this pointcut in the field of security through an example of a Web-based application. They have also provided the design of the dflow pointcut and its matching rules based on the origins of values. The dflow pointcut has been implemented as an extension to Aspect Sandbox (ASB) [75]. However, no formal semantics has been provided for this pointcut.

Alhadidi et al. [35] have presented the first formal framework for the dflow pointcut based on λ-calculus. In this work, dataflow tags are propagated statically to track data dependencies between λ-expressions. Compared to our framework, [35] makes use of the effect-based type system for propagating dataflow tags, matching pointcuts, and weaving advice. Though a static approach can help in reducing the runtime overhead, expressions in this approach need to be typed since matching depends primarily on types. The authors have also provided dynamic semantics and proved that it is consistent with the static semantics. The pointcut enclosed in a dflow pointcut is restricted to call and get pointcuts in this approach, while we consider the general case in our framework, i.e., the sub-pointcut of the dflow pointcut can be any pointcut.

9.7 Conclusion

In this chapter, we have provided formal semantics for aspect matching and weaving in λ-calculus. We chose CPS as the basis of our semantics because it provides a concise, accurate, and elegant description of aspect-oriented mechanisms. Using this style of semantics, one can easily notice that CPS and defunctionalization make join points explicit and facilitate the aspect matching and weaving mechanisms. For instance, we did not need to use any additional structure; the join points correspond exactly to continuation frames. We have addressed basic pointcuts, i.e., get, set, call, and exec pointcuts. These pointcuts are useful from a security perspective since they can pick out important points, where security mechanisms such as authorization, encryption, and decryption, may be added *before*, *after*, or *around* these points. In addition, we have extended our semantic framework with flow-based pointcuts, namely, cflow and dflow pointcuts, since they are widely used to detect and fix vulnerabilities related to information flow. The contribution presented in this chapter is a first step towards establishing a dynamic semantics for aspect matching and weaving based on CPS and defunctionalization. In the next chapter, we will apply the results of this work to our AOM framework to elaborate semantics for matching and weaving on executable UML models.

Chapter 10
Dynamic Matching and Weaving Semantics in Executable UML

In this chapter, we elaborate dynamic semantics for aspect matching and weaving in Executable UML (xUML) [134]. More precisely, we specify xUML models using the Action Language for Foundational UML (Alf) [156] proposed by OMG. In addition of being a standard, Alf is highly expressive. Moreover, Alf provides precise semantics for specifying detailed and executable behaviors within a UML model, such as creating class instances, establishing links between these instances, performing operations on variables and attributes, etc. Therefore, more security checks can be performed at the modeling phase and numerous flaws can get resolved before entering the implementation phase. This, in turn, significantly reduces costs and leads to more trustworthy software.

Existing AOM approaches that handle xUML models [92, 105, 213] mainly focus on providing a framework for executing the woven model for the purposes of simulation and verification. Moreover, these approaches are presented from a practical perspective; to date we are not aware of any work that explores the semantic foundations for aspect matching and weaving in xUML. It is our aim, in this chapter, to define such a semantics, particularly on executable activity diagrams. We elaborate the semantics in a frame-based CPS style by applying the results, presented in Chap. 9, on xUML models. As we have seen in Chap. 9, a semantics, based on CPS and defunctionalization, provides a precise and elegant description of aspect-oriented mechanisms. Furthermore, by expressing executable models in a frame-based representation, matching and weaving can be described in a simplified and unified way for both UML elements and action language constructs.

As we did in Chap. 9, we start by formalizing the matching and the weaving processes for basic pointcuts, i.e., `get`, `set`, `call`, and `exec` pointcuts. Then, we elaborate the semantics for the dataflow pointcut. Notice here that we match these pointcuts on both activity diagram elements and Alf expressions. For example, an operation call can be performed as a call operation action, which is an activity element, and as a function call inside Alf code. Consequently, our framework should be able to capture both points.

D. Mouheb et al., *Aspect-Oriented Security Hardening of UML Design Models*,
DOI 10.1007/978-3-319-16106-8_10

The remainder of this chapter is organized as follows. Section 10.1 introduces a motivating example. The syntax of activity diagrams and Alf is presented in Sect. 10.2, followed by their denotational semantics in Sect. 10.3. We transform the semantics into CPS in Sect. 10.4. Afterwards, Sect. 10.5 explores the semantics for matching and weaving. In Sect. 10.6, we extend the semantics with the dataflow pointcut. We discuss related work in Sect. 10.7. Finally, concluding remarks are represented in Sect. 10.8.

10.1 Example

To clarify our motivation, let us consider a simple example of a caching process as shown in Fig. 10.1. The caching executable activity diagram starts by executing the action *GetDataRequest*. This action is a UML accept action that awaits a data request. When a request is received, it checks whether the requested data is already cached or not. If yes, then the action *ReturnData*, which is a call operation action, is called and the requested data is returned. Otherwise, the action *Caching&ReturningData* is activated. This action is an opaque action whose behavior is specified using Alf action language. In this case, first the data is fetched and the cache is updated accordingly. Then the operation *ReturnData* is called and the requested data is returned.

Let us assume that our goal is to insert logging before calling the operation *Return-Data*. As it is highlighted in the example, this operation is called in two ways: as a call operation action and as an Alf expression. Therefore, the matching semantics should be able to capture both points. To do so, we provide a frame-based representation for both activity elements and Alf expressions and perform matching and weaving on frames.

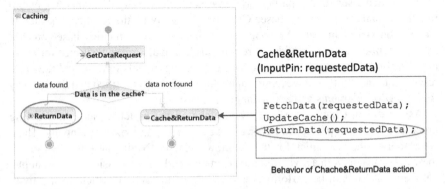

Fig. 10.1 Caching example

10.2 Syntax

In this section, we present the syntax of activity diagrams and Alf language. An activity diagram starts with an initial node ($\bullet$) that is connected to the subsequent nodes (n) through an edge ($\rightarrow$). A node can be either an executable node or a control node. For the sake of illustration, we choose a small subset of nodes that captures the essence of activity diagrams and omit complex features, such as concurrency and exception handling. The proposed syntax is shown in Fig. 10.2. The purpose of using labels is to uniquely refer to already defined nodes. In the following, we explain the activity constructs:

- The notation $\bullet \rightarrow n$ denotes an activity diagram, where $\bullet$ is the initial node and n is the subsequent flow of nodes.
- a is an action node, that can be either:

  - l : opaque (e), a labeled opaque action, where e is an Alf expression specifying the behavior of the action.
  - l : callOp (f), a labeled call operation action that invokes a function f.
  - l : read (x), a labeled read variable action that reads the value of x.
  - l : write (x), a labeled write variable action that updates the value of x.

- l : decision (e, n_1, n_2) denotes a labeled decision node having two alternative flows n_1 and n_2.
- l : merge $\rightarrow n$ denotes a labeled merge node that is followed by a flow of nodes n.
- l : $\odot$ denotes a labeled activity final node.
- $a \rightarrow n$ denotes an action that is followed by the subsequent flow of nodes n.
- l denotes a label that uniquely refers to a node.

ad	::=	$\bullet \rightarrow n$	**activity**
n	::=	a	**action**
	|	l : decision (e, n_1, n_2)	**decision**
	|	l : merge $\rightarrow n$	**merge**
	|	l : $\odot$	**activity final**
	|	$a \rightarrow n$	**node sequence**
	|	l	**label**
a	::=	l : opaque (e)	**opaque action**
	|	l : callOp (f)	**call operation**
	|	l : read (x)	**read variable**
	|	l : write (x)	**write variable**

Fig. 10.2 Syntax of activity diagrams

e	$::=$	c	constant
	$\vert$	x	variable
	$\vert$	$f(x) = e$	operation def.
	$\vert$	$f(e)$	operation call
	$\vert$	if e_1 then e_2 else e_3	conditional exp.
	$\vert$	$e_1 ; e_2$	exp. sequence
	$\vert$	new e	referencing
	$\vert$	$! \, e$	dereferencing
	$\vert$	$x := e$	assignment

Fig. 10.3 Syntax of Alf language

Figure 10.3 presents the syntax of Alf language. To keep the presentation simple and readable, we choose the main constructs of Alf and omit the object-oriented characteristic of the language. We consider the following expressions:

- Constants and variables
- Functional constructs
- Conditional expressions
- Sequential expressions
- Imperative features (referencing, dereferencing, and assignments). The expression new e allocates a new reference and initializes it with the value of e. The expression $! \, e$ reads the value stored at the location referenced by e.

10.3 Denotational Semantics

This section presents the denotational semantics of activity diagrams and Alf expressions. The functions and the types used in the semantics are defined in Fig. 10.4.

$\mathcal{A}[\![\_]\!]\_\_$	:	Activity $\rightarrow$ Env $\rightarrow$ Store $\rightarrow$ Result
$\eta[\![\_]\!]\_\_\_\_$	:	Node $\rightarrow$ Env $\rightarrow$ Store $\rightarrow$ Token $\rightarrow$ Value $\rightarrow$ Result
$\xi[\![\_]\!]\_\_$	:	Exp $\rightarrow$ Env $\rightarrow$ Store $\rightarrow$ Result
Result	:	Value $\times$ Store
Env	:	Identifier $\rightarrow$ Value
Store	:	Location $\rightarrow$ Value
Value	:	Boolean $\vert$ Natural $\vert$ String $\vert$ Unit $\vert$ Location $\vert$ Closure

Fig. 10.4 Semantic functions and types

10.3.1 Denotational Semantics of Activity Diagrams

The denotational semantics of activity diagrams is presented in Fig. 10.5. Given an activity diagram ad, a dynamic environment ε, and a store σ, the function $\mathcal{A}[\![\ \_\ ]\!]$ yields the computed value v and the updated store σ' after the termination of the activity execution. When an activity starts executing, a control token t is created and placed on the initial node. This token then propagates along the edges to the subsequent nodes. A node starts executing when it gets the required tokens and data values. Thus, the evaluation function for nodes $\eta[\![\ \_\ ]\!]$ takes a token t and a value v as inputs, in addition to the environment ε and the store σ. When the execution of a node terminates, it returns a value and the updated store that will be passed to the subsequent nodes.

In the following, we explain the semantics of each activity construct. The semantics of an opaque action, $l : \texttt{opaque}\,(e)$, depends on the semantics of its Alf expression e. A call operation action, $l : \texttt{callOp}\,(f)$, invokes the function f with the argument value v that it receives from its input. A read variable action, $l : \texttt{read}\,(x)$,

$$\mathcal{A}[\![\ \bullet \rightarrow n\ ]\!]\varepsilon\,\sigma = \textbf{let } t = createToken()\textbf{ in } \eta[\![\ n\ ]\!]\varepsilon\,\sigma\,t\,()\textbf{ end}$$

$$\eta[\![\ l : \texttt{opaque}\,(e)\ ]\!]\varepsilon\,\sigma\,t\,v = \xi[\![\ e\ ]\!]\varepsilon\,\sigma$$

$$\eta[\![\ l : \texttt{callOp}\,(f)\ ]\!]\varepsilon\,\sigma\,t\,v = \textbf{let } (\langle x,e,\varepsilon'\rangle,\sigma') = \xi[\![\ \varepsilon(f)\ ]\!]\varepsilon\,\sigma\textbf{ in}$$
$$\xi[\![\ e\ ]\!]\varepsilon'\dagger[x\mapsto v]\,\sigma'$$
$$\textbf{end}$$

$$\eta[\![\ l : \texttt{read}\,(x)\ ]\!]\varepsilon\,\sigma\,t\,v = \textbf{let } (\ell,\sigma') = \xi[\![\ x\ ]\!]\varepsilon\,\sigma\textbf{ in } (\sigma'(\ell),\sigma')\textbf{ end}$$

$$\eta[\![\ l : \texttt{write}\,(x)\ ]\!]\varepsilon\,\sigma\,t\,v = \textbf{let } (\ell,\sigma') = \xi[\![\ x\ ]\!]\varepsilon\,\sigma\textbf{ in } ((),\sigma'\dagger[\ell\mapsto v])\textbf{ end}$$

$$\eta[\![\ l : \texttt{decision}\,(e,n_1,n_2)\ ]\!]\varepsilon\,\sigma\,t\,v = \textbf{let } (v',\sigma') = \xi[\![\ e\ ]\!]\varepsilon\,\sigma\textbf{ in}$$
$$\textbf{if } (v')\textbf{ then } \eta[\![\ n_1\ ]\!]\varepsilon\,\sigma'\,t\,v$$
$$\textbf{else } \eta[\![\ n_2\ ]\!]\varepsilon\,\sigma'\,t\,v$$
$$\textbf{end}$$

$$\eta[\![\ l : \texttt{merge}\rightarrow n\ ]\!]\varepsilon\,\sigma\,t\,v = \eta[\![\ n\ ]\!]\varepsilon\,\sigma\,t\,v$$

$$\eta[\![\ l : \odot\ ]\!]\varepsilon\,\sigma\,t\,v = \textbf{let } b = destroyAllTokens()\textbf{ in } (v,\sigma)\textbf{ end}$$

$$\eta[\![\ a\rightarrow n\ ]\!]\varepsilon\,\sigma\,t\,v = \textbf{let } (v',\sigma') = \eta[\![\ a\ ]\!]\varepsilon\,\sigma\,t\,v\textbf{ in } \eta[\![\ n\ ]\!]\varepsilon\,\sigma'\,t\,v'\textbf{ end}$$

$$\eta[\![\ l\ ]\!]\varepsilon\,\sigma\,t\,v = \eta[\![\ \varepsilon(l)\ ]\!]\varepsilon\,\sigma\,t\,v$$

Fig. 10.5 Denotational semantics of activity diagrams

reads the value of the variable x from the store. A write variable action, l : write (x), updates the value of the variable x with the value v that it receives from its input. A decision node, l : decision (e, n_1, n_2), guides the flow depending on the value of the condition e. If e evaluates to true, the node n_1 is executed, otherwise the node n_2 is executed. A merge node, l : merge $\rightarrow n$, passes the token and the data that it receives to its subsequent node n. A final node, l : $\odot$, terminates the activity execution. Accordingly, all tokens in the activity are destroyed. Finally, the semantics of a label l depends on the semantics of the referenced node. Notice that the semantics of an edge is to transfer tokens and data values from the source node to the target node. In our syntax, a node is explicitly connected to its subsequent nodes (e.g., $a \rightarrow n$). Therefore, there is no need to separately define the semantics of an edge since it is taken care of during the evaluation of the nodes.

$$\xi[\![\, c \,]\!]\varepsilon\, \sigma = (c, \sigma)$$

$$\xi[\![\, x \,]\!]\varepsilon\, \sigma = (\varepsilon(x), \sigma)$$

$$\xi[\![\, f(x) = e \,]\!]\varepsilon\, \sigma = (\langle x, e, \varepsilon' \rangle, \sigma)$$

$$\xi[\![\, f(e) \,]\!]\varepsilon\, \sigma = \textbf{let}\ (v, \sigma') = \xi[\![\, e \,]\!]\varepsilon\, \sigma\ \textbf{in}$$
$$\qquad\qquad \textbf{let}\ (\langle x, e', \varepsilon' \rangle, \sigma'') = \xi[\![\, \varepsilon(f) \,]\!]\varepsilon\, \sigma'\ \textbf{in}$$
$$\qquad\qquad\qquad \xi[\![\, e' \,]\!]\varepsilon'\dagger[x \mapsto v]\, \sigma''$$
$$\qquad\ \textbf{end}$$
$$\textbf{end}$$

$$\xi[\![\, \text{if}\ e_1\ \text{then}\ e_2\ \text{else}\ e_3 \,]\!]\varepsilon\, \sigma = \textbf{let}\ (v, \sigma') = \xi[\![\, e_1 \,]\!]\varepsilon\, \sigma\ \textbf{in}$$
$$\qquad\qquad \textbf{if}\ (v)\ \textbf{then}\ \xi[\![\, e_2 \,]\!]\varepsilon\, \sigma'\ \textbf{else}\ \xi[\![\, e_3 \,]\!]\varepsilon\, \sigma'$$
$$\textbf{end}$$

$$\xi[\![\, e_1; e_2 \,]\!]\varepsilon\, \sigma = \textbf{let}\ (v, \sigma') = \xi[\![\, e_1 \,]\!]\varepsilon\, \sigma\ \textbf{in}\ \xi[\![\, e_2 \,]\!]\varepsilon\, \sigma'\ \textbf{end}$$

$$\xi[\![\, \text{new}\ e \,]\!]\varepsilon\, \sigma = \textbf{let}\ (v, \sigma') = \xi[\![\, e \,]\!]\varepsilon\, \sigma\ \textbf{in}$$
$$\qquad\qquad \textbf{let}\ \ell = alloc(\sigma')\ \textbf{in}\ (\ell, \sigma'\dagger[\ell \mapsto v])\ \textbf{end}$$
$$\textbf{end}$$

$$\xi[\![\, !\, e \,]\!]\varepsilon\, \sigma = \textbf{let}\ (\ell, \sigma') = \xi[\![\, e \,]\!]\varepsilon\, \sigma\ \textbf{in}\ (\sigma'(\ell), \sigma')\ \textbf{end}$$

$$\xi[\![\, x := e \,]\!]\varepsilon\, \sigma = \textbf{let}\ (v, \sigma') = \xi[\![\, e \,]\!]\varepsilon\, \sigma\ \textbf{in}$$
$$\qquad\qquad \textbf{let}\ (\ell, \sigma'') = \xi[\![\, x \,]\!]\varepsilon\, \sigma'\ \textbf{in}\ ((), \sigma''\dagger[\ell \mapsto v])\ \textbf{end}$$
$$\textbf{end}$$

Fig. 10.6 Denotational semantics of Alf language

10.3.2 Denotational Semantics of Alf Language

The denotational semantics of Alf language is presented in Fig. 10.6. Given an expression e, a dynamic environment ε, and a store σ, the dynamic evaluation function $\xi[\![\_]\!]$ yields the computed value v and the updated store σ'. Notice that in the case of a function definition $f(x) = e$, the computed value is a closure $\langle x, e, \varepsilon' \rangle$ capturing the function parameter x, the function body e, and the evaluation environment ε', which maps each free variable of e to its value at the time of the function declaration. The function *alloc* used in the semantics allocates a new cell in the store and returns a reference to it.

10.4 Continuation-Passing Style Semantics

In this section, we transform the previously defined denotational semantics into CPS. As we mentioned earlier, frame-based semantics allows describing matching and weaving processes in activity diagrams and Alf language in a precise and unified way. To help understanding this transformation, we proceed in two steps. First, we elaborate a CPS semantics by representing continuations as functions. Then, we provide a CPS semantics by representing continuations as frames.

10.4.1 Representation of Continuations as Functions

First, we modify the evaluation functions to take a continuation as an additional argument as shown in Fig. 10.7. As we did in the previous chapter, we translate the denotational semantics into CPS following the original formulation of the CPS transformation [84]. The CPS semantics of activity diagrams is presented in Fig. 10.8 and the CPS semantics of Alf is presented in Fig. 10.9.

$$
\begin{aligned}
&\mathcal{A}[\![\_]\!]\_\_\_ && : \text{Activity} \to \text{Env} \to \text{Store} \to \text{Cont} \to \text{Result} \\
&\eta[\![\_]\!]\_\_\_\_\_ && : \text{Node} \to \text{Env} \to \text{Store} \to \text{Token} \to \text{Value} \to \text{Cont} \to \text{Result} \\
&\xi[\![\_]\!]\_\_\_ && : \text{Exp} \to \text{Env} \to \text{Store} \to \text{Cont} \to \text{Result} \\
&\text{Cont} && : \text{Result} \to \text{Result} \\
&\text{Result} && : \text{Value} \times \text{Store}
\end{aligned}
$$

Fig. 10.7 Redefined semantic functions and types

$\mathcal{A}[\![\bullet \to n]\!] \varepsilon \, \sigma \, \kappa = \textbf{let} \, t \, = \, createToken() \, \textbf{in} \, \eta[\![n]\!] \varepsilon \, \sigma \, t \, () \, \kappa \, \textbf{end}$

$\eta[\![l : \texttt{opaque} \, (e)]\!] \varepsilon \, \sigma \, t \, v \, \kappa = \xi[\![e]\!] \, \varepsilon \, \sigma \, \kappa$

$\eta[\![l : \texttt{callOp} \, (f)]\!] \varepsilon \, \sigma \, t \, v \, \kappa = \xi[\![\, \varepsilon(f)]\!] \varepsilon \, \sigma \, (\lambda(v',\sigma'). \, \xi[\![e]\!] \varepsilon' \dagger [x \mapsto v] \, \sigma' \, \kappa)$
where $v' = \langle x, e, \varepsilon' \rangle$

$\eta[\![l : \texttt{read} \, (x)]\!] \varepsilon \, \sigma \, t \, v \, \kappa = \xi[\![x]\!] \varepsilon \, \sigma \, (\lambda(\ell,\sigma'). \, \kappa(\sigma'(\ell),\sigma'))$

$\eta[\![l : \texttt{write} \, (x)]\!] \varepsilon \, \sigma \, t \, v \, \kappa = \xi[\![x]\!] \varepsilon \, \sigma \, (\lambda(\ell,\sigma'). \, \kappa((),\sigma' \dagger [\ell \mapsto v]))$

$\eta[\![l : \texttt{decision} \, (e, n_1, n_2)]\!] \varepsilon \, \sigma \, t \, v \, \kappa =$
$\xi[\![e]\!] \varepsilon \, \sigma \, (\lambda(v',\sigma'). \, \textbf{if} \, (v') \, \textbf{then} \, \eta[\![n_1]\!] \varepsilon \, \sigma' \, t \, v \, \kappa \, \textbf{else} \, \eta[\![n_2]\!] \varepsilon \, \sigma' \, t \, v \, \kappa)$

$\eta[\![l : \texttt{merge} \to n]\!] \varepsilon \, \sigma \, t \, v \, \kappa = \eta[\![n]\!] \varepsilon \, \sigma \, t \, v \, \kappa$

$\eta[\![l : \odot]\!] \varepsilon \, \sigma \, t \, v \, \kappa = \textbf{let} \, b \, = \, destroyAllTokens() \, \textbf{in} \, \kappa(v,\sigma) \, \textbf{end}$

$\eta[\![a \to n]\!] \varepsilon \, \sigma \, t \, v \, \kappa = \eta[\![a]\!] \varepsilon \, \sigma \, t \, v \, (\lambda(v',\sigma'). \, \eta[\![n]\!] \varepsilon \, \sigma' \, t \, v'\kappa)$

$\eta[\![l]\!] \varepsilon \, \sigma \, t \, v \, \kappa = \eta[\![\, \varepsilon(l)]\!] \varepsilon \, \sigma \, t \, v \, \kappa$

Fig. 10.8 CPS semantics of activity diagrams: continuations as functions

10.4.2 Representation of Continuations as Frames

Using the defunctionalization technique [176], we transform the continuation functions, obtained from the previous step, into frames as shown in Fig. 10.10. In the following, we provide details about each frame:

- GetF does not store any value. It awaits a location and a store.
- SetF stores a value. It awaits a location and a store.
- CallF stores a function identifier and an environment. It awaits the value of the function argument.
- ExecF stores the value of the argument. It awaits a closure, which is the result of the evaluation of the function definition, and a store.
- IfF stores then and else expressions and an environment. It awaits the value of the condition and a store.
- DecisionF stores then and else nodes, an environment, a control token, and a value. It awaits the value of the condition and a store.
- ExpSeqF stores the next expression and an environment. It awaits the value of the first expression and a store.
- NodeSeqF stores the next node, an environment, and a control token. It awaits the output value of the first node and a store.

- AllocF does not store any value. It awaits the value to be stored in the newly allocated cell and a store.
- RhsF stores an identifier and an environment. It awaits a location and a store.

$$\xi[\![\, c \,]\!]\varepsilon\, \sigma\, \kappa = \kappa(c,\sigma)$$

$$\xi[\![\, x \,]\!]\varepsilon\, \sigma\, \kappa = \kappa(\varepsilon(x),\sigma)$$

$$\xi[\![\, f(x) = e \,]\!]\varepsilon\, \sigma\, \kappa = \kappa(\lambda(v,\kappa').\ [\![\, e \,]\!]\varepsilon\, \dagger\, [x \mapsto v]\, \sigma\, \kappa')$$

$$\xi[\![\, f(e) \,]\!]\varepsilon\, \sigma\, \kappa =$$
$$\xi[\![\, e \,]\!]\varepsilon\, \sigma\, (\lambda(v,\sigma').\ \xi[\![\, \varepsilon(f) \,]\!]\varepsilon\, \sigma'\, (\lambda(v',\sigma'').\ \xi[\![\, e' \,]\!]\varepsilon'\, \dagger\, [x \mapsto v]\sigma''\, \kappa))$$
where $v' = \langle x, e', \varepsilon' \rangle$

$$\xi[\![\, \text{if } e_1 \text{ then } e_2 \text{ else } e_3 \,]\!]\varepsilon\, \sigma\, \kappa =$$
$$\xi[\![\, e_1 \,]\!]\varepsilon\, \sigma\, (\lambda(v,\sigma').\ \textbf{if } (v) \textbf{ then } \xi[\![\, e_2 \,]\!]\varepsilon\, \sigma'\, \kappa \textbf{ else } \xi[\![\, e_3 \,]\!]\varepsilon\, \sigma'\, \kappa)$$

$$\xi[\![\, e_1; e_2 \,]\!]\varepsilon\, \sigma\, \kappa = \xi[\![\, e_1 \,]\!]\varepsilon\, \sigma\, (\lambda(v,\sigma').\ \xi[\![\, e_2 \,]\!]\varepsilon\, \sigma'\, \kappa)$$

$$\xi[\![\, \text{new } e \,]\!]\varepsilon\, \sigma\, \kappa = \xi[\![\, e \,]\!]\varepsilon\, \sigma\, (\lambda(v,\sigma').$$
$$\textbf{let } \ell = alloc(\sigma') \textbf{ in } \kappa(\ell,\sigma'\, \dagger\, [\ell \mapsto v])) \textbf{ end}$$

$$\xi[\![\, !\, e \,]\!]\varepsilon\, \sigma\, \kappa = \xi[\![\, e \,]\!]\varepsilon\, \sigma\, (\lambda(\ell,\sigma').\ \kappa(\sigma'(\ell),\sigma'))$$

$$\xi[\![\, x := e \,]\!]\varepsilon\, \sigma\, \kappa = \xi[\![\, e \,]\!]\varepsilon\, \sigma\, (\lambda(v,\sigma').\ \xi[\![\, x \,]\!]\varepsilon\, \sigma'$$
$$(\lambda(\ell,\sigma'').\ \kappa((),\sigma''\, \dagger\, [\ell \mapsto v])))$$

Fig. 10.9 CPS semantics of Alf language: continuations as functions

type GetF $= \{\}$
type SetF $= \{val : \text{Value}\}$
type CallF $= \{fun : \text{Identifier}; \ env : \text{Env}\}$
type ExecF $= \{arg : \text{Value}\}$
type IfF $= \{thenExp : \text{Exp}; \ elseExp : \text{Exp}; \ env : \text{Env}\}$
type DecisionF $= \{thenNode : \text{Node}; \ elseNode : \text{Node}; \ env : \text{Env};$
$\qquad\qquad\qquad token : \text{Token}; \ val : \text{Value}\}$
type ExpSeqF $= \{nextExp : \text{Exp}; \ env : \text{Env}\}$
type NodeSeqF $= \{nextNode : \text{Node}; \ env : \text{Env}; \ token : \text{Token}\}$
type AllocF $= \{\}$
type RhsF $= \{id : \text{Identifier}; \ env : \text{Env}\}$

Fig. 10.10 Frames

$\mathcal{A}[\![\, \bullet \to n \,]\!]\, \varepsilon\, \sigma\, \kappa = \mathbf{let}\; t \,=\, \mathit{createToken}()\;\mathbf{in}\;\eta[\![\, n \,]\!]\, \varepsilon\, \sigma\, t\, ()\, \kappa\; \mathbf{end}$

$\eta[\![\, l : \mathtt{opaque}\; (e) \,]\!]\, \varepsilon\, \sigma\, t\, v\, \kappa = \xi[\![\, e \,]\!]\, \varepsilon\, \sigma\, \kappa$

$\eta[\![\, l : \mathtt{callOp}\; (f) \,]\!]\, \varepsilon\, \sigma\, t\, v\, \kappa = \mathit{apply}(\mathit{push}(\mathsf{CallF}(f,\varepsilon),\kappa),(v,\sigma))$

$\eta[\![\, l : \mathtt{read}\; (x) \,]\!]\, \varepsilon\, \sigma\, t\, v\, \kappa = \xi[\![\, x \,]\!]\, \varepsilon\, \sigma\, (\mathit{push}(\mathsf{GetF}(),\kappa))$

$\eta[\![\, l : \mathtt{write}\; (x) \,]\!]\, \varepsilon\, \sigma\, t\, v\, \kappa = \xi[\![\, x \,]\!]\, \varepsilon\, \sigma\, (\mathit{push}(\mathsf{SetF}(v),\kappa))$

$\eta[\![\, l : \mathtt{decision}\; (e, n_1, n_2) \,]\!]\, \varepsilon\, \sigma\, t\, v\, \kappa = \xi[\![\, e \,]\!]\, \varepsilon\, \sigma(\mathit{push}(\mathsf{DecisionF}(n_1,n_2,\varepsilon,t,v),\kappa))$

$\eta[\![\, l : \mathtt{merge} \to n \,]\!]\, \varepsilon\, \sigma\, t\, v\, \kappa = \eta[\![\, n \,]\!]\, \varepsilon\, \sigma\, t\, v\, \kappa$

$\eta[\![\, l : \odot \,]\!]\, \varepsilon\, \sigma\, t\, v\, \kappa = \mathbf{let}\; b \,=\, \mathit{destroyAllTokens}()\;\mathbf{in}\;\kappa(v,\sigma)\; \mathbf{end}$

$\eta[\![\, a \to n \,]\!]\, \varepsilon\, \sigma\, t\, v\, \kappa = \eta[\![\, a \,]\!]\, \varepsilon\, \sigma\, t\, v\, (\mathit{push}(\mathsf{NodeSeqF}(n,\varepsilon,t),\kappa))$

$\eta[\![\, l \,]\!]\, \varepsilon\, \sigma\, t\, v\, \kappa = \eta[\![\, \varepsilon(l) \,]\!]\, \varepsilon\, \sigma\, t\, v\, \kappa$

Fig. 10.11 Frame-based semantics of activity diagrams

$\xi[\![\, c \,]\!]\, \varepsilon\, \sigma\, \kappa = \mathit{apply}(\kappa,(c,\sigma))$

$\xi[\![\, x \,]\!]\, \varepsilon\, \sigma\, \kappa = \mathit{apply}(\kappa,(\varepsilon(x),\sigma))$

$\xi[\![\, f(x) = e \,]\!]\, \varepsilon\, \sigma\, \kappa = \mathit{apply}(\kappa,(\langle x,e,\varepsilon'\rangle,\sigma))$

$\xi[\![\, f(e) \,]\!]\, \varepsilon\, \sigma\, \kappa = \xi[\![\, e \,]\!]\, \varepsilon\, \sigma\, (\mathit{push}(\mathsf{CallF}(f,\varepsilon),\; \kappa))$

$\xi[\![\, \mathtt{if}\; e_1\; \mathtt{then}\; e_2\; \mathtt{else}\; e_3 \,]\!]\, \varepsilon\, \sigma\, \kappa = \xi[\![\, e_1 \,]\!]\, \varepsilon\, \sigma\, (\mathit{push}(\mathsf{IfF}(e_2,e_3,\varepsilon),\kappa))$

$\xi[\![\, e_1; e_2 \,]\!]\, \varepsilon\, \sigma\, \kappa = \xi[\![\, e_1 \,]\!]\, \varepsilon\, \sigma\, (\mathit{push}(\mathsf{ExpSeqF}(e_2,\varepsilon),\kappa))$

$\xi[\![\, \mathtt{new}\; e \,]\!]\, \varepsilon\, \sigma\, \kappa = \xi[\![\, e \,]\!]\, \varepsilon\, \sigma\, (\mathit{push}(\mathsf{AllocF}(),\kappa))$

$\xi[\![\, !\, e \,]\!]\, \varepsilon\, \sigma\, \kappa = \xi[\![\, e \,]\!]\, \varepsilon\, \sigma\, (\mathit{push}(\mathsf{GetF}(),\kappa))$

$\xi[\![\, x :\, = e \,]\!]\, \varepsilon\, \sigma\, \kappa = \xi[\![\, e \,]\!]\, \varepsilon\, \sigma\, (\mathit{push}(\mathsf{RhsF}(x,\varepsilon),\kappa))$

Fig. 10.12 Frame-based semantics of Alf language

$\mathcal{F}[\![\, \mathsf{GetF}\ f\,]\!]\sigma\ v\ \kappa = apply(\kappa, (\sigma(v), \sigma))$

$\mathcal{F}[\![\, \mathsf{SetF}\ f\,]\!]\sigma\ v\ \kappa = apply(\kappa, ((), \sigma \dagger [v \mapsto f.val]))$

$\mathcal{F}[\![\, \mathsf{CallF}\ f\,]\!]\sigma\ v\ \kappa = \xi[\![\, (f.env)(f.fun)\,]\!](f.env)\ \sigma\ (push(\mathsf{ExecF}(v), \kappa))$

$\mathcal{F}[\![\, \mathsf{ExecF}\ f\,]\!]\sigma\ v\ \kappa = \xi[\![\, e\,]\!]\varepsilon' \dagger [x \mapsto f.arg]\ \sigma\ \kappa$ where $v = \langle x, e, \varepsilon' \rangle$

$\mathcal{F}[\![\, \mathsf{IfF}\ f\,]\!]\sigma\ v\ \kappa = \mathbf{if}\ (v)\ \mathbf{then}\ \xi[\![\, f.thenExp\,]\!](f.env)\ \sigma\ \kappa$
$\mathbf{else}\ \xi[\![\, f.elseExp\,]\!](f.env)\ \sigma\ \kappa$

$\mathcal{F}[\![\, \mathsf{DecisionF}\ f\,]\!]\sigma\ v\ \kappa = \mathbf{if}\ (v)\ \mathbf{then}\ \eta[\![\, f.thenNode\,]\!](f.env)\ \sigma\ (f.token)$
$(f.val)\ \kappa\ \mathbf{else}\ \eta[\![\, f.elseNode\,]\!](f.env)\ \sigma\ (f.token)\ (f.val)\ \kappa$

$\mathcal{F}[\![\, \mathsf{ExpSeqF}\ f\,]\!]\sigma\ v\ \kappa = \xi[\![\, f.nextExp\,]\!](f.env)\ \sigma\ \kappa$

$\mathcal{F}[\![\, \mathsf{NodeSeqF}\ f\,]\!]\sigma\ v\ \kappa = \eta[\![\, f.nextNode\,]\!](f.env)\ \sigma\ (f.token)\ v\ \kappa$

$\mathcal{F}[\![\, \mathsf{AllocF}\ f\,]\!]\sigma\ v\ \kappa = \mathbf{let}\ \ell = alloc(\sigma)\ \mathbf{in}\ apply(\kappa, (\ell, \sigma \dagger [\ell \mapsto v]))\ \mathbf{end}$

$\mathcal{F}[\![\, \mathsf{RhsF}\ f\,]\!]\sigma\ v\ \kappa = \xi[\![\, f.id\,]\!](f.env)\ \sigma\ (push(\mathsf{SetF}(v), \kappa))$

Fig. 10.13 Semantics of frames

The frame-based semantics of activity diagrams is presented in Fig. 10.11 and the frame-based semantics of Alf is presented in Fig. 10.12. Figure 10.13 shows the evaluation of the frames that are needed for computations. The primitive functions used in the semantics are the same as defined in the previous chapter.

10.5 Aspect Syntax and Semantics

In this section, we present our aspect extension to executable activity diagrams and elaborate its frame-based semantics. We start by presenting the aspect syntax. Then, we elaborate the matching and the weaving semantics.

Fig. 10.14 Proceed
Expression

e	$::=$	...	
		$\mid$ proceed (e)	**proceed**

```
type Aspect   = Advice list
type Advice   = {body : Exp; pc : Pointcut}
type Pointcut = GetPC | SetPC | CallPC | ExecPC | NotPC | AndPC
type GetPC    = {id : Identifier}
type SetPC    = {id : Identifier; val : Value}
type CallPC   = {id : Identifier; arg : Identifier}
type ExecPC   = {id : Identifier; arg : Identifier}
type NotPC    = {pc : Pointcut}
type AndPC    = {pc₁ : Pointcut; pc₂ : Pointcut}
```

Fig. 10.15 Aspect syntax

10.5.1 Aspect Syntax

An aspect includes a list of advice. An advice specifies actions to be performed when join points satisfying a particular pointcut are reached. An advice may also compute the original join point through a special expression named proceed. Hence, as shown in Fig. 10.14, we extend Alf syntax with an additional expression to denote the computation of the original join point with possibly a new argument e. The aspect syntax is denoted in Fig. 10.15.

Syntactically, an advice contains two parts (Fig. 10.15): (1) A body, which is an Alf expression, and (2) a pointcut, which designates a set of join points. An advice can be applied *before*, *after*, or *around* a join point. However, *before* and *after* advice can be expressed as *around* advice using the proceed expression. Hence, we consider all kinds of advice as *around* advice as this does not restrict the generality of the approach. We first consider basic pointcuts: GetPC, SetPC, CallPC, and ExecPC. The pointcut GetPC (respectively SetPC) picks out join points where the value of a variable is got from (respectively set to) the store. The pointcut CallPC (respectively ExecPC) picks out join points where a function is called (respectively executed).

10.5.2 Matching Semantics

Matching is a mechanism for identifying the join points targeted by the advice. In our approach, join points correspond to specific points in the execution of both activity diagrams and Alf expressions. However, since the semantics is in a frame-based style, both kinds of join points are continuation frames and arise naturally within the semantics. Therefore, our matching semantics examines whether a continuation frame satisfies a given pointcut or not, as shown in Fig. 10.16. In the following, we explain the matching rules.

$$
\begin{array}{l}
match\_pc : \text{Pointcut} \rightarrowtail \text{Frame} \rightarrow \text{Value} \rightarrow \text{Store} \rightarrowtail \text{Env} \rightarrow \text{Cont} \rightarrow \\
\text{Boolean} \\
\textbf{let } match\_pc\, p\, f\, v\, \sigma\, \varepsilon\, \kappa = \textbf{match } (p,f) \textbf{ with} \\
\quad (\text{GetPC } p, \text{GetF } f) \quad\Rightarrow \varepsilon(p.id) = v \\
\quad | \ (\text{SetPC } p, \text{SetF } f) \quad\Rightarrow \varepsilon(p.id) = v \\
\quad | \ (\text{CallPC } p, \text{CallF } f) \quad\Rightarrow p.id = f.fun \\
\quad | \ (\text{ExecPC } p, \text{ExecF } f) \Rightarrow \textbf{let } (v',\sigma') = \xi[\![\ \varepsilon(p.id)\ ]\!]\ \varepsilon\ \sigma\ \kappa \textbf{ in } v = v' \textbf{ end} \\
\quad | \ (\text{NotPC } p, \text{Frame } f) \ \Rightarrow \textbf{not } match\_pc(p.pc, f, v, \sigma, \varepsilon, \kappa) \\
\quad | \ (\text{AndPC } p, \text{Frame } f) \Rightarrow match\_pc(p.pc_1, f, v, \sigma, \varepsilon, \kappa) \textbf{ and} \\
\qquad\qquad\qquad\qquad\qquad\quad\ match\_pc(p.pc_2, f, v, \sigma, \varepsilon, \kappa) \\
\quad | \ \textbf{otherwise} \qquad\qquad\ \Rightarrow \textbf{false}
\end{array}
$$

Fig. 10.16 Matching semantics

Given a pointcut p, the current frame f, the current value v, a store σ, an environment ε, and a continuation κ, the matching semantics examines whether f matches p. Matching depends on three factors: the kind and the content of the frame f and the current value v that f receives. In the case of:

- GetPC, there is a match if f is a GetF frame and the location of the identifier given in p is equal to the location that f receives.
- SetPC, there is a match if f is a SetF frame and the location of the identifier given in p is equal to the location that f receives.
- CallPC, there is a match if f is a CallF frame and it holds a function identifier that is equal to the one given in p.
- ExecPC, there is a match if f is an ExecF frame and the evaluation of the function given in p is equal to the closure that f receives.
- NotPC, there is a match if f does not match the sub-pointcut of p.
- AndPC, there is a match if f matches both sub-pointcuts of p.

10.5.3 Weaving Semantics

The weaving semantics describes how to apply the matching advice at the identified join points. Since join points correspond to frames, advice body provides a means to modify the behavior of those frames. The weaving is performed automatically during the execution. Therefore, we redefine the apply function, as shown in Fig. 10.17, to take an aspect α and an environment ε into account. The weaving is done in two steps. When a frame is activated, we first check for a matching advice by calling the function $get\_matches$ (Fig. 10.18). If there is any applicable advice then the function $execute\_advice$, defined in Fig. 10.19, is called. Otherwise, the original computation is performed. In the following, we explain these two steps.

$apply$: Cont $\rightarrow$ (Value $\times$ Store) $\rightarrow$ Env $\rightarrow$ Aspect $\rightarrow$ (Value $\times$ Store)
let $apply \; \kappa \; (v, \sigma) \; \varepsilon \; \alpha =$ **match** κ **with**
$\quad [\,] \Rightarrow (v, \sigma)$
$\quad | \, f :: \kappa' \Rightarrow$ **let** $ms = get\_matches(f, v, \sigma, \varepsilon, \alpha, \kappa')$ **in**
$\qquad\qquad$ **if** $ms \;=\; [\,]$ **then** $\mathcal{F}[\![f]\!] \varepsilon \; \sigma \; v \; \alpha \; \kappa'$
$\qquad\qquad$ **else let** $argV =$ **match** f **with**
$\qquad\qquad\qquad$ SetF $f \qquad \Rightarrow f.val$
$\qquad\qquad\qquad | $ CallF $f \qquad \Rightarrow v$
$\qquad\qquad\qquad | $ ExecF $f \qquad \Rightarrow f.arg$
$\qquad\qquad\qquad | $ **otherwise** $\Rightarrow ()$
$\qquad\qquad\qquad$ **in** $execute\_advice(ms, f, argV, \sigma, \varepsilon, \alpha, \kappa')$
$\qquad\qquad$ **end**
$\quad$ **end**

Fig. 10.17 Redefined apply function

type MatchedAD $= \{arg :$ Identifier; $ad :$ Advice$\}$
$get\_matches \qquad :$ Frame $\rightarrow$ Value $\rightarrow$ Store $\rightarrow$ Env $\rightarrow$ Aspect $\rightarrow$ Cont
$\qquad\qquad\qquad\qquad \rightarrow$ MatchedAD list

let $get\_matches \, f \; v \; \sigma \; \varepsilon \; \alpha \; \kappa =$ **match** α **with**
$\quad [\,] \Rightarrow [\,]$
$\quad | ad :: \alpha' \Rightarrow$ **let** $p = ad.pc$ **in**
$\qquad\qquad$ **if** $match\_pc(p, f, v, \sigma, \varepsilon, \alpha, \kappa)$ **then**
$\qquad\qquad\quad$ **let** $arg =$ **match** p **with**
$\qquad\qquad\qquad$ SetPC $p \qquad\qquad \Rightarrow p.id$
$\qquad\qquad\qquad | $ CallPC $p \,|$ ExecPC $p \Rightarrow p.arg$
$\qquad\qquad\qquad | $ **otherwise** $\qquad \Rightarrow ()$
$\qquad\qquad\quad$ **in** MatchedAD$(arg, ad) :: get\_matches(f, v, \sigma, \varepsilon, \alpha', \kappa)$
$\qquad\qquad\quad$ **end**
$\qquad\qquad$ **else** $get\_matches(f, v, \sigma, \varepsilon, \alpha', \kappa)$
$\qquad\quad$ **end**

Fig. 10.18 Advice matching

10.5.3.1 Advice Matching

To get an applicable advice, we go through the aspect and check whether its enclosed
pointcuts match the current frame (Fig. 10.18). This is done by calling the function
$match\_pc$ defined previously in Fig. 10.16. In case there is a match, we return a
structure MatchedAD containing the advice itself and the pointcut arguments that
will pass values to the advice.

$execute\_advice$: MatchedAD list $\rightarrow$ Frame $\rightarrow$ Value $\rightarrow$ Store $\rightarrow$ Env
$\rightarrow$ Aspect $\rightarrow$ Cont $\rightarrow$ Result

let $execute\_advice\ ms\ f\ v\ \sigma\ \varepsilon\ \alpha\ \kappa =$ **match** ms **with**
$[\,] \Rightarrow apply(push(\mathsf{MarkerF}(),(push(f,\kappa))),(v,\sigma),\varepsilon,\alpha)$
$|m :: ms' \Rightarrow$ **let** $ad = m.ad$ **in**
$\quad\quad \xi[\![\ ad.body\ ]\!]\varepsilon \dagger [\&proceed \mapsto ms',\ \&jp \mapsto f, m.arg \mapsto v]\ \sigma\ \alpha\ \kappa$
end

Fig. 10.19 Advice execution

10.5.3.2 Advice Execution

Advice execution is shown in Fig. 10.19. It starts by evaluating the first applicable
advice. The remaining pieces of advice as well as the current frame are stored in the
environment by binding them to auxiliary variables $\&proceed$ and $\&jp$ respectively.
To evaluate the advice body, we define a new frame, AdvExecF, as follows:

type AdvExecF $= \{matches : \mathsf{MatchedAD}\ \mathtt{list};\ jp : \mathsf{Frame}\}$
$\mathcal{F}[\![\ \mathsf{AdvExecF}\ f\ ]\!]\varepsilon\ \sigma\ v\ \alpha\ \kappa = execute\_advice(f.matches, f.jp, v, \sigma, \varepsilon, \alpha, \kappa)$

The evaluation of the $\mathtt{proceed}$ expression is provided below. The value of its
argument is passed to the next advice or to the current join point if there is no further
advice. To execute the remaining pieces of advice, the frame AdvExecF is added to
the frame list.

$[\![\ \mathtt{proceed}\ (e)\ ]\!]\varepsilon\ \sigma\ \alpha\ \kappa = [\![\ e\ ]\!]\varepsilon\ \sigma\ \alpha\ (push(\mathsf{AdvExecF}(\varepsilon(\&proceed),\varepsilon(\&jp)),\kappa))$

When all the applicable pieces of advice are executed, the original computation,
i.e., the current frame is invoked. To avoid matching the currently matched frame
repeatedly, we introduce a new frame, MarkerF, which invokes the primary apply
function ($apply\_prim$).

type MarkerF $= \{\ \}$
$\mathcal{F}[\![\ \mathsf{MarkerF}\ f\ ]\!]\varepsilon\ \sigma\ v\ \alpha\ \kappa = apply\_prim(\kappa,(v,\sigma))$

10.6 Semantics of the Dataflow Pointcut

In this section, we explore the semantics of the $\mathtt{dflow}$ pointcut in xUML. As mentioned in the previous chapter, this pointcut is useful from a security perspective
since it can detect a considerable number of vulnerabilities related to information
flow, such as Cross-site Scripting (XSS) and SQL injection [86]. As defined below,
the $\mathtt{dflow}$ pointcut has a sub-pointcut pc and a unique tag that discriminates it from
other $\mathtt{dflow}$ pointcuts.

type DFlowPC $= \{pc : \mathsf{Pointcut};\ tag : \mathsf{Identifier}\}$

$\mathcal{F}[\![\ \mathsf{GetF}\ f\ ]\!]\varepsilon\ \gamma\ \sigma\ v\ \alpha\ \kappa = apply(\kappa, (\sigma(v), \sigma), \varepsilon, \gamma\dagger\,[\sigma(v) \mapsto \gamma(v)], \alpha)$

$\mathcal{F}[\![\ \mathsf{SetF}\ f\ ]\!]\varepsilon\ \gamma\ \sigma\ v\ \alpha\ \kappa = apply(\kappa, ((), \sigma\dagger\,[v \mapsto f.val]), \varepsilon, \gamma\dagger\,[v \mapsto \gamma(f.val)], \alpha)$

$\mathcal{F}[\![\ \mathsf{CallF}\ f\ ]\!]\varepsilon\ \gamma\ \sigma\ v\ \alpha\ \kappa = \xi[\![\ (f.env)(f.fun)\ ]\!](f.env)\gamma\ \sigma\ \alpha(push(\mathsf{ExecF}(v), \kappa))$

$\mathcal{F}[\![\ \mathsf{ExecF}\ f\ ]\!]\varepsilon\ \gamma\ \sigma\ v\ \alpha\ \kappa =$
$\xi[\![\ e\ ]\!](\varepsilon'\dagger\,[x \mapsto f.arg])\ (\gamma'\dagger\,[\varepsilon(x) \mapsto \gamma(f.arg)])\ \sigma\ \alpha\ (push(\mathsf{DflowF}(\gamma), \kappa))$
where $v = \langle x, e, \varepsilon', \gamma' \rangle$

$\mathcal{F}[\![\ \mathsf{IfF}\ f\ ]\!]\varepsilon\ \gamma\ \sigma\ v\ \alpha\ \kappa = \mathbf{if}\ (v)\ \mathbf{then}\ \xi[\![\ f.thenExp\ ]\!](f.env)\ \gamma\ \sigma\ \alpha\ \kappa$
$\mathbf{else}\ \xi[\![\ f.elseExp\ ]\!](f.env)\ \gamma\ \sigma\ \alpha\ \kappa$

$\mathcal{F}[\![\ \mathsf{DecisionF}\ f\ ]\!]\varepsilon\ \gamma\ \sigma\ v\ \alpha\ \kappa =$
$\mathbf{if}\ (v)\ \mathbf{then}\ \eta[\![\ f.thenNode\ ]\!](f.env)\ \gamma\ \sigma\ (f.token)\ (f.val)\ \alpha\ \kappa$
$\mathbf{else}\ \eta[\![\ f.elseNode\ ]\!](f.env)\ \gamma\ \sigma\ (f.token)\ (f.val)\ \alpha\ \kappa$

$\mathcal{F}[\![\ \mathsf{ExpSeqF}\ f\ ]\!]\varepsilon\ \gamma\ \sigma\ v\ \alpha\ \kappa = \xi[\![\ f.nextExp\ ]\!](f.env)\ \gamma\ \sigma\ \alpha\ \kappa$

$\mathcal{F}[\![\ \mathsf{NodeSeqF}\ f\ ]\!]\varepsilon\ \gamma\ \sigma\ v\ \alpha\ \kappa = \eta[\![\ f.nextNode\ ]\!](f.env)\ \gamma\ \sigma\ (f.token)\ v\ \alpha\ \kappa$

$\mathcal{F}[\![\ \mathsf{AllocF}\ f\ ]\!]\varepsilon\ \gamma\ \sigma\ v\ \alpha\ \kappa = \mathbf{let}\ \ell = alloc(\sigma)\ \mathbf{in}$
$apply(\kappa, (\ell, \sigma\dagger\,[\ell \mapsto v]), \varepsilon, \gamma\dagger\,[\ell \mapsto \gamma(v)], \alpha)\ \mathbf{end}$

$\mathcal{F}[\![\ \mathsf{RhsF}\ f\ ]\!]\varepsilon\ \gamma\ \sigma\ v\ \alpha\ \kappa = \xi[\![\ f.id\ ]\!](f.env)\ \gamma\ \sigma\ \alpha\ (push(\mathsf{SetF}(v), \kappa))$

$\mathcal{F}[\![\ \mathsf{AdvExecF}\ f\ ]\!]\varepsilon\ \gamma\ \sigma\ v\ \alpha\ \kappa = execute\_advice(f.matches, f.jp, v, \sigma, \varepsilon, \gamma, \alpha, \kappa)$

$\mathcal{F}[\![\ \mathsf{MarkerF}\ f\ ]\!]\varepsilon\ \gamma\ \sigma\ v\ \alpha\ \kappa = apply\_prim(\kappa, (v, \sigma))$

$\mathcal{F}[\![\ \mathsf{DFlowF}\ f\ ]\!]\varepsilon\ \gamma\ \sigma\ v\ \alpha\ \kappa = apply(\kappa, (v, \sigma), \varepsilon, f.tag\_env\dagger\,[v \mapsto getTags(\gamma)], \alpha)$

Fig. 10.20 Semantics of frames with the `dflow` pointcut

In order to track dependencies between values, we use a tagging environment γ that maps values to tags. Tag propagation is performed dynamically during the execution of the activity diagram and Alf expressions. In particular, this is done at the frames side (Fig. 10.20). Notice that the functions now take the tagging environment γ as an additional argument. Notice also that in the case of an ExecF frame, the closure $\langle x, e, \varepsilon', \gamma' \rangle$ is extended with a tagging environment γ' to capture the tags generated during the function execution. In addition, we define a marker frame DflowF that is used for tag propagation in the case of a function call. The DflowF frame stores a tagging environment before entering a function call and awaits the result of the call.

type DflowF = {*tag_env* : Env}

In the following, we explain the tag propagation rules for the affected frames:

- In the case of a GetF frame, the tags of the location v propagate to the value stored at that location.
- In the case of a SetF frame, the tags of the value of the right-hand side of an assignment propagate to the location of the assignment identifier.
- In the case of an ExecF frame, the tags of the argument value $f.arg$ propagate to the value of the variable x. In addition, the tags of the argument and the tags that are generated during the function execution propagate to the result of the function. For this reason, we use a DflowF frame to access the result of the function call and restore the tagging environment after returning from the call. The function $getTags(\gamma)$ used in $\mathcal{F}[\![$ DFlowF $f\ ]\!]$ retrieves all the tags stored in the tagging environment γ.
- In the case of an AllocF frame, the tags of v propagate to the created location ℓ.

The matching semantics of the dflow pointcut is presented in Fig. 10.21. A join point frame f matches a dflow pointcut that contains a pointcut pc and a tag t if: (1) The frame f matches the pointcut pc of the dflow pointcut, or (2) the set of tags

---

type JpF = GetF | SetF | CallF | ExecF
let *match_pc* $p\,f\ v\ \sigma\ \varepsilon\ \gamma\ \alpha\ \kappa$ = **match** (p,f) **with**
...
| (DFlowPC p, JpF f) $\Rightarrow$ **let** $(b,\gamma') = match\_pc(p.pc, f, v, \sigma, \varepsilon, \gamma, \alpha, \kappa)$ **in**
                   let $val =$ **match** f **with**
                      GetF $f\ \Rightarrow\ v$
                      SetF $f\ \Rightarrow\ f.val$
                      CallF $f\ \Rightarrow\ $ **let** $(v', \sigma') = \xi[\![\ \varepsilon(f.fun)\ ]\!]\varepsilon\ \gamma\ \sigma\ \alpha\ \kappa$
                               in
                                v'
                           end
                      ExecF $f\ \Rightarrow\ v$
                  in
                  if (b)
                  then $(\texttt{true}, \gamma'\ \dagger\ [val \mapsto \gamma'(val) \cup \{p.tag\}])$
                  else let $val' =$ **match** f **with**
                          CallF $f\ \ \Rightarrow\ v$
                          otherwise $\ \Rightarrow\ val$
                      in $(p.tag \in \gamma'(val'), \gamma')$
                      end
                end
              end

Fig. 10.21 Matching semantics of the dflow pointcut

of the value that the frame f awaits (captured by the variable val') contains the tag t. In case a frame f matches the pointcut pc of the dflow pointcut, the tag t propagates to the value associated with the frame f (captured by the variable val).

Example To illustrate the dflow pointcut in xUML, let us consider the *Search-Page* activity diagram presented in Fig. 10.22. The activity starts by accepting a search request. Then, the searched phrase is extracted by the action *GetQuery*. If the requested phrase is empty, an error message is generated. Otherwise, the action *Search* is executed and the result message, containing both the requested phrase and the search result, is generated. Finally, the generated message is printed on the web page.

The presented example is vulnerable to XSS attacks since the untrusted input, received from the user, has not been sanitized before being placed into the contents of the web page. Therefore, it enables an attacker to inject malicious scripts into the web page and reveal confidential information. To fix this vulnerability, we need to sanitize the untrusted input and all the data that originated from it before printing them on the web page. The dflow pointcut can be remarkably used to address this problem. Indeed, the dflow pointcut, dflow(p), picks out all points in the activity execution where values are dependent on the join points that are previously picked out by p. Therefore, by defining pointcut p as CallPC(*GetQuery*), the pointcut dflow(p)

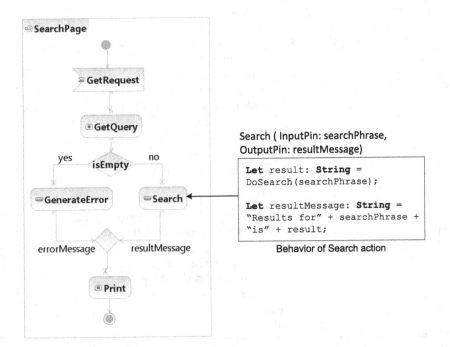

Fig. 10.22 Search page activity diagram

picks all join points that are originated from the search phrase, which is the user input. Below, we provide a sanitizing aspect for fixing the discussed vulnerability.

Aspect (Pointcuts and Advice):

$$
\begin{aligned}
\mathsf{CallPC}\ p_1 &= \{id = GetQuery;\ arg = x\} \\
\mathsf{DFlowPC}\ p_2 &= \{pc = p_1;\ tag = t\} \\
\mathsf{CallPC}\ p_3 &= \{id = Print;\ arg = y\} \\
\mathsf{AndPC}\ p_4 &= \{pc_1 = p_2;\ pc_2 = p_3\} \\
\mathsf{Advice}\ a &= \{body = \texttt{proceed}\ (Sanitize(y));\ pc = p_4\}
\end{aligned}
$$

Briefly, the aspect captures points where the function *Print* is called with an argument that is originated from the user input. The aspect first sanitizes the argument by calling the function *Sanitize* and then calls the function *Print* with the sanitized argument. The join points targeted by this aspect are matched based on the following:

- The call to the function *GetQuery* (Fig. 10.22) matches the pointcut p_2 since it matches the sub-pointcut p_1. Consequently, the tag t of the dflow pointcut (p_2) is added to the tagging environment of the function *GetQuery*, and is given to the result of the function evaluation.
- Then, if the search phrase is not empty then the action *Search* and its enclosing Alf code are executed. According to the tag propagation rules for assignment and call operation expressions, the values of the variables *result* and *resultMessage*, used in the Alf expressions, get the tag t.
- Subsequently, the call to the function *Print* matches p_4 since it matches both sub-pointcuts of p_4 (p_2 and p_3). More precisely, the call to the function *Print* matches the pointcut p_3 as p_3 is a call to the function *Print*. In addition, the call to the function *Print* matches the pointcut p_2 as the value of its argument (*resultMessage*) has the tag t. Therefore, the sanitizing advice will be woven at this point.

10.7 Related Work on Aspect Semantics in xUML

Existing AOM approaches that handle xUML models are presented from a practical perspective [92, 105, 213]. In addition, they mainly focus on providing a framework for executing the woven model for the purposes of simulation and verification. In the following, we provide an overview of these approaches.

Fuentes and Sánchez [92] have proposed a dynamic weaver for aspect-oriented executable UML models. A UML profile, called AOEM, is elaborated to support aspect-oriented concepts. Advice pieces are modeled as activity diagrams and injected into the base model as structured activities. Pointcuts, that intercept message sending and receiving, are specified using sequence diagrams. The weaving process is defined as a chain of model transformations. However, no model transformation language is used. Instead, Java and standards, like XSLT and XPath, are used to directly manipulate the XMI representation of the models. In addition, this approach does not support action languages.

Zhang et al. [213] have presented Motorola WEAVR, a tool for weaving aspects into executable UML state machines. Motorola WEAVR is one of the stable weavers that is developed in an industrial environment. In addition, it concentrates on executable modeling, and therefore it is more suited to detailed design. Motorola WEAVR supports two types of join points that are action and transition. Aspect interference is handled by allowing precedence relationships to be specified at the modeling level. However, this weaver is based on the Telelogic TAU G2 [10] implementation. Therefore, it is tool-dependent and not portable. In addition, the graphical representation of the woven models is not supported by the tool; the woven models cannot be manually inspected.

Jackson et al. [105] have introduced an approach for specifying and weaving executable class diagrams and sequence diagrams. This weaver is based on Kermeta action language [143] for defining precise behaviors and providing executability. However, it only supports weaving of executable class diagrams, as all behavioral diagrams, such as sequence diagrams, are defined as methods. Furthermore, Kermeta has been designed for specifying meta-model behaviors and it is not as expressive as UML action languages.

10.8 Conclusion

In this chapter, we have presented a formal semantics for aspect matching and weaving in xUML models expressed using the standard Alf language. We have elaborated frame-based CPS semantics since this style of semantics allows formalizing aspect-oriented mechanisms in a precise and elegant way. In fact, one can easily notice that CPS and defunctionalization make join points explicit and facilitate aspect matching and weaving. In addition, by expressing the semantics of activity diagrams and Alf constructs in a frame-based representation, the matching and the weaving processes are performed in a unified way for both activity diagrams and Alf constructs.

We have addressed useful pointcuts from a security perspective that pick out join points where functions are called and executed, and where variables are get and set. These pointcuts are useful since they detect important points, where security mechanisms, such as, authorization, encryption, and decryption, may be added *before*, *after*, or *around* these points. In addition, we have elaborated semantics for the dataflow pointcut. This pointcut identifies join points based on data dependencies between values, and therefore allowing the detection of vulnerabilities related to information flow.

This contribution is very useful in the field of software security hardening since it targets matching and weaving on precise and detailed specifications that are, at the same time, high-level and independent of any programming language. Such a semantics allows capturing more join points that cannot be easily identified on high-level and abstract UML models. Therefore, numerous flaws can get resolved before entering the implementation phase, which significantly reduces costs and leads to more trustworthy software. The proposed semantics is a first step towards a complete semantic framework, where more security-related pointcuts can be addressed together with their semantic foundations.

Chapter 11
Conclusion

With the increasing complexity and pervasiveness of today's software systems, security should be integrated to software since the first stages of the development life cycle. In this context, model-driven engineering is a promising approach to early software security hardening. This approach aims at alleviating the complexity of software development by shifting the development efforts from the code level to the modeling level, where models are first-class entities and are considered in every step of the software development life cycle. Moreover, because of the pervasive nature of security concerns and the lack of security knowledge among developers, there is a clear need for a systematic way to integrate those concerns into the software development process. In this respect, aspect-oriented modeling is the most appropriate paradigm. Indeed, by separating security concerns from the main functionalities, software developers can make use of the expertise of security specialists and systematically integrate security solutions into design models. In this setting, we have elaborated an AOM framework for specifying and systematically integrating security hardening solutions into UML design models.

For the specification of security aspects, we have devised, in Chap. 6, a UML profile allowing the specification of common aspect-oriented primitives and covering the main UML diagrams, i.e., class diagrams, state machine diagrams, sequence diagrams, and activity diagrams. The proposed profile allows specification of security solutions for high-level security requirements, such as, confidentiality, integrity, authentication, access control, etc. It supports adaptations, which add new elements *before*, *after*, or *around* join points, and remove existing elements. In addition, we have defined a UML-specific pointcut language that provides high-level and user-friendly primitives to designate UML join points. Regarding the join point model, in activity diagrams, we consider not only executable nodes but also various control nodes to allow modeling crosscutting concerns that are needed with alternatives, loops, exceptions, and multi-threaded applications. In state machine diagrams, we consider not only static states, but also we capture states that dynamically depend on the triggered transitions. For purposes of reuse, the aspects can be designed as generic solutions, then specialized to a particular application.

© Springer International Publishing Switzerland 2015
D. Mouheb et al., *Aspect-Oriented Security Hardening of UML Design Models*,
DOI 10.1007/978-3-319-16106-8_11

Furthermore, we have designed and implemented, in Chap. 7, a weaving framework to specialize the security aspects and automatically inject them into base models. The weaver covers all the diagrams that are supported in our approach. In addition, it supports all kinds of adaptations that can be specified using our AOM profile presented in Chap. 6. The adoption of a model-to-model transformation to implement the weaving process helped in generating the weaving rules in an automatic way without having to manipulate the internal representation of UML models. Moreover, the adoption of the standard OCL language for evaluating the pointcuts allowed us to match a wide set of join points belonging to various UML diagrams. Besides, the adoption of the standard QVT language for implementing the adaptation rules extends portability of the designed weaver to all tools supporting QVT language. To get the full advantages of this comprehensive and portable framework, we have developed it as a plug-in to IBM-RSA tool. To demonstrate the viability and the relevance of our framework, we have used it to experiment adding various security mechanisms in mid-size open source projects such as SIP communicator and OpenSAF. The supported security mechanisms are those related to high-level security requirements such as access control, authentication, authorization, etc. Finally, to validate the correctness of our weaving methods, we can provide the woven model, together with the needed security properties, to verification and validation tools [69, 126], that will verify the woven model against the specified security properties.

From a theoretical point of view, our contribution is two fold: First, we have elaborated formal specifications, in an operational style, for matching and weaving in UML activity diagrams. The purpose of elaborating this semantics is to derive algorithms for implementing our weaving adaptations presented in Chap. 7. In this respect, a syntax of activity diagrams together with their corresponding adaptations have been defined to express the matching and the weaving semantic rules. Afterwards, we have derived algorithms for matching and weaving and proved the correctness and the completeness of these algorithms with respect to the defined semantic rules. To the best of our knowledge, this is the first contribution in handling formal specifications for adaptation weaving, specifically for *around* adaptations with or without *proceed*. We have elaborated the semantics for activity diagrams mainly because of their richness in terms of actions and control nodes that can be captured as join points. However, a formal semantics for matching and weaving for the other diagrams, i.e., class diagrams, state machine diagrams, and sequence diagrams, can be provided in the same vein as for activity diagrams.

Second, to be able to address advanced security concerns such as information flow vulnerabilities, we have extended our weaving framework to include xUML models expressed using the standard Alf language. Indeed, xUML allows to specify detailed and precise behaviors that include variables, assignments, operation calls, etc. We have elaborated a semantics for matching and weaving in xUML following a CPS/frame-based style because this style of semantics provides a concise, accurate, and elegant description of aspect-oriented mechanisms. Indeed, CPS and defunctionalization make join points explicit, and therefore allow the aspect matching and weaving in a straightforward manner. In addition, by expressing the semantics of activity diagrams and Alf language in a frame-based representation, the matching and the weaving processes are performed in a unified way for both activity diagram elements and Alf expressions. We have addressed useful pointcuts from a security perspective that pick out join points where functions are called and executed, and where variables are get and set. In addition, we have elaborated semantics for flow-based pointcuts, which are useful to detect and fix vulnerabilities related to information flow. Using a CPS/frame-based style simplified greatly the specification of the matching and the weaving semantics for this kind of pointcuts, which is an advantage compared to expressing them in an operational style, where lots of implementation details need to be specified. Regarding the implementation of the matching and the weaving in xUML, it is not addressed in this book mainly because of the lack of tools that support the execution of Alf expressions.

In the following, we evaluate our framework from different perspectives as follows:

- *User Friendliness*: To facilitate the use of our framework, we have proposed a pointcut language in a textual representation to designate join points in a user-friendly way. It is important to mention here that the process of translating the textual pointcuts into OCL is completely automatic and without any user intervention. On the other hand, the added or the replaced-by elements, specified by adaptations, are graphically represented using the concrete syntax of the modeling language. The use of the concrete syntax makes our framework broadly applicable because no experience with meta-modeling is required from developers. This facilitates using the framework by modelers who are unlikely to have enough knowledge about UML abstract syntax. Moreover, the framework allows visualizing the woven model easily.
- *Formality*: We have explored two styles of semantics for the formalization of the matching and the weaving processes. First, we used a structured operational style, in which our semantics is defined using deductive proof systems. Second, we used a denotational style, in which our semantics is defined using CPS and defunctionalization. Our main target is the activity diagram. However, the formal definitions for the other diagrams can be provided in the same vein that we provide them for activity diagrams. Klein et al. [118] have proposed formal definitions for matching and weaving. However, their approach is limited to the detection of join points for basic or combined sequence diagrams. Generic AOM approaches based on graph transformation [138, 206] have a formal underpinning, but this is an advantage of using graph transformations.
- *Expressiveness*: Our framework is more expressive than previous ones, in the sense that it supports a large set of modifications of UML models since it views model weaving as simply as model transformation. Moreover, the elements allowed as join points are more than in many previous approaches. However, the approaches that are based on graph transformation, such as MATA [206] and GeKo [138], are considered more expressive because they allow any modeling element to be a join point. Another point to mention is that MATA supports sequence pointcuts, that is, an aspect may match against a sequence of messages or a sequence of transitions.

We do not address this pointcut in this book. However, this can be achieved in the future by instrumenting OCL to identify specific sequences of model elements.

- *Extensibility and Portability*: In our framework, aspect adaptations are specified using a UML profile. This mechanism allows extending UML metamodel elements, by means of stereotypes, without changing UML metamodel. Therefore, new AOM extensions for security hardening can be easily added to our framework by extending our AOM profile with the needed stereotypes and their associated tagged values. In addition, since profiles are standard UML extensions, almost any UML modeling framework can store and manipulate them. Moreover, the defined architecture for the weaving framework facilitates the extension of the transformation tool to support a wider range of UML diagrams. Indeed, new transformations can be easily plugged-in without going through the hassle of modifying and altering the existing architecture. Additionally, since QVT mapping rules are defined based on UML meta-elements, our framework is portable to any UML modeling framework and to other tools supporting QVT language [3–5, 8, 9, 11].

- *Reusability*: In our framework, security aspects can be designed as generic templates independently of the application specificities. Generic aspects are important to define libraries of reusable aspects for special purposes such as security hardening. Since generic pointcuts, as part of generic aspects, have no concrete specification, an aspect needs to be specialized to a specific application before it can be woven into base models. To this end, we have provided a weaving interface that exposes the generic pointcuts to the developer. After mapping all the generic pointcuts to their corresponding elements in the base model, the application-dependent aspect is automatically generated by the defined framework. It is important to mention here that aspects in our framework can be generic and specific as well. The modeler chooses the kind of aspects that fulfils his/her needs.

The work presented in this book can be further pursued by identifying and elaborating new AOM extensions, i.e., pointcut and advice primitives, together with their semantic foundations, for security hardening. An example of such extensions is tracematches [36]. Tracematches support matching a sequence of consecutive events rather than individual join points. At the modeling level, this pointcut can help in capturing, for instance, a sequence of messages in sequence diagrams or a sequence of transitions in state machine diagrams. Tracematches are important from a security perspective because some vulnerabilities involve a sequence of events, such as transactions and race conditions [47]. Once new primitives have been identified, our AOM framework can be extended with the newly-defined pointcuts and advices. This means extending our AOM profile with the needed stereotypes along with their associated tagged values, as well as extending our weaving framework with the needed transformation rules. It is also important to explore the definition of AOM security primitives for executable models, and in particular, in UML action languages. Furthermore, the work that we did on UML can be extended to other modeling languages, such as Systems Modeling Language (SysML) [147], to address security hardening in systems engineering.

From a theoretical perspective, our framework can be extended by elaborating the matching and the weaving semantics in other UML diagrams, such as, class diagrams, sequence diagrams, and state machine diagrams. In addition, we have seen that CPS/frame-based style is an elegant and interesting venue for the formalization of aspect-oriented constructs. Therefore, it is important to investigate the formalization of other security primitives using this style of semantics. Another interesting work is to explore the equivalence between CPS/frame-based semantics and the practical techniques that are used to implement matching and weaving, such as the shadow concept in AOP [98].

References

1. ATLAS Transformation Language (ATL) (2012), Available at: https://eclipse.org/atl/. Last visited: Nov 2012
2. Jitsi (formerly SIP Communicator) (2012), Available at: https://jitsi.org/. Last visited: Nov 2012
3. Medini QVT (2012), Available at: http://projects.ikv.de/qvt/. Last visited: Nov 2012
4. Model To Model (M2M) (2012), Available at: http://www.eclipse.org/m2m/. Last visited: Nov 2012
5. ModelMorf Registration Form (2012), Available at: http://121.241.184.234/trddc_website/ModelMorf/ModelMorf.htm. Last visited: Nov 2012
6. Open Architecture Ware (2012), Available at: http://www.itemis.com/itemis-ag/services-and-solutions/eclipse-modeling/language=en/35056/openarchitectureware-oaw. Last visited: Aug 2012
7. OptimalJ (2010), Available at: http://en.wikipedia.org/wiki/OptimalJ. Last visited: May 2010
8. SmartQVT (2012), Available at: http://sourceforge.net/projects/smartqvt/. Last visited: Nov 2012
9. Software Architecture Design, Visual UML & Business Process Modeling—From Borland (2012), Available at: http://www.borland.com/us/products/together/. Last visited: Nov 2012
10. Telelogic TAU G2 (2012), Available at: http://www-01.ibm.com/support/docview.wss?uid=swg21380572. Last visited: Nov 2012
11. UMT-QVT Homepage (2012), Available at: http://umt-qvt.sourceforge.net/. Last visited: Nov 2012
12. Make Your Software Behave: Preventing Buffer Overflows (2010), Available at: http://www.ibm.com/developerworks/library/s-overflows/
13. MSC34-C, Do Not Use Deprecated and Obsolete Functions—Secure Coding—CERT Secure Coding (2010), Available at: https://www.securecoding.cert.org/confluence/display/c/VOID+MSC34-C.+Do+not+use+deprecated+and+obsolete+functions
14. Service Availability Forum (2010), Available at: http://www.saforum.org/
15. The Open Service Availability Framework (OpenSAF) (2010), Available at: http://www.opensaf.org/
16. OCaml for Scientists (2011), Available at: http://caml.inria.fr/pub/docs/manual-ocaml
17. Kermeta—Breathe life into your metamodels (2012), Available at: http://www.kermeta.org/
18. CERT C Secure Coding Standard (2009), Available at: https://www.securecoding.cert.org/confluence/display/c/CERT+C+Coding+Standard, June 2009
19. CERT C++ Secure Coding Standard (2009), Available at: https://www.securecoding.cert.org/confluence/pages/viewpage.action?pageId=637, June 2009

© Springer International Publishing Switzerland 2015
D. Mouheb et al., *Aspect-Oriented Security Hardening of UML Design Models*,
DOI 10.1007/978-3-319-16106-8

20. Law of Demeter (2009), Available at: http://www.c2.com/cgi/wiki?LawOfDemeter, June 2009
21. The CERT Sun Microsystems Secure Coding Standard for Java (2009), Available at: http://www.oracle.com/technetwork/java/seccodeguide-139067.html, June 2009
22. Community:JBoss.org:Community (2009), Available at: https://developer.jboss.org/, Mar 2009
23. Aspicere2, more AOP for C (2009), Available at: http://mcis.polymtl.ca/~bram/aspicere/, Oct 2009
24. US Department of Homeland Security Coding Rules (2009), Available at: https://buildsecurityin.us-cert.gov/articles/knowledge/coding-practices, Oct 2009
25. Java Metadata Interface 1.0. Sun Microsystems, Inc. (2010), Available at: http://java.sun.com/products/jmi/. Last visited: Apr 2010
26. M.S. Ager, O. Danvy, J. Midtgaard, A functional correspondence between monadic evaluators and abstract machines for languages with computational effects. Theor. Comput. Sci. **342**, 4–28 (2005)
27. G.J. Ahn, M.E. Shin, UML-based representation of role-based access control, in *Proceedings of the 9th IEEE International Workshop on Enabling Technologies: Infrastructure for Collaborative Enterprises (WETICE'2000)* (IEEE Computer Society, Gaithersburg, 2000), pp. 195–200
28. O. Aldawud, T. Elrad, A. Bader, UML profile for aspect-oriented modeling, in *Proceedings of the OOPSLA Workshop on Aspect Oriented Programming* (2001)
29. O. Aldawud, T. Elrad, A. Bader, UML profile for aspect-oriented software development, in *Proceedings of the 3rd International Workshop on Aspect-Oriented Modeling with UML (AOM@AOSD'03)* (2003)
30. C. Alexander, S. Ishikawa, M. Silverstein, *A Pattern Language: Towns, Buildings, Construction* (Oxford University Press, New York, 1977)
31. M. Alférez, N. Amálio, S. Ciraci, F. Fleurey, J. Kienzle, J. Klein, M.E. Kramer, S. Mosser, G. Mussbacher, E.E. Roubtsova, G. Zhang, Aspect-oriented model development at different levels of abstraction, in *ECMFA*. Lecture Notes in Computer Science, vol. 6698, ed. by R.B. France, J.M. Küster, B. Bordbar, R.F. Paige (Springer, Berlin, 2011), pp. 361–376
32. K. Alghathbar, D. Wijeskera, Consistent and complete access control policies in use cases, in *Proceedings of the 6th International Conference UML 2003. Model Languages and Applications*, San Francisco, CA, USA, pp. 373–387 (2003)
33. D. AlHadidi, N. Belblidia, M. Debbabi, Security crosscutting concerns and AspectJ, in *Proceedings of the 2006 International Conference on Privacy, Security and Trust (PST'06)* (ACM, New York, 2006), p. 1
34. D. Alhadidi, N. Belblidia, M. Debbabi, P. Bhattacharya, An AOP extended lambda-calculus, in *Proceedings of the Fifth IEEE International Conference on Software Engineering and Formal Methods (SEFM'07)* (IEEE Computer Society, Washington, 2007), pp. 183–194
35. D. Alhadidi, A. Boukhtouta, N. Belblidia, M. Debbabi, P. Bhattacharya, The dataflow pointcut: a formal and practical framework, in *Proceedings of the 8th ACM International Conference on Aspect-Oriented Software Development (AOSD'09)* (ACM, New York, 2009), pp. 15–26
36. C. Allan, P. Avgustinov, A.S. Christensen, L. Hendren, S. Kuzins, O. Lhoták, O. de Moor, D. Sereni, G. Sittampalam, J. Tibble, Adding trace matching with free variables to AspectJ. SIGPLAN Not. **40**, 345–364 (2005)
37. Ch. Allan, P. Avgustinov, A.S. Christensen, L. Hendren, S. Kuzins, O. Lhoták, O. de Moor, D. Sereni, G. Sittampalam, J. Tibble, Adding trace matching with free variables to AspectJ, in *Proceedings of the 20th Annual ACM SIGPLAN Conference on Object-Oriented Programming, Systems, Languages, and Applications, OOPSLA'05* (ACM, New York, 2005), pp. 345–364
38. J.H. Allen, S. Barnum, R.J. Elison, G. McGraw, N.R. Mead, *Software Security Engineering: A Guide for Project Managers* (Addison-Wesley Professional, Boston, 2008)
39. A.W. Appel, *Compiling with Continuations* (Cambridge University Press, New York, 2006)

40. Aspect-Oriented Modeling Workshop (2012), Available at: http://www.aspect-modeling.org/. Last visited: Nov 2012

41. Aspect-Oriented Software Development (2010), Available at: www.aosd.net. Last visited: May 2010

42. A. Bandara, H. Shinpei, J. Jurjens, H. Kaiya, A. Kubo, R. Laney, H. Mouratidis, A. Nhlabatsi, B. Nuseibeh, Y. Tahara, T. Tun, H. Washizaki, N. Yoshioka, Y. Yu, Security patterns: comparing modeling approaches. Technical report, Department of Computing, Faculty of Mathematics, Computing and Technology. The Open University (2009)

43. E. Barra, G. Genova, J. Llorens, An approach to aspect modelling with UML 2.0, in *Proceedings of the 5th International Workshop on Aspect-Oriented Modeling (AOM'04)*, Lisbon, Portugal (2004)

44. M. Basch, A. Sanchez, Incorporating aspects into the UML, in *Proceedings of the 3rd International Workshop on Aspect-Oriented Modeling (AOM'03)*, Boston, MA (2003)

45. D. Bell, L. LaPadula, Secure computer systems: mathematical foundations model. M74-244, Mitre Corporation (1975)

46. M. Bishop, How attackers break programs and how to write programs more securely, in *Proceedings of SANS 2002 Annual Conference* (2002)

47. M. Bishop, M. Dilger, Checking for race conditions in file accesses. Comput. Syst. **9**(2), 131–152 (Spring 1996)

48. B. Blakley, C. Heath, Members of the open group security forum. Security design patterns. Technical Report G031, Open Group (2004)

49. R. Bodkin, Enterprise security aspects, in *Proceedings of the 4th Workshop on AOSD Technology for Application-Level Security* (2004)

50. A. Bogdanov, S.J. Garland, N.A. Lynch, Mechanical translation of I/O automaton specifications into first-order logic, in *Proceedings of the 22nd IFIP WG 6.1 International Conference* Houston, pp. 364–368 (2002)

51. M. Brambilla, *Model-Driven Software Engineering (MDE)* (Morgan & Claypool Publishers, San Rafael, 2012)

52. G. Brose, M. Koch, K.P. Lohr, Integrating access control design into the software development process, in *Proceedings of the 6th Biennial World Conference on the Integrated Design and Process Technology (IDPT'02)*, Pasadena, CA (2002)

53. G. Bruns, R. Jagadeesan, A. Jeffrey, J. Riely, μABC: a minimal aspect calculus, in *Proceedings of the International Conference on Concurrency Theory*. LNCS, vol. 3170 (Springer, London, 2004), pp. 209–224

54. M.T. Chan, L.F. Kwok, Integrating security design into the software development process for E-commerce systems. Inf. Manag. Comput. Secur. **9**(3), 112–122 (2001)

55. C. Chavez, C. Lucena, A metamodel for aspect-oriented modeling, in *Proceedings of the 1st International Workshop on Aspect-Oriented Modeling with UML (AOM'02)*, Enschede, The Netherlands (2002)

56. M.H. Chunlei, C. Wang, L. Zhang, Toward a reusable and generic security aspect library, in *Proceedings of the AOSD Technology for Application-level Security (AOSDSEC'04)* (2004)

57. A. Church, A formulation of the simple theory of types. J. Symb. Log. **5**(2), 56–68 (1940)

58. Cigital, Case study: finding defects early yields enormous savings (White paper) (2003)

59. S. Clarke, E. Baniassad, *Aspect-Oriented Analysis and Design: The Theme Approach* (Addison-Wesley, Boston, 2005)

60. C. Clifton, G.T. Leavens, MiniMAO: an imperative core language for studying aspect-oriented reasoning. Sci. Comput. Program. **63**(3), 321–374 (2006)

61. Y. Coady, G. Kiczales, M. Feeley, G. Smolyn, Using AspectC to improve the modularity of path-specific customization in operating system code, in *Proceedings of Foundations of Software Engineering* (ACM, New York, 2001), pp. 88–98

62. Z. Cui, L. Wang, X. Li, D. Xu, Modeling and integrating aspects with UML activity diagrams, in *Proceedings of the Symposium on Applied Computing (SAC'09)*, ed. by S.Y. Shin, S. Ossowski (ACM, New York, 2009), pp. 430–437

63. K. Czarnecki, S. Helsen, Classification of model transformation approaches, in *OOPSLA'03 Workshop on Generative Techniques in the Context of Model-Driven Architecture*, Anaheim, CA, USA (2003)

64. K. Czarnecki, S. Helsen, Feature-based survey of model transformation approaches. IBM Syst. J. **45**(3), 621–645 (2006)

65. L. Dai, K. Cooper, Modeling and analysis of non-functional requirements as aspects in a UML based architecture design, in *Proceedings of the 6th International Conference on Software Engineering, Artificial Intelligence, Networking and Parallel/Distributed Computing and First ACIS International Workshop on Self-Assembling Wireless Networks* (IEEE Computer Society, Washington, 2005), pp. 178–183

66. D.S. Dantas, D. Walker, G. Washburn, S. Weirich, AspectML: a polymorphic aspect-oriented functional programming language. ACM Trans. Program. Lang. Syst. **30**, 14:1–14:60 (2008)

67. O. Danvy, A. Filinski, Abstracting control, in *Proceedings of the 1990 ACM Conference on LISP and Functional Programming, LFP'90* (ACM, New York, 1990), pp. 151–160

68. O. Danvy, L.R. Nielsen, Defunctionalization at work, in *Proceedings of the 3rd ACM SIGPLAN International Conference on Principles and Practice of Declarative Programming, PPDP'01* (ACM, New York, 2001), pp. 162–174

69. M. Debbabi, F. Hassaïne, Y. Jarraya, A. Soeanu, L. Alawneh, *Verification and Validation in Systems Engineering—Assessing UML/SysML Design Models* (Springer, Berlin, 2010)

70. S. Demathieu, C. Griffin, S. Sendall, Model Transformation with the IBM Model Transformation Framework (2012), Available at: http://www.ibm.com/developerworks/rational/library/05/503_sebas/. Last visited: Nov 2012

71. S.D. Djoko, R. Douence, P. Fradet, D. Le Botlan, CASB: Common Aspect Semantics Base—AOSD Europe Deliverable No. 41 (2006)

72. T. Doan, L.D. Michel, S.A. Demurjian, A formal framework for secure design and constraint checking in UML, in *Proceedings of the International Symposium on Secure Software Engineering (ISSSE'06)*, Washington, DC (2006)

73. C. Dougherty, K. Sayre, R.C. Seacord, D. Svoboda, K. Togashi, Secure design patterns. Technical Report, CMU/SEI-2009-TR-010, ESC-TR-2009-010, Software Engineering Institute, Carnegie Mellon University (2009)

74. C. Dutchyn, Specializing continuations: a model for dynamic join points, in *Proceedings of the 6th International Workshop on Foundations of Aspect-Oriented Languages* (ACM, New York, 2007), pp. 45–57

75. C. Dutchyn, G. Kiczales, H. Masuhara, Aspect SandBox (2002), Available at: http://www.cs.ubc.ca/labs/spl/projects/asb.html

76. C. Dutchyn, D.B. Tucker, S. Krishnamurthi, Semantics and scoping of aspects in higher-order languages. Sci. Comput. Program. **63**, 207–239 (2006)

77. T. Elrad, R.E. Filman, A. Bader, Aspect-oriented programming: introduction. Commun. ACM **44**(10), 29–32 (2001)

78. P. Epstein, R.S. Sandhu, Towards a UML based approach to role engineering, in *Proceedings of the 4th ACM Workshop on Role-Based Access Control* (ACM, New York, 1999), pp. 135–143

79. J. Evermann, A meta-level specification and profile for AspectJ in UML. J. Object Technol. **6**(7), 27–49 (2007)

80. M. Fabro, J. Bezivin, F. Jouault, E. Breton, G. Gueltas, AMW: a generic model weaver, in *Proceedings of the 1ère Journée sur l'Ingénierie Dirigée par les Modèles (IDM'05)* (2005)

81. E.B. Fernández, A methodology for secure software design, in *Proceedings of the International Conference on Software Engineering Research and Practice (SERP'04)*, pp. 130–136 (2004)

82. E.B. Fernandez, R. Warrier, Remote authenticator/authorizer, in *Proceedings of the 10th Conference on Pattern Languages of Programs (PLoP'03)* (2003)

83. D. Ferraiolo, R. Sandhu, S. Gavrila, R. Kuhn, R. Chandramouli, Proposed NIST standard for role-based access control. ACM Trans. Inf. Syst. Secur. **4**(3), 224–274 (2001)

84. M.J. Fischer, Lambda calculus schemata, in *Proceedings of the ACM Conference on Proving Assertions About Programs* (ACM, New York, 1972), pp. 104–109

85. F. Fleurey, B. Baudry, R. France, S. Ghosh, A generic approach for automatic model composition, in *Proceedings of the Workshop on Aspect-Oriented Modeling (AOM'07)* (Springer, Berlin, 2007), pp. 7–15

86. Fortify, Software Security, Protect Your Software at the Source (2011), Available at: http://www.fortify.com/resoures/download-rats.htm

87. J.C. Foster, V. Osipov, N. Bhalla, N. Heinen, *Buffer Overflow Attacks: Detect, Exploit, Prevent* (Syngress Publishing, Rockland, 2005)

88. B. De Fraine, M. Südholt, V. Jonckers, StrongAspectJ: flexible and safe pointcut/advice bindings, in *Proceedings of the 7th International Conference on Aspect-Oriented Software Development, AOSD'08* (ACM, New York, 2008), pp. 60–71

89. R. France, I. Ray, G. Georg, S. Ghosh, Aspect-oriented approach to early design modeling. IEE Proc.—Softw. **151**(4), 173–186 (2004)

90. R. France, B. Rumpe, Model-driven development of complex software: a research roadmap, in *FOSE'07: Future of Software Engineering* (IEEE Computer Society, Washington, 2007), pp. 37–54

91. L. Fuentes, P. Sanchez, Elaborating UML 2.0 profiles for AO design, in *Proceedings of the International Workshop on Aspect-Oriented Modeling (AOM'06)* (2006)

92. L. Fuentes, P. Sánchez, Dynamic weaving of aspect-oriented executable UML models. Trans. Asp.-Oriented Softw. Dev. **5560**, 1–38 (2009)

93. S. Gao, Y. Deng, H. Yu, X. He, K. Beznosov, K. Cooper, Applying aspect-orientation in designing security systems: a case study, in *Proceedings of International Conference of Software Engineering and Knowledge Engineering* (2004)

94. G. Georg, R.B. France, I. Ray, An aspect-based approach to modeling security concerns, in *Critical Systems Development with UML—Proceedings of the UML'02 Workshop*, ed. by J. Jürjens, M.V. Cengarle, E.B. Fernandez, B. Rumpe, R. Sandner (Institut für Informatik, Technische Universität München, 2002), pp. 107–120

95. G. Georg, S.H. Houmb, I. Ray, Aspect-oriented risk-driven development of secure applications, in *Proceedings of the 20th Annual IFIP WG 11.3 Working Conference on Data and Applications Security (DBSec'06)*. Lecture Notes in Computer Science, vol. 4127, ed. by E. Damiani, P. Liu (Springer, Berlin, 2006), pp. 282–296

96. M.J.C. Gordon, *Programming Language Theory and its Implementation—Applicative and Imperative Paradigms*. Prentice Hall International Series in Computer Science (Prentice Hall, Upper Sadle River, 1988)

97. I. Groher, M. Voelter, XWeave: models and aspects in concert, in *Proceedings of the Workshop on Aspect-Oriented Modeling (AOM'07)* (ACM, New York, 2007), pp. 35–40

98. E. Hilsdale, J. Hugunin, Advice weaving in AspectJ, in *Proceedings of the 3rd International Conference on Aspect-Oriented Software Development (AOSD'04)* (ACM, New York, 2004), pp. 26–35

99. K. Soo Hoo, A.W. Sudbury, A.R. Jaquith, Tangible ROI through secure software engineering. Secur. Bus. Q.: Spec. Issue Return Secur. Invest. **2**, 1–4 (2001)

100. A. Hovsepyan, S. Baelen, Y. Berbers, W. Joosen, Generic reusable concern compositions, in *Proceedings of the 4th European Conference on Model Driven Architecture (ECMDA-FA'08)* (Springer, Berlin, 2008), pp. 231–245

101. M. Huang, Ch. Wang, L. Zhang, Toward a reusable and generic security aspect library, in *AOSDSEC: AOSD Technology for Application-Level Security*, ed. by B. De Win, V. Shah, W. Joosen, R. Bodkin, March 2004

102. M. Huth, M. Ryan, *Logic in Computer Science: Modelling and Reasoning About Systems* (Cambridge University Press, New York, 2004)

103. IBM-Rational Software Architect (2012), Available at: http://www.ibm.com/software/awdtools/architect/swarchitect/. Last visited: Nov 2012

104. ISO/IEC17799, Information Technology—Security Techniques—Code of Practice for Information Security Management (2000)

105. A. Jackson, J. Kleinand, B. Baudry, S. Clarke. KerTheme: testing aspect oriented models, in *Proceedings of the ECMDA Workshop on Integration of Model Driven Development and Model Driven Testing* (2006)

106. R. Jagadeesan, A. Jeffrey, J. Riely. A calculus of untyped aspect-oriented programs, in *Proceedings of the European Conference on Object-Oriented Programming* (Springer, Berlin, 2003), pp. 54–73

107. J.M. Jézéquel, Model Transformation Techniques (2010), Available at: http://people.irisa.fr/ Jean-Marc.Jezequel/enseignement/ModelTransfo.pdf. Last visited: May 2010

108. F. Jouault. Eclipse QVT Operational (2008), Available at: http://www.eclipse.org/mmt/? project=qvto

109. L. Brown Jr, F.L. Brown, J. Divietri, G.D. De Villegas, E.B. Fernandez, The authenticator pattern, in *Proceedings of the 10th Conference on Pattern Languages of Programs (PLoP'03)* (Wiley, Chichester, 1999), p. 6

110. J. Jürjens, *Secure Systems Development with UML* (Springer, Berlin, 2004)

111. J. Jürjens, S.H. Houmb, Dynamic secure aspect modeling with UML: from models to code, in *MoDELS*. Lecture Notes in Computer Science, vol. 3713, ed. by L.C. Briand, C. Williams (Springer, Berlin, 2005), pp. 142–155

112. M. Kande, J. Kienzle, A. Strohmeier, From AOP to UML—a bottom-up approach, in *Proceedings of the 1st International Workshop on Aspect-Oriented Modeling with UML*, Enschede, The Netherlands (2002)

113. G. Kiczales, E. Hilsdale, J. Hugunin, M. Kersten, J. Palm, W.G. Griswold, An overview of AspectJ, in *Proceedings of the 15th European Conference on Object-Oriented Programming (ECOOP'01)* (Springer, London, 2001), pp. 327–353

114. G. Kiczales, J. Lamping, A. Menhdhekar, C. Maeda, C. Lopes, J.-M. Loingtier, J. Irwin, Aspect-oriented programming, in *Proceedings of the 11th European Conference on Object-Oriented Programming (ECOOP'97)*, vol. 1241, ed. by M. Akşit, S. Matsuoka (Springer, Berlin, 1997), pp. 220–242

115. D.M. Kienzle, M.C. Elder, D. Tyree, J. Edwards-Hewitt, Security Patterns Repository, Version 1.0 (2006), Available at: http://citeseerx.ist.psu.edu/viewdoc/download?doi=10.1.1.103. 1391&rep=rep1&type=pdf

116. J. Kienzle, W. Al, Abed, F. Fleurey, J.M. Jézéquel, J. Klein, Aspect-oriented design with reusable aspect models. Trans. Asp.-Oriented Softw. Dev. **7**, 272–320 (2010)

117. J. Kienzle, W. Al Abed, J. Klein, Aspect-oriented multi-view modeling, in *AOSD*, ed. by K.J. Sullivan, A. Moreira, C. Schwanninger, J. Gray (ACM, New York, 2009), pp. 87–98

118. J. Klein, F. Fleurey, J.M. Jézéquel, Weaving multiple aspects in sequence diagrams. Trans. Asp.-Oriented Softw. Dev. **3**, 167–199 (2007)

119. A.G. Kleppe, J. Warmer, W. Bast, *MDA Explained: The Model Driven Architecture: Practice and Promise* (Addison-Wesley Longman, Boston, 2003)

120. Cigital Labs, An aspect-oriented security assurance solution. Technical Report AFRL-IF-RS-TR-2003-254, Cigital Labs, Dulles, Virginia, USA (2003)

121. P.J. Landin, A generalization of jumps and labels, in *Report UNIVAC Systems Programming Research* (1965)

122. M.-A. Laverdiére, A. Mourad, A. Soeanu, M. Debbabi, Control flow based pointctus for security hardening concerns, in *Proceedings of the Joint iTrust and PST Conferences on Privacy, Trust Management and Security*, Moncton, New Brunswick, Canada (2007)

123. M. Laverdière, A. Mourad, A. Hanna, M. Debbabi, Security design patterns: survey and evaluation, in *Proceedings of the Canadian Conference on Electrical and Computer Engineering (CCECE'06)* (IEEE, 2006), pp. 1605–1608

124. Y. Ledru, R. Laleau, M. Lemoine, S. Vignes, D. Bert, V. Donzeau-Gouge, C. Dubois, F. Peureux. An attempt to combine UML and formal methods to model airport security, in *Proceedings of the 18th International Conference on Advanced Information Systems Engineering (CAISE'06)*, Luxembourg, pp. 47–50 (2006)

125. B.A. Lieberman, *The Art of Software Modeling* (Auerbach Publication, Boca Raton, 2006)

126. V. Lima, C. Talhi, D. Mouheb, M. Debbabi, L. Wang, M. Pourzandi, Formal verification and validation of UML 2.0 sequence diagrams using source and destination of messages. Electron. Notes Theor. Comput. Sci. **254**, 143–160 (2009)
127. T. Lodderstedt, D. Basin, J. Doser, SecureUML: a UML-based modeling language for model-driven security, in *Proceedings of the International Conference on the Unified Modeling Language (UML'02)*. Lecture Notes in Computer Science, vol. 2460 (Springer, London, 2002), pp. 426–441
128. T. Lodderstedt, D. Basin, J. Doser, Model-driven security: from UML models to access control infrastructures. ACM Trans. Softw. Eng. Methodol. (TOSEM) **15**(1), 39–91 (2006)
129. H. Masuhara, Y. Endoh, A. Yonezawa, A fine-grained join point model for more reusable aspects, in *Proceedings of the 4th Asian Symposium on Programming Languages and Systems (APLAS'06)*. Lecture Notes in Computer Science, vol. 4279, ed. by N. Kobayashi (Springer, Berlin, 2006), pp. 131–147
130. H. Masuhara, K. Kawauchi, Dataflow pointcut in aspect-oriented programming, in *Proceedings of the First Asian Symposium on Programming Languages and Systems (APLAS'03)*. Lecture Notes in Computer Science, vol. 2895, ed. by A. Ohori (Springer, Berlin, 2003), pp. 105–121
131. H. Masuhara, G. Kiczales, C. Dutchyn, A compilation and optimization model for aspect-oriented programs, in *Proceedings of the 12th International Conference on Compiler Construction (CC'03)* (Springer, Berlin, 2003), pp. 46–60
132. H. Masuhara, G. Kiczales, C. Dutchyn, A compilation and optimization model for aspect-oriented programs, in *Proceedings of the 12th International Conference on Compiler Construction (CC'03)* (Springer, Berlin, 2003), pp. 46–60
133. G. Mcgraw, *Software Security: Building Security In*. Addison-Wesley Software Security Series (Addison-Wesley Professional, Boston, 2006)
134. S.J. Mellor, M.J. Balcer, *Executable UML: A Foundation for Model-Driven Architecture* (Addison-Wesley Professional, Boston, 2002)
135. T. Mens, P. Van Gorp, A taxonomy of model transformation. Electron. Notes Theor. Comput. Sci. **152**, 125–142 (2006)
136. W. De Meuter, N. Boyen, An informal tour on denotational semantics. Technical Report vub-prog-tr-94-08, Programming Technology Lab, Vrije Universiteit Brussel (1994)
137. C. Montangero, M. Buchholtz, L. Perrone, S. Semprini, For-LySa: UML for authentication analysis, in *Global Computing: IST/FET International Workshop (GC'04)*. Lecture Notes in Computer Science, vol. 3267 (Springer, Berlin, 2005), pp. 93–106
138. B. Morin, J. Klein, O. Barais, J.M. Jézéquel, A generic weaver for supporting product lines, in *Proceedings of the Workshop on Software Architectures and Mobility (EA'08)* (ACM, New York, 2008), pp. 11–18
139. F. Mostefaoui, J. Vachon, Formalization of an aspect-oriented modeling approach, in *Proceedings of the International Conference on Formal Methods* (2006)
140. A. Mourad, M.A. Laverdière, M. Debbabi, Security hardening of open source software, in *Proceedings of the 2006 International Conference on Privacy, Security and Trust (PST'06)* (ACM, New York, 2006), p. 1
141. A. Mourad, M.A. Laverdière, M. Debbabi, A high-level aspect-oriented based framework for software security hardening. Inf. Secur. J: A Glob. Perspect. **17**(2), 56–74 (2008)
142. H. Mouratidis, P. Giorgini, *Integrating Security and Software Engineering: Advances and Future Visions* (IGI Publishing, Hershey, 2007)
143. P.A. Muller, F. Fleurey, J.M. Jézéquel, Weaving executability into OO meta-languages, in *International Conference on Model Driven Engineering Languages and Systems*. LNCS, vol. 3713 (Springer, Heidelberg, 2005), pp. 264–278
144. National Computer Security Center, Department of Defense, A Guide to Understanding Discretionary Access Control in Trusted Systems. NCSC-TG-003 (1987)
145. Object Management Group, Business Process Model and Notation (BPMN) Version 1.2 Specification (2009)

146. Object Management Group, Common Warehouse Metamodel (CWM) Version 1.1 Specification (2009)
147. Object Management Group, Systems Modeling Language, Version 1.2 (2010)
148. Object Management Group (OMG), Model Driven Architecture Guide, Version 1.0.1 (2003), Available at: http://www.omg.org/cgi-bin/doc?omg/03-06-01
149. Object Management Group (OMG), Object Constraint Language, Version 2.2 (2010)
150. Object Management Group (OMG), Meta Object Facility (MOF) 2.0 Query/View/Transformation Specification, Version 1.1 (2011), Available at: http://www.omg.org/spec/QVT/1.1/
151. Object Management Group (OMG). Meta Object Facility Specification, Version 2.4.1. (2011), Available at: http://www.omg.org/spec/MOF/2.4.1/
152. Object Management Group (OMG). Unified Modeling Language (OMG UML): Superstructure, Version 2.4.1. (2011), Available at: http://www.omg.org/spec/UML/2.4.1/Superstructure/
153. Object Management Group (OMG). Object Constraint Language Specification, Version 2.3.1. (2012) Available at: http://www.omg.org/spec/OCL/2.3.1/
154. J. Oikarinen, D. Reed, RFC1459: Internet Relay Chat Protocol (IRC) (1993)
155. OMG, Unified Modeling Language: Infrastructure, Version 2.3 (2010), Available at: http://www.omg.org/spec/UML/2.3/Infrastructure/PDF/
156. Object Management Group (OMG), Action Language for Foundational UML (ALF): Concrete Syntax for UML Action Language (2011), Available at: http://www.omg.org/spec/ALF/
157. Object Management Group (OMG), Semantics of a Foundational Subset for Executable UML Models (fUML) (2011), Available at: http://www.omg.org/spec/FUML/
158. D. Orleans, K. Lieberherr, DJ: dynamic adaptive programming in Java, in *Proceedings of the Third International Conference on Meta-level Architectures and Separation of Crosscutting Concerns (Reflection'01)*, Kyoto, Japan (Springer, London, 2001), p. 8
159. H. Ossher, P. Tarr, Multi-dimensional separation of concerns and the hyperspace approach, in *Proceedings of the Symposium on Software Architectures and Component Technology: The State of the Art in Software Development* (Kluwer, Berkeley, 2000), pp. 293–323
160. H. Ossher, P. Tarr, Hyper/J: multi-dimensional separation of concerns for Java, in *Proceedings of the 23rd International Conference on Software Engineering (ICSE'01)* (IEEE Computer Society, Washington, 2001), pp. 821–822
161. F. Painchaud, D. Azambre, M. Bergeron, J. Mullins, R.M. Oarga, SOCLe: integrated design of software applications and security, in *Proceedings of the 10th International Command and Control Research and Technology Symposium (ICCRTS'05)*, McLean, VA, USA (2005)
162. Palo Alto Research Center, The AspectJ programming guide: AspectJ langage semantics: join points (2009), Available at: http://www.eclipse.org/aspectj/doc/released/progguide/semantics.html, May 2009
163. J. Pavlich-Mariscal, T. Doan, L. Michel, S. Demurjian, T. Ting, Role slices: a notation for RBAC permission assignment and enforcement, in *Proceedings of the 19th Annual IFIP WG 11.3*, Connecticut, USA, pp. 40–53 (2005)
164. J. Pavlich-Mariscal, L. Michel, S. Demurjian, Enhancing UML to model custom security aspects, in *Proceedings of the 11th International Workshop on Aspect-Oriented Modeling (AOM@AOSD'07)* (2007)
165. R. Pawlak, L. Duchien, G. Florin, F. Legond-Aubry, L. Seinturier, L. Martelli, A UML notation for aspect-oriented software design, in *Proceedings of the 1st International Workshop on Aspect-Oriented Modeling with UML (AOM'02)*, Enschede, The Netherlands (2002)
166. S. Perdita, R. Pooley, *Using UML: Software Engineering with Objects and Components*. Object Technology Series (Addison-Wesley Longman, Boston, 1999)
167. K. Philippe, The 4+1 view model of architecture. IEEE Softw. **12**(6), 42–50 (1995)
168. K. Pohl, G. Böckle, F.J. van der Linden, *Software Product Line Engineering: Foundations, Principles and Techniques* (Springer, New York, 2005)
169. G. Popp, J. Jürjens, G. Wimmel, R. Breu, Security-critical system development with extended use cases, in *Proceedings of the 10th Asia-Pacific Software Engineering Conference (APSEC'03)*, pp. 478–487 (2003)

170. R. Chitchyan et al., Survey of analysis and design approaches. Technical Report-AOSD-Europe-ULANC-9 (2005)
171. D.J. Pearce, R. Ramachandran, I. Welch, AspectJ for multilevel security, in *Proceedings of the AOSD Workshop on Aspects, Components, and Patterns for Infrastructure Software (ACP4IS'06)*, 21st March 2006, Bonn, Germany, pp. 13–17 (2006)
172. R. Ramachandran, D.J. Pearce, I. Welch, AspectJ for multilevel security, in *Proceedings of the AOSD Workshop on Aspects, Components, and Patterns for Infrastructure Software (ACP4IS'06)*, pp. 13–17 (2006)
173. I. Ray, R. France, N. Li, G. Georg, An aspect-based approach to modeling access control concerns. Inf. Softw. Technol. **46**(9), 575–587 (2004)
174. I. Ray, N. Li, D.K. Kim, R. France, Using parameterized UML to specify and compose access control models, in *Proceedings of the 6th IFIP TC-11 WG 11.5 Working Confrence on Integrity and Internal Control in Information Systems (IICIS'03)*, Lausanne, Switzerland (2003)
175. Y.R. Reddy, S. Ghosh, R.B. France, G. Straw, J.M. Bieman, N. McEachen, E. Song, G. Georg, Directives for composing aspect-oriented design class models. Trans. Asp.-Oriented Softw. Dev. **3880**, 75–105 (2006)
176. J.C. Reynolds, Definitional interpreters for higher-order programming languages, in *Proceedings of the ACM Annual Conference, ACM'72*, vol. 2 (ACM, New York, 1972), pp. 717–740
177. J.C. Reynolds, The discoveries of continuations. J. Lisp Symb. Comput., Spec. Issue Contin. **6**(3–4) (1993)
178. A. Rodriguez, E. Fernandez-Medina, M. Piattini, Security requirement with a UML 2.0 profile, in *ARES'06: Proceedings of the First International Conference on Availability, Reliability and Security* (IEEE Computer Society, Washington, 2006), pp. 670–677
179. S. Romanosky, Enterprise security design patterns, in *Proceedings of the European Conference on Pattern Languages of Programs (EuroPLoP'02)* (2002)
180. J. Rosenberg, H. Schulzrinne, G. Camarillo, A. Johnston, J. Peterson, R. Sparks, M. Handley, E. Schooler, RFC3261: Session Initiation Protocol (SIP) (2002)
181. P. Saint-Andre, RFC3920: Extensible Messaging and Presence Protocol (XMPP): Core (2004)
182. A. Schauerhuber, W. Schwinger, E. Kapsammer, W. Retschitzegger, M. Wimmer, G. Kappel, A survey on aspect-oriented modeling approaches. Technical Report, Vienna University of Technology (2007)
183. D.A. Schmidt, *Denotational Semantics: A Methodology for Language Development* (Wm. C. Brown, Dubuque, 1988)
184. M. Schumacher, E. Fernandez-Buglioni, D. Hybertson, F. Buschmann, P. Sommerlad, *Security Patterns: Integrating Security and Systems Engineering*. Wiley Software Patterns Series (Wiley, Chichester, 2006)
185. M. Schumacher, U. Roedig, *Security Engineering with Patterns*. Lecture Notes in Computer Science (LNCS), vol. 2754 (Springer, Heidelberg, 2001)
186. S. Sendall, W. Kozaczynski, Model transformation: the heart and soul of model-driven software development. Softw. IEEE **20**(5), 42–45 (2003)
187. P. Slowikowski, K. Zielinski, Comparison study of aspect-oriented and container managed security, in *Proceedings of the ECCOP Workshop on Analysis of Aspect-Oriented Software* (2003)
188. E. Song, R. Reddy, R. France, I. Ray, G. Georg, R. Alexander, Verifiable composition of access control and application features, in *Proceedings of the 10th ACM Symposium on Access Control Models and Technologies, SACMAT'05* (ACM, New York, 2005), pp. 120–129
189. O. Spinczyk, A. Gal, W. Schröder-Preikschat, AspectC++: an aspect-oriented extension to the C++ programming language, in *Proceedings of the 40th International Conference on Tools Pacific (CRPIT'02)*, Darlinghurst, Australia, pp. 53–60 (2002)
190. T. Stahl, M. Völter, *Model-Driven Software Development: Technology, Engineering, Management* (Wiley, Chichester, 2006)

191. D. Stein, S. Hanenberg, R. Unland, A UML-based aspect-oriented design notation for AspectJ, in *Proceedings of the 1st International Conference on Aspect-Oriented Software Development (AOSD'02)* (ACM, New York, 2002), pp. 106–112

192. P. Stevens, R. Pooley, *Using UML: Software Engineering With Objects and Components*. Object Technology Series (Addison-Wesley Longman, Boston, 1999)

193. J.E. Stoy, *Denotational Semantics: The Scott-Strachey Approach to Programming Language Theory* (MIT Press, New York, 1981)

194. C. Strachey, C.P. Wadsworth, *Continuations: A Mathematical Semantics for Handling Full Jumps*. Technical Monograph PRG-11, Oxford University Computing Laboratory (1974)

195. D. Thomsen, D. O'Brien, J. Bogle, Role-based access control framework for network enterprises, in *Proceedings of the 14th Annual Computer Security Applications Conference (ACSAC'98)* (IEEE Computer Society, Washington, 1998), p. 50

196. M. Tkatchenko, G. Kiczales, Uniform support for modeling crosscutting structure, in *Model Driven Engineering Languages and Systems*. Lecture Notes in Computer Science, vol. 3713, ed. by L. Briand, C. Williams (Springer, Berlin, 2005), pp. 508–521

197. S. Tlili, X. Yang, R. Hadjidj, M. Debbabi, Verification of CERT secure coding rules: case studies, in *On the Move to Meaningful Internet Systems: OTM 2009*, pp. 913–930 (2009)

198. B. Unhelkar, *Verification and Validation for Quality of UML 2.0 Models* (Wiley, Chichester, 2005)

199. J. Viega, J.T. Bloch, P. Chandra, Applying aspect-oriented programming to security. Cutter IT J. **14**, 31–39 (2001)

200. J.L. Vivas, J.A. Montenegro, J. Lopez, Towards a business process-driven framework for security engineering with the UML, in *Proceedings of the 6th Information Security Conference (ISC'03)*, Bristol, UK. Lecture Notes in Computer Science, vol. 2851 (Springer, Berlin, 2003), pp. 381–395

201. D. Walker, S. Zdancewic, J. Ligatti, A theory of aspects, in *ICFP'03*, vol. 38 (ACM, New York, 2003), pp. 127–139

202. M. Wand, G. Kiczales, C. Dutchyn, A semantics for advice and dynamic join points in aspect-oriented programming. ACM Trans. Program. Lang. Syst. **26**, 890–910 (2004)

203. J. Warmer, A. Kleppe, *The Object Constraint Language: Getting Your Models Ready for MDA* (Addison-Wesley Longman, Boston, 2003)

204. T. Weilkiens, *System Engineering with SysML/UML: Modeling, Analysis, Design* (Morgan Kaufmann, San Francisco, 2008)

205. T. Weilkiens, B. Oestereich, *UML 2 Certification Guide: Fundamental & Intermediate Exams* (Morgan Kaufmann, San Francisco, 2006)

206. J. Whittle, P.K. Jayaraman, A.M. Elkhodary, A. Moreira, J. Araújo, MATA: a unified approach for composing UML aspect models based on graph transformation. Trans. Asp.-Oriented Softw. Dev. VI **6**, 191–237 (2009)

207. B. De Win, Engineering application level security through aspect-oriented software development. Ph.D. Thesis, Katholieke Universiteit, Leuven (2004)

208. H. Yan, G. Kniesel, A. Cremers, A meta-model and modeling notation for AspectJ, in *Proceedings of the 5th International Workshop on Aspect-Oriented Modeling (AOM'04)*, Lisbon, Portugal (2004)

209. N. Yoshioka, H. Washizaki, K. Maruyama, A survey on security patterns. Prog. Inform. **5**, 35–47 (2008)

210. Y. Younan, W. Joosen, F. Piessens, Code injection in C and C++: a survey of vulnerabilities and countermeasures. Technical Report CW386, Departement of Computer Science, Katholieke Universiteit Leuven, July 2004

211. G. Zhang, H. Baumeister, N. Koch, A. Knapp, Aspect-oriented modeling of access control in web applications, in *Proceedings of the 6th Workshop on Aspect Oriented Modeling (AOM'05)* (2005)

212. G. Zhang, M.M. Hölzl, HiLA: high-level aspects for UML state machines, in *MoDELS Workshops*. Lecture Notes in Computer Science, vol. 6002, ed. by S. Ghosh (Springer, Berlin, 2009), pp. 104–118

213. J. Zhang, T. Cottenier, A. Berg, J. Gray, Aspect composition in the motorola aspect-oriented modeling weaver. J. Object Technol., Spec. Issue AOM 6(7), 89–108 (2007)
214. P. Ziemann, M. Gogolla, An extension of OCL with temporal logic, pp. 53–62 (2002)
215. A. Zisman, A static verification framework for secure peer-to-peer applications, in *Second International Conference on Internet and Web Applications and Services (ICIW'07)*, p. 8 (2007)

Index

© Springer International Publishing Switzerland 2015   233
D. Mouheb et al., *Aspect-Oriented Security Hardening of UML Design Models*,
DOI 10.1007/978-3-319-16106-8

Printed in the United States
By Bookmasters

Printed in the United States
By Bookmasters